ENDURING TRAUMA THROUGH THE LIFE CYCLE

ENDURING TRAUMA
THROUGH THE LIFE CYCLE

Edited by
Eileen McGinley and
Arturo Varchevker

KARNAC

First published in 2013 by
Karnac Books Ltd
118 Finchley Road
London NW3 5HT

British Library Cataloguing in Publication Data

A C.I.P. for this book is available from the British Library

ISBN-13: 978-1-78049-105-9

Typeset by V Publishing Solutions Pvt Ltd., Chennai, India

Printed in Great Britain

www.karnacbooks.com

CONTENTS

v

ABOUT THE EDITORS AND CONTRIBUTORS

Michael Brearley is a psychoanalyst in London and was until recently president of the British Psychoanalytical Society. He teaches, writes, and gives talks on psychoanalysis, on team building and motivation, and continues to write occasionally on cricket. Earlier, he was a lecturer in philosophy at the University of Newcastle-upon-Tyne, and played cricket professionally, captaining Middlesex for twelve years, and England for thirty-one Tests. He wrote *The Art of Captaincy* (London: Hodder and Stoughton, 1985) and has been President of the MCC.

Ronald Britton is a distinguished fellow and training and supervising analyst of the British Psychoanalytical Society. He has been president of the British Society and vice-president of the International Psychoanalytical Association. He was formerly chair of the Children and Families Department at the Tavistock Clinic, London. He is an internationally renowned author, and his books include *The Oedipus Complex Today*, with M. Feldman and E. O'Shaughnessy, edited by J. Steiner (London: Karnac, 1988); *Belief and Imagination: Explorations in Psychoanalysis* (London; Routledge, 1998); and *Sex, Death and the Superego: Experiences in Psychoanalysis* (London: Karnac, 2003).

Catalina Bronstein MD (née Halperin) is a visiting professor in the Psychoanalysis Unit at University College London. She is a fellow and training and supervising analyst of the British Psychoanalytical Society. She works as a child, adolescent, and adult psychoanalyst in private practice and also at the Brent Adolescent Centre. Until recently, she was the London editor of the *International Journal of Psychoanalysis*. She lectures in Britain and abroad, and has written numerous papers, chapters in books, and monographs on a wide variety of topics. She edited *Kleinian Theory: A Contemporary Perspective* (London: Whurr, 2001).

Sara Flanders is a fellow and training and supervising analyst of the British Psychoanalytical Society. She has worked for many years at the Brent Adolescent Centre, seeing adolescents in therapeutic consultation and intensive therapy. She edited *The Dream Discourse Today* (London: Routledge, 1993) and co-edited, with Dana Birksted Breen and Alain Gibeault, *Reading French Psychoanalysis* (London: Routledge, 2010).

Isky Gordon is Emeritus Professor of Neuro-Imaging at the Institute of Child Health, University College London. He was on the Board of Dignity in Dying from 2005 to 2011. He has been on the steering group of Health Professionals for Assisted Dying since its inception in 2009. He is a keen photographer, with recent exhibitions in London Town Hall and Riverside Studios.

Francis Grier is a fellow and training and supervising analyst of the British Psychoanalytical Society and a member of the Society of Couple Psychoanalytic Psychotherapists. He has edited *Brief Encounters with Couples: Some Analytical Perspectives* (London: Karnac, 2001) and *Oedipus and the Couple* (London: Karnac, 2005), both part of the Tavistock Clinic Series. He has written several other papers, including "Lively and deathly intercourse", in *Sex, Attachment and Couple Psychotherapy: Psychoanalytic Perspectives* (Ed. C. Clulow, London: Karnac, 2009).

Eileen McGinley is a fellow of the British Psychoanalytical Society and works in full-time private psychoanalytic practice in London. She was previously a consultant psychiatrist in psychotherapy at the Maudsley Hospital, where she convened a course on borderline psychopathology. She has edited, with Arturo Varchevker, two other books in the Psychoanalytic Forum series: *Enduring Loss: Mourning, Depression and Narcissism Through the Life Cycle* (London: Karnac, 2010) and *Enduring Migration Through the Life Cycle* (London: Karnac, 2013).

Nick Midgley is a child and adolescent psychotherapist. He trained at the Anna Freud Centre in London, where he now works as a clinician and as programme director of the MSc in Developmental Psychology and Clinical Practice. He is an honorary senior lecturer at the Centre for Psychoanalytic Studies, University of Essex, and is joint editor of *Child Psychotherapy and Research: New Directions, Emerging Findings* (London: Routledge, 2009) and *Minding the Child: Mentalization Based Interventions with Children, Young People and Families* (London: Routledge, 2012). He is the author of the book *Reading Anna Freud* (London: Routledge, New Library of Psychoanalysis, 2012).

Nicholas Stargardt is an intellectual and social historian of modern Germany. He is the first scholar to write a history of Germany in the Second World War through children's eyes, drawing on their pictures and games, diaries, letters, psychiatric files. His book *Witnesses of War: Children's Lives under the Nazis* was first published in 2005 (London: Cape). Currently completing a new social history of Germany in the Second World War, he is Professor of Modern European History at Oxford and a fellow of Magdalen College.

Joanne Stubley is a member of the British Psychoanalytical Society and works as a consultant psychiatrist in psychotherapy at the Tavistock Clinic. She leads the adult section of the Tavistock Trauma Service, and has extensive experience of working with individuals, groups, and organisations who have experienced trauma. She is actively involved in teaching and training in this field, with a particular interest in complex trauma.

Judith Trowell is Professor of Child Mental Health at Worcester and Honorary Consultant Psychiatrist at the Tavistock Clinic in London. She is co-leader of the MA in Child Protection and Family Support, and co-leader of research projects in child protection and child sexual abuse. She is an expert witness in family law, particularly child protection. Professor Trowell is a fellow of the British Psychoanalytical Society, and is both an adult and child psychoanalyst.

Arturo Varchevker is a fellow of the British Psychoanalytical Society, where he developed and chairs the Psychoanalytic Forum. He teaches in the UK and abroad, and his main area of interest in psychoanalysis is internal migration and psychic change. He is a marital and family therapist with a special interest in domestic violence and the impact of migration. He has edited, with Edith Hargreaves, *In Pursuit of Psychic Change: The Betty Joseph Workshop* (East Sussex: Brunner-Routledge, 2004) and, with Eileen McGinley, two other books in the Psychoanalytic Forum series, *Enduring Loss: Mourning, Depression and Narcissism Through the Life Cycle* (London: Karnac, 2010) and *Enduring Migration Through the Life Cycle* (London: Karnac, 2013).

INTRODUCTION

Eileen McGinley

This book grew out of a series of talks given by the Psychoanalytic Forum of the British Psychoanalytical Society entitled "Trauma Through the Life Cycle". Its aim is not to give a comprehensive account of the subject of psychic trauma, which is a broad and complex one, incorporating different aspects of mental life and psychological functioning. Rather, the book aims to highlight some specific clinical challenges and technical issues that arise when working with traumatised individuals at different stages of life. The authors show how their differing theoretical psychoanalytic perspectives influence and inform their clinical approaches. By considering trauma at different stages of life, we can reflect on the origins of psychic trauma and what makes a traumatic situation traumatic, how infantile trauma has long-lasting effects on the developing mind and object-relating, and on the way in which traumatic situations from the past can become reactivated intra-psychically at later stages through the process of deferred action or *après coup*.

Some of the major themes of the present collection are highlighted.

The nature of psychic trauma, unconscious phantasy, and "Nachträglichkeit"

There is no one single understanding of what constitutes psychic trauma. When trauma became linked to the concept of anxiety in Freud's watershed paper of 1926, "Inhibitions, symptoms and anxiety", the notion of a "traumatic situation" acquired a much broader meaning than previously, incorporating intra-psychic mechanisms and unconscious factors, as well as the contribution of external factors. The concept of trauma became inextricably bound up with the theory of anxiety, of drives, and of intra-psychic conflict.

Laplanche and Pontalis have defined a traumatic situation as "an event in the subject's life defined by its intensity, by the subject's incapacity to respond adequately to it, and by the upheaval and long-lasting effects that it brings about in the psychical organization" (Laplanche & Pontalis, 1973, p. 465). They go on to qualify that the traumatic situation "derives its traumatic force from psychical conflict that prevents its integration into his conscious life. Its effectiveness derives from the phantasies it activates and from the influx of instinctual excitation it provokes" (Laplanche & Pontalis, 1973, p. 468).

These concepts have been particularly discussed in the chapters by Bronstein, Britton, and Stubley.

Catalina Bronstein, in her chapter "Nobody died! Trauma in adolescence", starts with Freud's 1926 paper and emphasises two theoretical perspectives that inform her clinical approach both to trauma and to adolescence as a developmental phase. One is that the effects of traumatic events cannot be considered as if they were isolated psychic phenomena that need to be addressed in a special way. This approach leads her to consider traumas alongside all other manifestations of the patient's psychic life. She distinguishes between the traumatic event and the reaction to the trauma, and shows both as making a contribution to what constitutes the traumatic situation. She argues against taking too narrow a view of reconstructing a traumatic situation, both because of the risk of colluding with the defensive use this can serve for both patient and analyst, but also because the complexity of the interplay of unconscious phantasy, anxieties, and internal object relations gets lost if we think only in terms of "reconstruction of trauma". (The clinical studies by both Stubley and Britton in the book also take up this point.) Bronstein uses the same approach to the impact of developmental stages as she does to the effects of trauma, in that the impact of developmental stages are not considered separately from other psychic processes.

Bronstein's is the first chapter in the book to introduce the term "*Nachträglichkeit*", that is, Freud's term for the notion of deferred action. Freud postulated two phases in the constitution of a traumatic situation, one occurring at an earlier time when an event is registered by the psyche but has no traumatic effect, and a second phase, occurring at a later time when the individual is able to understand it and becomes highly conflicted, which gives rise to symptoms. The impact of newly met anxiety-laden situations can re-activate the affective states of helplessness and fear originally connected with the earlier situation. When considering the developmental background in which the trauma is perceived, what might be considered traumatic at one stage need not be perceived or experienced as traumatic at another.

Bronstein gives two rich clinical vignettes illustrating both trauma and adolescent development. In the first, a traumatic assault on an adolescent young man exposes other anxieties, fears, and conflicts related to the onset of a potentially life-threatening illness some years earlier. The impact this has on the adolescent's growing individuation and separateness and independence from his family is described. She borrows from the Barangers' ideas that traumatic events are ones that are experienced as an actualisation of the subject's worst fears and anxieties (Baranger, Baranger & Mom, 1988), a concept expanded by Britton in his description of the return of inchoate fears. Of the patient's experience, she writes, "I think that the 'traumatic experience' lent meaning and signification to a series of phantasies and experiences that were linked to a view of himself and of his Oedipal objects." From her description, we can see that although the traumatic assault led to some psychic disruption in this young man, he had sufficient ego strength that therapeutic intervention led to him being able to work through both the trauma and the anxieties connected with his growing independence.

The second example she gives is of a more troubled adolescent, who approached adolescence in an already disturbed state of mind and for whom adolescence itself had the potential to be experienced as being traumatic. Bronstein does not conceptualise that adolescent development in itself is traumatic, but that the inevitable psychic disruptions and conflicts associated with the onset of puberty and adolescence can prove too much for the immature mind. In the example she gives,

manic and omnipotent thinking had served to protect the young man
from unbearable pre-Oedipal and Oedipal conflicts and anxieties he
could not resolve. His omnipotence made it difficult for him to face the
painful realities with which his developing mind and body were confronting him, as puberty impinged on his delicate psychic equilibrium
(Bronstein, 2010).

Her two examples highlight that the consequences of a traumatic
event will vary from person to person depending on the state of maturity of the ego when a traumatic event occurs and that some traumata
are recoverable from, whereas some produce such disorganisation of
the mind that the long-term effects are irreparable.

Ronald Britton, in his chapter "External danger and internal threat",
distinguishes between endogenous and exogenous aspects of trauma,
and compares Freud's concept of deferred action, *Nachträglichkeit,* or
après coup, to his post-Kleinian version of the role of deferred action in
traumatic experience. He adopts the notion of a "traumatic situation"
as incorporating intra-psychic mechanisms and unconscious factors,
as well as the contribution of external factors. But by tracing Freud's
understandings and revisions of the source of traumatic neuroses from
his early papers on hysteria in 1893 to his revised theory of anxiety as
expounded in "Inhibitions, symptoms and anxiety" (Freud, 1926d), he
makes the distinction between the ego's anxiety provoked by the external danger and the surge of automatic anxiety connected with that traumatic situation where the ego is defenceless. That is to say, that there is
both an external danger and an internal threat; the ego is attacked from
within by instinctual fears and excitations, just as it is from without.

Britton takes a different view in this chapter from Freud concerning
the origin of the deferred action of trauma, in that for Freud *Nachträgli-*
chkeit inferred that a trauma got its force from current drives applied to
past memories, whereas for Britton, the extra power and disturbance
of a trauma comes from the resurrection of infantile phantasy evoked
by later events. I think both mechanisms are true and present in varying degrees according to the maturity of the ego when the trauma is
received. That is, a traumatic situation can activate anxieties associated
with infantile phantasies of a more primitive nature associated with
paranoid-schizoid fears, as well as anxieties associated with the integration of the meaning of past memories as they become less fragmented
as the ego matures. The pain and anxieties are more connected then
with depressive position functioning. Some traumas are so great they

lead to disorganisation of the mind no matter what state the ego was in when first encountering the trauma. Other traumatic situations have the potential to be less disorganising and none can escape the painful depressive working through of a trauma if some reparation is to be achieved.

In this chapter, Britton points out that very little is to be found under the heading of psychogenic trauma in the later writings of Melanie Klein, or post-Kleinian writers, not because they have regarded it as unimportant, but because Klein subsumed trauma into her central theory of development. Klein's view was that there was an innate fear from the outset, a fear of annihilation of life (Klein, 1952). In keeping with Klein and Money-Kyrle (1955), Britton regards the deepest terror met with in traumatic situations as being the terror of annihilation or disintegration, corresponding to Bion's notion of a "nameless dread" (Bion, 1962, p. 95) and Freud's concept of "traumatic anxiety". For many of us, these fears are deeply repressed, or occasioned upon briefly in dreams or fiction. But under certain circumstances (and I think here Britton is referring to circumstances or events that prove to be overwhelming to the ego, and thus traumatogenic), if these primitive phantasies become indistinguishable from external reality, then they are experienced as traumatic in themselves. In the more severe cases of borderline functioning where there has been little repression, the situation is more persistent and intransigent. It is not the loss of an object that is feared, but the loss of sanity itself.

Britton compassionately conveys the dilemma for the deeply traumatised patient who fears recurrence of a disordered state of mind when defences are breeched and who fears the process of recovery as a new danger. In those states, the very process of thinking itself becomes feared as the source of danger, where to think is associated with annihilation of the self. At times, the traumatic memory can be used defensively to act like a rigid container, or pathological organisation, binding what would otherwise be an overwhelming state of disintegration, an idea further elaborated by Jo Stubley in her chapter.

In this chapter, Britton seems to be postulating two aspects of endogenous trauma. One is the shattering dissolution of pre-existing unconscious belief systems that underpinned the individual's sense of safety and assumption of the rightness of things. He suggests that the disruption that can produce this can come from the inside as well as the outside; that trauma can be endogenous as well as exogenous.

He also seems to postulate that the power of an endogenous trauma results from the resurgence of primitive inchoate phantasies associated with an overwhelming terror of annihilation and fear of the loss of sanity.

Joanne Stubley entitles her chapter "The Kraken awakens: the re-emergence of traumatic experiences when defences break down". She imaginatively uses the tale of the mythical creature, the Kraken, the monster who only becomes visible to man when it is awoken in a fury from the ocean deep, only to die roaring on the surface, as a metaphor for the re-emergence of traumatic memories into conscious awareness. She describes her work with a middle-aged man who was re-experiencing traumatic events from his distant past in such a way "that he was living in a kind of dual reality where past and present were intertwined and at times he was not fully able to distinguish which reality he was reacting to". This vivid clinical example allows her to explore a central concept when considering trauma, namely the nature of time and temporality.

Freud considered that most repression seen in our therapeutic work were cases of repression by deferred action, *après coup*. By this, he meant that experiences and memories were revised at a later date when the individual reached a new stage of maturity. Stubley emphasises that the notion of *après coup* links up with the function of repetition. "What is new about my theory is the thesis that memory is present not once but several times over, that it is laid down in various species of indication" (Freud, 1926d).

Stubley's patient had used defences commonly seen in traumatised individuals, namely the encapsulation of his traumatic experiences inside a defensive structure of disavowal and manic omnipotence. In so doing, the traumatic experiences had not been available to the passage of time, to the work of mourning. When his psychic defences broke down, he re-experienced, or experienced for the first time with much affective force, the situations that he had previously not been able to bear. It was likely that he feared the dissolution of his mind and fragmentation by the overwhelming nature of the experience. His failure to mourn his lost objects had instead resulted in his identifying with his dead and damaged objects, leading to a kind of limbo where he was unable to be fully alive or in contact with himself and with the passage of time. To do so would be to risk knowing about temporality, with its potential for loss and separation, and hence mourning.

Stubley shows the need in working with the traumatised individual for the therapist to be able to move flexibly from thinking about the specificity of the trauma, and its place as an historic event, to its meaning and representation in phantasy and what it symbolises in the unconscious. Of screen memories, she writes, "they may cover both past and present, holding on to an experience of time that stresses trauma rather than history". This highlights the concrete, repetitious, and frozen-in-time or timeless nature of trauma. Its effects remain unmodified and monstrous unless what is past can be mourned and temporality and the passage of time acknowledged.

I think that Stubley's patient would link with Bronstein's view that for the patient she described, the "traumatic experience" brought both past and present into conscious awareness and challenged the meaning and signification of a series of unconscious phantasies and experiences that were linked to a view of himself and of his Oedipal objects.

The impact of trauma on Oedipal issues and psycho-sexual development

The working through of Oedipal issues comes to the fore at the end of latency and the onset of puberty and involves the disillusionment of long-held phantasies and the loss and mourning of one stage of life for the prospects and uncertainties of another. The reality of bodily changes impinges on the psyche, and separation and individuation from Oedipal objects becomes more pressing. In the chapters by Flanders and Midgley, they consider how trauma impacts on the resolution of Oedipal issues and on psycho-sexual development.

Sara Flanders considers the traumatogenic potential of development itself in her chapter "What's so traumatic about adolescence?". She elaborates Freud's move from his theory of seduction as the root cause of neurotic disorders of sexual life towards the more complex evolution of sexuality as a product of development (Freud, 1926d). She considers the clinical usefulness of the notion of a primary seduction, as proposed by Laplanche and Pontalis (1968), who suggested that the intrusion of adult sexuality into each mother–child relation is in itself of a traumatic nature, the impact of the adult's unconscious on the child the universal seduction which lays the foundation for the relationship to sexuality within the individual. This is accentuated when there are powerful projective mechanisms coming from a more disturbed parent.

She discusses two different clinical cases. The first is a young adolescent woman with an eating disorder who was rigid and controlling in her thinking. Flanders postulates that the adolescent's lack of wherewithal to sustain the shocks of pubertal change was the product of maternal projective intrusions throughout her life. Flanders goes on to highlight what seemed to me to be several of the factors associated with what constitutes a traumatic situation. She writes:

> She seemed to have little in her mind to help her when she met any difficulty at all, let alone the difficulties faced in relation to the intensities of sexual relationship. She reflected a maternal object who found her otherness unthinkable, a maternal object difficult to separate from because mentally she did not really acknowledge her daughter's separateness, a maternal object who had not been able to facilitate a space for thinking (Bion, 1962). She was a poor ally in the struggle to accept reality, one might say she psychologically abandoned her daughter to face reality alone.

This resonates with both Balint and Khan's ideas that what is traumatic is not so much the event itself, but how it is subsequently dealt with and whether there is a containing environment that will help ameliorate the subsequent impact of the trauma (Balint, 1969; Khan, 1963). Khan's idea of "cumulative trauma" incorporates the idea of repeatedly experiencing an object that is not only intrusive, but one that repeatedly fails to provide adequate containment. For Freud, the original exposure to helplessness, ultimately to death if the primary caretaker is lost, is the original trauma to which some are exposed far more painfully and damagingly than others, but no one escapes completely. Primitive anxieties of annihilation, associated with the fears of abandonment, remain unmodified. Thus, in the case of Flander's adolescent young woman, when faced with separation from the primary object of dependence, despite incestuous anxiety, she clung to her mother, and experienced an intolerable reawakening of the pubertal crisis (Gutton, 1998). Her way of meeting anxiety was, as Flanders describes, to explode into frenzies of bingeing and vomiting.

In her second vignette, Flanders describes an adolescent young man who struggled with acute incestuous anxiety, preoccupying thoughts of suicide, fear of madness, and homosexual anxiety. He also needed help with the incestuous anxiety which, Flanders writes, "Is the burden of any adolescent, but particularly for any adolescent who has not had to abandon the project of being his mother's idealised partner until the changes in the body break in upon this *modus vivendi*." However, like the case of the latency child described by Midgley, this adolescent also had to contend with the impact of paternal abandonment and the psychotic breakdown which totally debilitated his father's functioning as an adult. This resulted in the absence of a father who could facilitate his separation from the subjective immersion in his relationship with his mother, and the working through of mourning the losses associated with growing up.

As in Bronstein's paper on adolescence, Flanders seems to highlight that in some instances, the strain of adolescent development has pathological consequences on the developing psyche, but that adolescent development, although disruptive, is not of itself pathological (though many parents might not agree with this!).

Nick Midgley considers the Oedipal conflicts of a traumatised latency child for whom the absence of a good father figure leaves the child open and vulnerable to the considerable intrusiveness and cruelty of his mother. In his chapter "A soul in bondage", he describes in detail his work with a ten-year-old boy abused and neglected by his mother. He subtly shows that traumatic abuse can be both direct, involving acts of cruelty and intrusiveness directed at the child, but can also be indirect, with neglect and abandonment having traumatic sequelae on the child's development. This combination often results in a sadomasochistic attachment to the mother and subsequent transference objects, where relating to a cruel object is preferred to abandonment. As with Flanders' clinical examples where there was the absence of a father, for Midgley's child there was also the lack of a father to provide any safe triangular space where the Oedipal conflicts could be worked through. The therapist saw himself as providing a space where the needs of the child could be met and contained, away from the mother's, and also as providing a role model for the child in the absence of a real father. Where the therapy broke down was at the point at which the child was confronted with what seemed like an impossible psychological task, that of choosing between his loyalty to his pathological relationship with his mother or to him developing separately from her with the help of his therapist. I thought he had at that point to choose between the certainty of how he related to his mother, and that even though she was monstrous, she was at least his monster and one he knew, to facing the uncertainty and insecurity of relating to a new object.

This chapter also reminded me that in the work with children, the added difficulty is that the child is often still very physically and mentally dependent on the abusive and neglectful parent, so that psychological separation often feels too catastrophic in its outcome, either to the child, or the child's feared effects it will have on the parent. These relate to fears of fragmentation and survival, more schizoid fears. There are also conflictual Oedipal issues, whereby the child has often taken the place of partner to one of the parents, which may also be psychologically difficult to relinquish. It highlights the ambivalence of the child, both wanting a loving father who could help with mother, but also not wanting a father who comes between him and his mother. I see these as more depressive position conflicts and fears we all hesitate over at some points in our lives.

Manifest psychological sequelae to trauma and PTSD

Several of the chapters focus less on the intra-psychic meaning of a trauma situation, and focus more on some of the manifest psychological sequelae of the traumatic event.

In the opening chapter to the book, *Judith Trowell* describes the enduring impact of a particular type of trauma, namely child sexual abuse. She gives a full account of the wide-ranging psychological sequelae of the traumatic event, which although she discusses in the context of child abuse, are also relevant to other types of trauma occurring when the ego is immature. She also outlines the psychopathological consequences of the trauma, which include the development of psychological symptoms and the syndrome of post-traumatic stress disorder, behavioural problems, relationship and sexual difficulties, and the development of psychiatric disorders. She particularly highlights the long-lasting effects of defensive splitting and dissociation on the developing ego. She briefly discusses how this impacts on the development of sexual identity and the working through of Oedipal issues for the child. Her two clinical vignettes are of her work with two deeply traumatised children and show how difficult it can be to make meaningful contact with the traumatised person and are a testament to the difficulties and intensity of the work.

Arturo Varchevker looks at some of the manifestations of trauma from the other end of the age span, namely, in old age. In his chapter "Passengers, next station is old age—are you ready?", he explores some of the ways traumata are manifest in old age, both where there has been healthy development and where there have been developmental disturbances. Drawing heavily on Freud's classic paper "Mourning and melancholia" (1917e), he sees the individual's capacity for mourning losses, which are an inevitable part of older life, as central to how the individual faces old age and approaching death. Where there is a failure to mourn, other pathological defences may become manifest, such as a manic flight from reality, melancholia, or a narcissistic denial of the reality of the ageing process, both physical and mental.

He gives examples of how a trauma experienced in later life can reactivate earlier experiences related to helplessness and frailty and a sense of catastrophic change. One example is of an older woman's reaction to a fall, a common occurrence and almost an occupational hazard of old age. The fall reactivated feelings of helplessness and overwhelming anxieties that did not seem in keeping with the severity of her injuries, and which led her to think she would be better off dead. Varchevker links this to a much earlier period when she felt there was a lack of a stable containing figure in her life and so felt abandoned and left to deal with the trauma on her own. This is an instance of when an event does not seem objectively too damaging, yet subjectively can reactivate earlier experiences that were felt to be traumatic, infusing the situation with infantile or primitive phantasies that make it hard to bear.

Varchevker considers the defensive use of past traumatic events to avoid present stressors, a concept written about by both Joanne Stubley and Catalina Bronstein. This is a difficult area clinically as the symptoms of post-traumatic stress disorder (PTSD) may initially overwhelm the person in ways not in their control. There are times, though, when the individual seems unable to face new anxiety-provoking situations, and when the old but familiar symptoms related to a trauma are held on to and used as a shield against any further impingement of reality, or any other external demands being made. The analyst needs to keep in mind the person's previous capacities, and assess whether these are being temporarily overwhelmed by the strains of the new situation, or whether they have been more disrupted and disorganised leading to more permanent loss.

Isky Gordon writes on a topic that most of us are resistant to contemplating, namely that with old age comes the fact that life is closer to the end as death approaches. In his chapter "Immortality versus mortality: why are the elderly different?", he considers that our society denies death, and that the fear of death and nothingness has led most societies to develop a concept of an afterlife to avoid facing death as an end. Death is fought against and resisted, and not seen as a natural and expected limitation of life. In our society, death is also removed from the community and home, with dying taking place in institutions. He compares Western attitudes to death to those in Mexico, where death remains incorporated within society, and the celebration of the Day of the Dead and the use of photographs as *memento mori* serve as reminders of mortality and the inevitability of death.

He goes on to consider the potential traumatic effects of how those with terminal illnesses are treated, and the prolongation of suffering by denying the inevitability of death. He makes the important distinction between a fear of death and a fear of dying. Often, the dying person is able to face the prospect of death, but is afraid of the process of dying, with fears of loss of dignity and self-reliance and of pain. The chapter concerns mainly those dying of cancer. Although the process of dying is better understood, and hospices offer greater care for the dying person, Gordon argues from a personal standpoint for the legalisation of medically assisted dying as a possibility for the terminally ill. He argues that the prolongation of the life of the other at all costs seems to have taken precedence over the pain and suffering they have to endure in not being allowed to die.

The final parts of the book reflect on trauma as seen in couple work, and on trauma and society.

Trauma and the couple

Francis Grier, in his chapter "The hidden traumas of the young boarding school child as seen through the lens of adult couple therapy", addresses the nature of the cumulative trauma of the child who is sent away early to boarding school and its effects on the developing adult's capacity for intimate couple relationships. It adds psychoanalytic insights to the growing body of work on the subject.

He firstly gives a detailed account of the boarding school "system" for those young children, often as young as six years old, who were sent to become boarders in a school that was far away from home, often in a different country and culture to the one in which they were born. There is both the acute trauma of being suddenly wrenched from the security of their attachments, as well as the cumulative trauma of the unremitting sense of premature separation and loss without any good objects to help them through it. What he describes as the "system" seems to me to have many of the characteristics of a pathological organisation as described by Rosenfeld and Steiner (Rosenfeld, 1971; Steiner, 1981, 1993). The child is placed in a perverse world where the natural emotional responses to loss, mourning, and attachments are frowned upon and denigrated, and a cold detachment from emotions idealised. The difficult child is the one who complains, questions the system, or exhibits any pain and suffering, the compliant child being preferred. A blind eye is turned to maltreatment, bullying, and abuse. Like Rosenfeld's mafia-like gang, adherence to the organisation promises great privileges, whereas dissension risks punishment or expulsion from the privileged group.

A major aspect of the system Grier describes is of a masculine, phallic-dominated world without the modifying influence of maternal and feminine care. The child feels a hatred and resentment towards the mother for having abandoned him. Out of this pathological situation, fear, hatred, and mistrust of women develops, often hidden beneath idealisation of them, which is transferred to the adult's capacity to form secure and loving intimate relationships.

In the second part of his chapter, Grier describes in detail some of the psychological sequelae of this hidden trauma from his analytic work with a couple who both had childhood experiences of boarding school, the man in a direct way, and the woman in an indirect way. The factors that mitigate for and against the working through of the trauma are discussed. The slow, painful and painstaking nature of the work with the traumatised is also evident from his clinical work.

Trauma and society

These chapters by the psychoanalyst Michael Brearley and the historian Nicholas Stargardt were presented together at the conference on "Society and Trauma" and an enriching exchange of ideas occurred between the authors on the day. Stargardt took notes which were later expanded and formed the basis of the discussion piece at the end.

Michael Brearley approaches the topic of social trauma in an unusual way, bringing together both the concept of trauma as a psychological event affecting the individual, and trauma as it affects societies and groups—the concept of social and collective trauma. As well as looking at the psychological sequelae of trauma, he brings in the notion that the working through of a trauma can lead to unexpected strengthening of the ego if there is not too much disruption to psychic functioning. He also introduces the notion of reparation.

Brearley recognises that we are all to a greater or lesser extent subject to traumas as part of the human condition. In his chapter, he cites from literature and history to give individual examples of how we deal with traumas, what strengths we need to call on to help us through, how reparation can transform a traumatic experience in a healing way, and how grievance and revenge, natural components of the response to a trauma, need to be pulled back from for reparation to occur. He also reminds us that the perpetrators of trauma and violence to others can also be traumatised by the realisation of what they have done.

Turning to society, he gives four different aspects of societal traumas. In the first, he examines Jonathan Lear's account of the Crow Indians of North America (Lear, 2007) who lost their cultural identity and way of life in an enforced restriction of their nomadic existence. This example showed how distinctions could be made in individual responses to the trauma, how each individual of the tribe suffered the experience in their own unique way, some able to mourn the loss and psychologically adapt and develop, whereas others could not, producing an aggregation of the traumas. He distinguished this from the life-threatening blow made on the tribe's way of life, producing a cultural trauma.

His second example, concerning language and cultural trauma, looks at the enforced removal of native children in the colonies to schools where they were punished if they spoke their own language (Brody, 2001). He uses Wittgenstein's idea that to lose one's language is to lose a form of life. With the enforced loss of language, the impact of trauma comes not so much from it being felt as painful, but more related to a loss of identity, and in the case of societal traumas, a loss of the collective sense of identity.

In his third example, he explores a central aspect of trauma, elucidated more fully in the chapter by Britton, namely the shattering of the subject's internal structure, a structure provided by concepts and that of object relationships. However, Brearley explores this not from the perspective of individual psychology, but that of the social group and considers how a traumatic event for the group comes to be subsequently reconfigured in history. He uses Gregorio Kohon's work on the retelling of the Disaster at Masada (Kohon, 2007) to show how, over time, "the past is revised while the present is historicised".

Finally, Brearley combines his cricket expertise with his psychoanalytic insights to give an example of how a societal trauma could in time be overcome and transcended. He cites the success of the West Indian cricketers, who came from a society in which they were enslaved and denigrated, yet who were able to adopt something of value from the culture of their oppressors, namely the game of cricket. He sees their success as an example of a reparative move to a more depressive position functioning, and a working through of the trauma, as opposed to being stuck in a paranoid reaction, endless grievance, or masochistic submission.

Nicholas Stargardt is an intellectual and social historian of modern Germany. His chapter "A German trauma: the experience of the Second World War in Germany", continues his study of the childhood experiences of children in Germany during the war. He is sceptical of the oft-used term "collective trauma", mainly because he thinks it stymies the detailed evaluation of any given event, and reduces its complexity with too broad a sweep. He also warns against the tendency to consider traumatised individuals as victims, and writes, "recognition as a victim can also have a curiously disempowering effect, as historical subjects who were trying to make calculations in terrible predicaments are turned into the passive objects of history".

Rather than using the term "collective trauma", Stargardt is more interested in the concept of emotional rupture. This is when the emotional impact of a traumatic situation impinges itself on the individual, threatening the integrity of the psychic structures on which they have previously relied. Like Brearley's notion of how a traumatic event is subsequently reconfigured, Stragardt gives examples of where subjective and objective experiences could only be fragmentary, and only later pieced together to form a more coherent narrative.

It is, I think, very clear from his account of individual experiences of children in the Second World War in Germany that the term "collective trauma" does not do justice to the complexity of the situation. Perhaps what was most shocking about reading some of his accounts of individual experiences was how people came to be treated or mistreated and dehumanised according to "collective" categories being imposed on them. The German children of a war-torn world had to learn to survive in a dangerous world, one in which the social order of decent humanity was destroyed. To be a child of the Jewish ghetto, or of the concentration camps, was particularly hazardous. The identification with the aggressor in their play was most painful to read. Tales of children learning to survive by stealing and cheating, drinking, and sexual promiscuity would be common in any war-torn country. But the added sense of persecution and paranoia for those living in a pathological organisation where perversity and totalitarianism were the norm also took a psychological toll on those trying to survive in a murderous culture. How could one protect one's good objects under such a state, and even worse psychologically, how could one recognise and trust who one's good objects were?

> Near the end of his chapter, Stargardt says:
> The war was not just something that had happened to children. As they strove to survive in it and to parent their parents, it also tore apart their inner emotional world. Through their games, children simultaneously protected themselves from and adapted to a reality in which they recognised their enemies as the image of victorious strength and their parents as impotent failure. Children's games as much as their other precocious activities, demonstrated that they were not just the mute and traumatised witnesses to this war.

This description seems to me to be psychologically astute, and points to the fact that a paranoid-schizoid response is called for in the face of persecution. But as Stargardt had earlier emphasised, this process is not a passive one, even though psychologically required.

Stargardt concludes his chapter with what I think is also one of the central questions when considering any traumatic situation, namely, what happens when the war is over? How does a person mourn what happened when the threat of external danger is over, face their own guilt, and give up a sense of omnipotence for the uncertainties of human frailty? As many of the chapters in the book attest, the psychological effects of trauma last far beyond the traumatic event, and as Brearley writes, recovery involves facing the painful facts of the trauma and of oneself.

References

Balint, M. (1969). Trauma and object relationship. *International Journal of Psycho-Analysis, 50*: 429–435.

Baranger, M., Baranger, W. & Mom, J. M. (1988). The infantile psychic trauma from Us to Freud: pure trauma, retroactivity and reconstruction. *International Journal of Psycho-Analysis, 69*: 113–128.

Bion, W. R. (1962). *Learning from Experience*. London: Karnac.

Brody, H. (2001). *The Other Side of Eden: Hunters, Farmers and the Shaping of the World*. New York: North Point Press.

Bronstein, C. (2010). Two modalities of manic defenses: their function in adolescent breakdown. *International Journal of Psycho-Analysis, 91*: 583–600.

Freud, S. (1893a). On the psychical mechanism of hysterical phenomena. *S.E. 3*. London: Hogarth.

Freud, S. (1917e). Mourning and melancholia. *S.E. 14*. London: Hogarth.

Freud, S. (1918b). From the history of an infantile neurosis. *S.E. 17*. London: Hogarth.

Freud, S. (1926d). Inhibitions, symptoms and anxiety. *S.E. 20*. London: Hogarth.

Freud, S. (1937c). Analysis terminable and interminable. *S.E. 23*. London: Hogarth.

Gutton, P. (1998). The pubertal, its sources and fate. In: M. Perret-Catipovic & F. Ladame (Eds.), *Adolescence and Psychoanalysis*. London: Karnac.

Khan, M. (1963). The concept of cumulative trauma. *Psychoanalytic Studies of the Child, 18*: 286–306.

Klein, M. (1952). Some theoretical conclusions regarding the emotional life of the infant. In: R. Money-Kyrle, B. Joseph, E. O'Shaughnessy & H. Segal (Eds.), *The Writings of Melanie Klein*, Vol. 3 (pp. 61–93). London: Hogarth, 1975.

Klein, M. (1958). On the development of mental functioning. In: R. Money-Kyrle, B. Joseph, E. O'Shaughnessy & H. Segal (Eds.), *The Writings of Melanie Klein*, Vol. 3 (pp. 236–246). London: Hogarth, 1975.

Kohon, G. (2007). The Aztecs, Masada and the compulsion to repeat. In: R. J. Perelberg (Ed.), *Time and Memory*. London: Karnac.

Laplanche, J. & Pontalis, J. B. (1968). Fantasy and the origins of sexuality. *International Journal of Psycho-Analysis, 49*: 1–18.

Laplanche, J. & Pontalis, J. B. (1973). *The Language of Psycho-Analysis* [Translated by D. Nicholson-Smith]. London: The International Psycho-Analytical Library, 1983.

Lear, J. (2007). Working through the end of civilisation. *International Journal of Psycho-Analysis, 88*: 291–308.

Money-Kyrle, R. (1955). An inconclusive contribution to the theory of the death instinct. In: D. Meltzer & E. O'Shaughnessy (Eds.), *The Collected Papers of Roger Money-Kyrle*. Perthshire: Clunie Press, 1978.

Rosenfeld, H. (1971). A clinical approach to the psychoanalytic theory of the life and death instincts: an investigation into the aggressive aspects of narcissism. *International Journal of Psycho-Analysis, 52*: 169–178. [Reprinted in E. Spillius & B. Joseph (Eds.), *Melanie Klein Today*, Vol. 1: *Mainly Theory*. London: Routledge, 1988.]

Stargardt, N. (2005). *Witnesses of War: Children's Lives under the Nazis*. London: Jonathan Cape.

Steiner, J. (1981). Perverse relationships with part of the self: a clinical illustration. *International Journal of Psycho-Analysis, 63*: 241–251.

Steiner, J. (1993). *Psychic retreats; pathological organisations in psychotic, neurotic and borderline patients*. London: Routledge.

PART I

CHILDHOOD

The emotional impact of abusive experiences in childhood, particularly sexual abuse

Judith Trowell

In the late 1970s and early 1980s, the occurrence of childhood sexual abuse began to be widely recognised. The Cleveland Inquiry report was published in the United Kingdom in 1988, and in this Lord Elizabeth Butler-Sloss confirmed that sexual abuse did indeed occur and existed. Until then, many in society did not believe this to be so. What is important is to ask whether it matters that sexual abuse actually happens to children. We know about the Oedipal conflict and the enormous power of the associated phantasies. But the actual physical enactment of the act of adult–child sexuality—masturbation, oral, anal, or vaginal intercourse, and then all the various other sexual acts some children experience—is a very different psychological trauma from the effect of phantasy. Violation of the actual body, and the accompanying threats to ensure silence and secrecy, are damaging in a way that differs from phantasies. The fear of violence and the actual violence that so frequently accompanies the abuse are also very different from the phantasy of destruction of murderous rage.

We have become much clearer about the problems and behaviour associated with childhood sexual abuse. Beitchman and colleagues have undertaken two extensive reviews. The first (Beitchman, Zucker, Hood, Dacosta & Akman, 1991) looked at forty-two different studies to draw out the short-term effects; the second (Beitchman, Zucker, Hood, Dacosta & Akman, 1992) reviewed the long-term effects. These effects have been summarised by Cotgrove and Kolvin (1996) as four main long-term associations with child sexual abuse:

1. Psychological symptoms consisting of depression, anxiety, low self-esteem, guilt, sleep disturbance, and dissociative phenomena.
2. Problem behaviours including self-harm, drug use, prostitution, and running away.
3. Relationships and sexual problems—social withdrawal, sexual promiscuity, and re-victimisation.
4. Psychiatric disorders, particularly eating disorders, sexualisation, post-traumatic stress disorder, and borderline personality disorder.

We have also become increasingly aware, as the children and adults abused as children have been able to speak about their experiences and seek help, that the therapeutic work needed is very complex and difficult. In order to understand and think about the emotional impact of this abuse and how to work therapeutically, we have learned that it is vital to draw on the understanding of child development and of sexuality and aggression that is central in object relations psychoanalytic theory. Psychoanalytic theory has a significant contribution to make to the work—in particular, the understanding of transference, countertransference, and early mechanisms for trying to manage intense feelings such as splitting, denial, projection, and projective identification—because they are used so extensively by these individuals and their families.

Child sexual abuse

Sexual abuse is defined in the United Kingdom by the Department of Health (Schechter & Roberge, 1976) as "the involvement of dependent developmentally immature children in sexual activities that they do not truly comprehend and to which they are unable to give informed consent, and that violate the social taboos of family roles".

In this chapter, what is being considered is contact sexual abuse, which means that the child or the adult as a child has touched or been touched by the abuser. The acts have been kept secret and may involve bribery, threats, or violence, and some children may have been involved in multiple sexual abuse with groups of children and adults. The abuse may have occurred once or lasted over a period of years with variable frequency.

It is important to always remember that sexual abuse is not a psychiatric disorder, it is a psychosocial event, and the mental health sequelae vary from individual to individual. What to us seems horrendous abuse may not profoundly impact on the survivor; lesser abuse may leave the victim very damaged.

Assessment

When we started work in this area, we mainly saw adolescent girls and women abused as children. Over the years, we have seen more and more younger children, down to 6/12, and more boys and men abused as children or adolescents.

The only definite diagnosis is made when semen or seminal fluid is found. So most abuse is diagnosed on the balance of probabilities. The child bleeding from the anus or vagina, or bruising in the area, are pretty clear signs. Colposcopy can be used and this may show signs invisible to the naked eye. However, most cases are diagnosed on the basis of the history and the interviews with the individual.

Adults can recall abuse, and often siblings or friends can corroborate events. A man in his fifties recently talked to me of abuse lasting several years by his older brother's best friend. The friend used to offer to read a bedtime story and abused him. But back then, he felt special, "the chosen one". Only later did he realise. Of course, there are no physical signs in these retrospective accounts, but often others can confirm.

One needs to be careful, given the "false memory syndrome", regarding an individual who has become convinced they were abused. Such individuals often have no corroborating details, and this arouses my suspicion. Survivors talk of gazing at the ceiling and describe the lights or the wall covering, the situations where it occurred, floating out of their bodies and looking down. There are usually some details that imply an authentic account.

Adolescents can be very vocal about what has happened but suddenly embarrassed to give precise details. They can sometimes draw or tell it in the third person—as a story. We have learned over the years that most assessments only reveal a small amount of what really happened; a fuller account emerges later in treatment.

Children and adolescents need to know that the therapist can bear to hear it. Often, we say, "other boys and girls have told us that bad things happened to them, they were touched in private places, or made to do things they didn't want, has this ever happened to you?"

I have assessed many individuals, but also had to assist in Ireland in an extensive way in a case in which many children were involved. I also went to Orkney where there were fifteen children potentially abused, and have been leading teams working with boys from a church choir and two boys' special church residential schools.

Many of these young people have been terrified to talk, and most only allow glimpses of what has occurred. Later, they report it takes six months to a year before they really dare trust anyone.

However, one has to make some judgements, and generally we give up to four sessions and the individual can in that time convey enough. Often, when seen in a group, they can talk more. But if one is aware there may be court proceedings, group interviews are not permitted. Small children often need a "safe", trusted person with them or just outside the door, to speak. We have reasonable accounts from three-year-olds.

But one must always bear *not knowing* and that, for many, uncertainty remains. More and more assessment interviews must not be allowed. I use dolls (pipe cleaner), play dough, cellotape, felt tips and paper, small animals and string, whether with children or adults. They need to be doing something and cannot just sit and talk.

This whole internal ferment is going on for the child around each significant relationship. The child, not surprisingly, becomes very confused. They have to make sense of real experiences of loss and separation, and at the same time be trying to adjust to their present set of relationship standards, expectations, and do all the mental work of appraising their internal representations, real or fantasy. Not surprisingly, many of them do not have the mental or emotional energy to do this.

Identity is based on these internal representations. Older children, despite being relieved to be away from the external reality of their home, carry it with them in their minds. All of them may have to settle for either siding with and idealising the internal representations of mother or father, or rejecting them and living in fear of retaliation, retribution, and intense feelings of disloyalty.

Interventions

We concluded from our work that the individuals, children or adults, need a menu of treatments. Debriefing does not seem to be helpful—the belief that it must be talked about. Some individuals need to talk—some flood one with it and have to be helped to slow down and reflect. Others do not want or cannot talk; to force them is wrong. Some need help to manage themselves and their behaviour, some need medication initially for depression or post-traumatic stress disorder. Art or music therapy may be helpful.

What is so important is, when they are ready, to offer help for the deep emotional pain, confusion, and distress. Psychoanalytic work is vital to help them recover, because the emotional impact of the abuse is like an intra-psychic abscess that poisons all aspects of the individual's internal life. We cannot *cure* them, they will be left scarred, but the wound can heal; it does not need to be a raw, suppurating wound.

Many such patients start once weekly, terrified of being in a room one to one. Gradually, frequency can be increased. Some manage a group, and from every group of six, then two or three need individual work. The families or partners of patients need help also, as there are consequences for them, and there may also be issues raised from their own pasts.

Psychological sequelae of sexual abuse

There is a persistent and frequently unresolved question: has abuse occurred, is it real—reality—or is it imagination, or is it some form of phantasy, conscious or unconscious? Is it possible to understand this? Trying to understand childhood trauma and its impact on thinking and memory, we have to consider post-traumatic stress disorder (PTSD), some features of which are applicable to child sexual abuse. In PTSD, there can be flashbacks, the person is awake, conscious, and is suddenly dramatically and vividly back, in the mind, in the very stressful situation, re-experiencing the events. Also they can have flashback dreams, in which they dream the re-experiencing, and if they awake during this "action-replay" dream, their confusion and distress is even greater than with the awake re-experiencing. Experiencing a flashback, being able to distinguish phantasy from reality when the phantasy had, in fact, been a real experience, is very distressing.

But there are other features of PTSD that also need to be considered and can be helpful in understanding why children, or the child inside the adult, function in the way they do after traumatic experiences. Part of PTSD is what is known as psychogenic amnesia—the memories are pushed out of consciousness. This may be done so successfully that individuals are aware there are things that they cannot remember, but they do not know what those things are. Alongside this goes an inability to concentrate, a lack of emotional involvement, a loss of liveliness sometimes described as feeling of numbness. It is not surprising, therefore, that individuals appear to be confused and uncertain about what has happened to them. It is also not surprising that their emotional reactions may be rather flat, that they do not show the level of distress or anger that might be expected.

It is easy to understand how rather flat accounts that do not have great detail in them lead to questions about whether the abuse occurred or not. Why it is so difficult to confirm or refute abuse in the absence of physical signs begins to make sense; the difficulty of staying with the uncertainty as far as the legal system is concerned is a large part of the problem. Post-traumatic stress disorder also involves avoidance and dissociation. The abuse victim appears to be somewhat vacant or blanks out, will pause and then change the subject completely during an interview. This is partly conscious avoidance but also seems to be a process occurring in the preconscious or the upper levels of the unconscious. Memories and experiences that are too painful and distressing are blanked out, and the individual becomes very adept at doing this so that the interviewer may hardly notice the pauses and the switches in themes or diversions.

But PTSD does not explain why sexually abusive experiences cause so many difficulties. Psychoanalytic theory is needed to try to understand the persistent and long-term problems.

Childhood sexual abuse can be seen as the abusing adult's "madness" being forced into the mind of the child, and it penetrates deep into the unconscious: the child's mind is "raped". The mental mechanisms used to deal with the overwhelming trauma are splitting, denial, projection, projective identification, introjection (introjective identification), and manic flight. Experiences, thoughts, feelings are split off; they may then be projected or they may be denied. Understanding these processes and the phantasies that accompany them is crucial in the understanding of childhood sexual abuse.

One of the things that seems to happen in sexual abuse is that the split-off denied experience forms a bubble, which can become encapsulated. It may be a very small bubble if it was an experience that did very little damage, or it may be a very large bubble if there was major emotional/psychic trauma. This bubble may then sink—a denied split-off fragment that, like an abscess, can give off undetected poison—and the person may be impaired in a number of ways: their learning capacities, their capacity to make relationships, or their complete hold on reality. Alternatively, the split-off experience, the encapsulated bubble, may be quite large and encompass quite an area of mental life and functioning and cause considerable impairment. The impairment may be significant in the area of learning, in developing relationships, or on the individual's hold on reality, but for all of them there is impairment, a block on their normal development.

If the individual has had good-enough early experiences and their development had been proceeding satisfactorily, then the abuse and its resulting split-off and denied aspects can be dealt with using displacement, disavowal, or dissociation; in a way, the child gets on with their life, and it is as if the abuse never happened. But the protective processes may fail at some point, and then awareness re-emerges: for example, when trying to make intimate relationships, when pregnant or giving birth, when their child is the age they were when the abuse took place, or during the course of seeking help for something altogether different.

Where the abusive experience was extensive and early childhood experiences were not good enough, then the split-off, denied abusive experiences seem almost to take over the whole person, leaving very little mental or emotional energy available for current life. Unconscious phantasies dominate and spill out in bizarre and disconcerting ways, for the individual and for those around them. It appears that the individual is using projection and projective identification as a means of struggling to return to some psychic equilibrium. The individual can go on to become a borderline personality or to be overtly psychotic; the ability to establish relationships and the capacity to function can be very limited.

Some clinical examples to illustrate the therapeutic intensity of the work with an abused child

"Phillipa"

Phillipa, an early adolescent aged fourteen years, was referred by an outside psychiatrist for treatment; she was doing extremely well at school, spending hours there, and was reluctant to leave to go home.

She was very small and uncared for but was very friendly with teachers; child sexual abuse was discovered when she talked to the deputy head, saying her father came to her room at night.

She was the eldest of three children, with a younger brother and then a sister. Since her sister's birth, when Phillipa was five years old, mother and father had been having problems. Mother adored her younger brother and sister. Phillipa had to help in the house, run errands, and give father his meals as her mother was busy with the other two children. Phillipa was very fond of her father; her father began to cuddle Phillipa a lot, then to visit her bedroom for cuddles, then to get into her bed. They had intercourse; at the start, this was anal and was then vaginal for about the last three years.

The therapy

Phillipa was fostered by a teacher at school. She was very angry: "Why do I need to come? I only come because I'm made to. What do you know? What could you do—nothing. You haven't been abused—have you." I was totally useless, there was no point in her coming. In spite of this, I arranged to see her; the contempt, derision, sarcasm, denigration, went on and on. She knew more than I did about everything, was more intelligent than I was; she was relentlessly sneering and mocking. Then she began to flaunt her sexual knowledge and to be quite provocative. She talked in a very erotic and sexualised way, becoming excited and seductive so that sometimes it felt as though she could masturbate me with her words. I began to dread her visits, her words, to dislike her intensely. And yet here was this small, vulnerable child/woman who seemed desperately to need help. I felt ground down and useless. I learned that the foster mother felt that she couldn't get near her, and the foster father was extremely uncomfortable.

The feeling of hopelessness and despair led me to talk about her mother, and she became more and more repulsive. I felt that she resembled a poisonous snake. I began to talk about terror and fear and panic and feeling trapped. This later produced a dramatic response. She began to talk and talk about her terror and sense of being trapped in her family, in her bed, with her father. She had coped by pulling the sheets up to her chin, putting her arms and head out of the top, and not knowing what went on below. She insisted that she had completely cut off. She began to have terrifying night terrors—dreams that were a repetition of the abuse. She talked about her father coming home drunk, how he hated himself, how she was left to get him undressed and into bed, how one day she couldn't support him and he fell and injured himself—she was very upset but relieved. In the room with me, she began to weep. For several weeks, she wept and wept through each session. Now, she was talking to her foster mother, but when Phillipa wept for three weeks almost continuously, I think everyone wondered what I was doing to her in the sessions.

Around this time, she started to have symbolic dreams, nightmares of her father in a coffin: either he was dead and it was her fault, or he was being buried alive and only she knew it. She wept for her father, finding it hard to be in touch with any anger or rage and her wish to kill her father. They were both victims, he should not have done it; but her hatred of her mother was intense, vitriolic.

She also still woke up frequently at night, screaming, having felt something hard pressing against her and feeling terrified, convinced that it was her father beside her and his erect penis, and that she "knew" intercourse would follow. We understood these dreams as "memories", whereas the other dreams were more usual symbolic dreams which we could struggle to understand. It now felt that she had become a person, not a walking mind; but the pain and despair were very powerful, and at times she raged at me for having done this to her, put her in touch with feelings, tortured her. Finally, she was able to rage at her father as well as show her pity for him. She had some compassion for her mother, whom she realised wasn't aware of the abuse and who had probably been quite depressed. We then had to work on her feelings of triumph over her mother and myself and how hard it was to be a teenage girl.

"Susan"

Susan, aged nine and a half years, was at primary school and was referred by the social services department. She was one of four children. Her mother had left when Susan was small. The elder two children were placed in a foster home. Susan and her youngest brother, about eighteen months old, were placed in another foster home; this was a family with six foster children, where the parents were fostering full-time. A short-term foster child, a girl, there whilst her mother was in hospital, when back at home told her own father about Mr X, the foster father, touching her, Susan, and other girls; this child's father told social services. All the children were removed.

Mr X had begun touching Susan when she was small, soon after she arrived, initially masturbation of her, then mutual masturbation, then vaginal intercourse over the last few years.

Susan was in an ESN school and had been moved there after nursery class. No reason had been found for her quite serious learning difficulties.

Assessment showed a very flat, unresponsive child, and she had hearing problems—how much was she hearing, how much was subnormality or depression? Recurrent ear infections had left her virtually completely deaf in her right ear and partially deaf in the left. She was unable to cope in a group, unresponsive to counselling in school, and not speaking to her new foster parents.

The therapy

Susan was offered twice-weekly treatment. There were weeks of saying very little, with apparently no response from her to anything. Then I became aware of her eyes, which were quite alert, watchful, usually hidden by her hair; she never appeared to look at me and still looked stupid. I was aware of feeling more and more depressed and said this to her, and how hopeless it all felt.

She began to talk with rage and hatred about her ex-foster mother, the terrible food, the hours of slaving away doing work in the house and garden, the terrible pain in her ears, and never being taken to the doctor.

At times, she was very hostile and suspicious of me. She had further ear infections, and she told me that I was there in the night hitting her about the head, making her vomit, forcing burnt food, stale going-off food, down her, standing over her until she ate it. She had difficulty in sorting out me in her dreams and me at the clinic. It seemed I was seen as the cruel foster mother.

Material from a session after six months of therapy

Susan came in and sat opposite me across the room—she could not sit further away. She had come to the room rather reluctantly but had not resisted. She did not show any interest in the paper or plasticine as she had previously begun to do. She sat without any eye contact and without saying a word. I caught her looking around the room, and her eyes seemed to be darting this way and that. I said: "It seems to be hard today." No reply. I said: "Is it horrid here today?" Susan said nothing but nodded her head. I said: "Why horrid?" Susan looked at me for a moment. I said: "I was puzzled. Was it horrid here in the clinic or outside, at school, in the foster home, before?" After quite a long pause, Susan said: "You hit me". I felt very shaken—what had I done, when, why couldn't I remember? I asked: "When do you think I hit you?" Susan said very firmly: "You hit me". "Tell me", I said. She said: "Night time, night time, you hit me, wake me up hitting me." She was now holding her head in both hands and thrashing in her chair from side to side. "You hit me, I wake up. Why, why you hit me? Pain, hurt." She began to cry and, with her heels on the floor, pushed her chair as far away from me as possible. She was looking at me with fear and rage. I said: "Susan is very afraid and very angry with Dr Trowell. But Dr Trowell is in the clinic, not in your house. Perhaps Susan had bad dreams." "No", she shouted: "You hit me, you hit me, you bad."

I felt worried and a bit panicky. What if outside people could hear, what if her foster parents or social worker thought I was abusing her? Had I hit her? What had I done and perhaps forgotten? I said: "Maybe Susan had a bad dream, a dream that was remembering bad things?" Susan paused and then said: "She hit me, like you hit me, she hit me." I said: "And in the night it all gets muddled up." Silence. Then I said: "It must be very scary not knowing, is Mrs X there, are you back there and she is hurting you, or is it me, Dr Trowell. Maybe because you missed Dr Trowell and wanted me to be there." "No", she said, "You hit me, you bad. You make me eat bad things. Don't take me to doctor's. Need doctor make ears better. Don't take me. Bad." I said: "I think Susan gets in a muddle. It all gets muddled up. Mrs X, myself, her new foster mum and her real mum. So much pain and hurt. Missing pain, earache pain, and then all the pain with Mr and Mrs X hitting and hurting. It was very hard to sort it out." She began to sob. After a while, I said: "Maybe the hardest thing could be sort of wanting to be hit, wanting the pain, because then Susan knew someone was there. Susan wasn't all by herself." She left tearful and down.

During this session, I had been very thrown. I needed to check with myself and reassure myself that I hadn't hit her as far as I could remember. I also felt briefly furious with her for disconcerting me. I wanted to shake her and say, "Don't be so stupid. I never hit you. How dare you say that." Susan's conviction when she came in that I had hit her seemed fixed—or was it my anxiety that made it seem so? Certainly, it was very hard indeed to hold on to the capacity to think and not know the answers, to stay with uncertainty.

Towards the end of the first year, she began to talk about her foster father. She wept a great deal. He hadn't been cruel; she had felt bad, dirty, knew it was wrong, and it was also good, being held, being touched, stroked; no-one else did, except she and her brother, but hardly ever. The inside bit was awful and all the mess and the smell. She thought everyone could smell it, knew it, everyone at school. Now he was in trouble and she felt sad, glad it had all stopped, but she sort of missed him. He had a terrible time with Mrs X; she was a right cow.

Now she was sobbing for her natural mother—where was she, why had she walked out, and, to a lesser extent, why hadn't their natural father kept them (she still saw him)? At school, she began to learn, to ask questions; she started to try to write—for example, her name—and she drew. She began to read, about families and animals, and later to use small numbers and add up. Susan developed a real talent for drawing and painting and using clay, making animal models. She was a real star in the school kitchen and she loved cookery. She began to read in earnest—recipes and the instructions on the kiln at school.

We now went over and over the sexual abuse, her sexual feelings for girls and women and myself, her shame, her longing for babies. She wondered if she was normal—could she have them? Would she ever have normal relationships with men? My reactions were very powerful and at times difficult to cope with: despair, fear, guilt, anger, the seduction of being the good, idealised, abandoning mother—the ease with which I could have been the cruel, sadistic foster mother.

Thoughts about the development of sexual identity

In undertaking this work, an issue that has emerged is the development of identity, particularly sexual identity. At the start of treatment, very often the central issue appeared to be "are they a person and are they sane?". They have dreams, day-dreams, possibly hallucinations that involve terrifying fantasies. The processes of coping take all the psychic energy, using projective identification to get rid of the unbearable, the unthinkable, and then having to manage the terror of retaliation, possible attacks, and persecution. But then, gradually, questions about sexuality and sexual identity come to the forefront and need to be thought about and understood.

Psychosexual development as understood psychoanalytically plays a very important part in this understanding (see Trowell, 1997a, 1997b). In particular, Melanie Klein's early papers (1932a, 1932b) are very helpful. She describes how baby boys and girls are aware of their bodies, their genitalia, as a source of pleasure very early on, boys with their penile erection and their wish to thrust forward, to penetrate, and girls with their sense of something precious inside. She suggests that alongside the Oedipal longing for the parent of the opposite sex and the reverse Oedipal longing for the parent of the same sex, there is for both small boys and girls a sense of the power and importance of "mother", the main female carer. Mother who cares and nurtures is also feared. (See Baker Miller, 1976; Freud, 1905e, 1931b; Jukes, 1993.)

This is a complicated and complex situation for the child. Mother is loved and longed for but is also hated for depriving, for failing to meet needs, and for involvement with others. The child then fears mother's retaliation for this hatred. But, in addition, mother who has the source of life inside her, all the babies, all the penises, is feared because she is expected to wish to attack. The boy child expects mother in her envy to wish to take over his penis, and the girl child expects mother in her envy to attack the child's "womb" as a potential rival to her own (see Klein, 1932a, 1932b; Heimann, 1951). These are all normal phantasies and fears that have to be worked through, and with a loving, caring mother, the envy, fear, and terror is slowly made bearable.

However, in abusive situations, there appear to be times when the child thinks that mother knew what was happening and wanted him or her to be damaged or, if not actually wanting damage inflicted, certainly failed to prevent it happening. This is an internal phantasy that becomes a thought and has nothing to do with the external reality of the circumstances of the abuse. During childhood and puberty, these issues are repeatedly reworked. Puberty for girls is particularly crucial, the onset of menstruation provoking considerable anxiety in the girl— "Have I been damaged inside?" The girl needs the "mother" to be particularly supportive and to take pride in the girl's emerging sexuality as she struggles with all the fantasies. Sexual abuse at this age, with the fantasy that mother's envy could not bear a rival and that she wanted her daughter to be damaged, seems to be a crucial factor in why sexual abuse can be so damaging.

Slowly, then, in treatment, the sexual development, sexual identity, emerges as an issue (see Breen, 1993; Mitchell & Rose, 1982). Trying to understand the process is slow and difficult, but common themes have begun to emerge. Body gender seems to be the earliest to emerge; by this, one is considering physical gender based on genitalia and, later, secondary sexual characteristics such as breasts and fat distribution. This gives rise to an awareness that "I am a boy" or "I am a girl", maleness and femaleness.

Children usually know their body gender early on, probably before speech is well developed, although what exactly is understood is not clear. What follows next is an awareness of oneself as a boy or girl in one's mind: one's self as an internal object has a gender attribution. This gives rise to a sense of masculinity or femininity, one of which predominates in most people. Thus, a person may have a male physical body but could have either a male or female gender in the mind. The internal object "self"—one's awareness of masculinity or femininity, one's mind gender—is conveyed non-verbally as well as verbally. It is not clear how this develops, but it appears that it takes place largely in the context of interactions and relationships with those around, plus intra-uterine and hormonal factors. Alongside the relationships in the external world, the internal object relationships appear to be very significant—for example, the mother and father internalisation from the main carers, and their internalised carers from their childhood, all in interaction with unconscious phantasies.

Early on, at primary school, children are working through the Oedipal phase and are preoccupied with the possible choice of a partner—homosexual, heterosexual, or bisexual—at some time in the future. The sexual orientation fluctuates, and this fluctuation returns in adolescence (Limentani, 1989). Small children do not usually experiment in reality, although this may happen in adolescence. Childhood sexual abuse may influence this developmental phase.

Very closely linked with sexual orientation is object choice, but it is helpful for the girls and boys and the therapists to keep this as a separate phase. If a person decides that he or she is heterosexual, there is then a second stage, which involves the generational boundary. A man may have had as his sexual orientation female partners, but are they to be women or girls? A woman may settle on a homosexual orientation: does she then want as her sexual partners girls or women? There is often an assumption on the part of therapists, patients, and citizens that homosexuality involves the choice of children as objects. This does not appear to be so, and it is important to keep this distinction. "Does this mean that they wanted sex with girls or with women?", is a frequent question. There are the issues of guilt, of shame, of not knowing, which need to be acknowledged, and it seems to be helpful to talk about the fear and anxiety about homosexuality and object choice so that this can be thought about and worked on.

If this phase can be negotiated, there is often a considerable step forward, with the emerging of creativity. Patients can discover a capacity to be in touch with feelings and have an active intelligence which arises from recognition of their internal parental couple (see Chasseguet-Smirgel, 1985).

In the final years at primary school and on into adolescence, these creative thoughts begin to link with the possibility of babies—real babies or intellectual babies, emotional babies, new ventures, new activities. Maternal or paternal feelings are then followed by thoughts of actual motherhood, fatherhood, and, if there is to be a real baby, child-care, parenting. Many individuals who were sexually abused as children find this whole phase very difficult. They may, in fact, by the physical act of intercourse, become pregnant and have a child, but the mental work to prepare for the care of a child is missing.

Thoughts on working through Oedipal issues

Are there particular problems, following sexual abuse for boys and girls, with the resolution of the Oedipal conflict? Boys abused by older boys or men are often initially in a state of turmoil and confusion, the violation of their body, penetration of the anus, has a profound impact. Many of them ask why they were chosen: did they invite the assault? Sadomasochism can be part of the abuse and, if this was part of their parenting, it easily becomes embedded in their personality structure. Turning to mother consciously becomes impossible: the shame, humiliation, and, for some, the excitement inhibits them. Unconsciously, the Oedipal conflict is not resolved unless previous parenting was good enough and there is a solid intra-psychic structure already. Many boys use splitting, denial, and projection, and some use disavowal. This can be more dangerous, as they know abuse is wrong but then, when their needs surface, they act. So they can "believe" what they are doing is a consensual sexual relationship. Most boys we have seen have no internal creative parental couple, no sense of a combined parental object, no coming together of their male and female internal objects.

They may forcefully relinquish an attachment to mother, may reject father or be in identification with father. This does not mean they become paedophiles, and they may be straight or gay. It may leave them predatory in terms of seeking sex, with no concern for their male or female partner. Attunement and differentiation has been lost.

When phantasies become reality, the usual Oedipal resolution is lost—it has happened! This also applies to girls, but for girls whose abuser is male, there is the possibility of safety with mother. If mother is abusive, then they too have the betrayal and shame, but the disintegration usually turns inwards—"it must be my fault"—with the path leading to self-harm or mental health difficulties. It seems that physical abuse, sexual abuse, and neglect can have similar outcomes in the internal world, although sexual abuse often has more self-destructive sequelae.

Conclusions

Starting from the experience of working with traumatised girls, ideas have been developed about the impact of trauma on these individuals and on those trying to work with them. Post-traumatic stress disorder can follow abuse; it is partly a means of managing the unbearable thoughts and feelings but also, if there is frequent re-experiencing, seems to fixate the experience.

Understanding the intra-psychic phantasies and ways of dealing with these overwhelming experiences with current psychoanalytic ideas enable the individual to be helped with psychoanalytic psychotherapy and psychoanalytically informed case management. Similarly, the confusion and distress about their psychosexual development can be understood, relieved, and assisted.

What has become increasingly obvious in this area of work is that the therapy must be in stages. The post-traumatic stress disorder must be recognised and treated. The children need to be helped to give words to the sensations, the experiences they have been through—the smells, sights, sounds, physical sensations—and to talk about their feelings about what has happened. But doing so leaves them with all the unconscious trauma, confusion, and distress untouched. This will need to be treated; it may be immediately, but some children may prefer to have a space and then begin the deeper psychoanalytic therapy work. Most, at some point in their lives, need the intra-psychic pain, conflicts, and confusion to be struggled with and resolved as far as possible, but in order to undertake this difficult and distressing psychoanalytic work, they need to be in a family or substitute setting that can support them through the work.

Different psychoanalytic theories have provided different concepts to try to make sense of this material and to try to help children understand what has happened to them. Trying to integrate some of these ideas in order to help these individuals and enable us to understand has been challenging and rewarding.

References

Baker Miller, J. (1976). *Towards a New Psychology of Women*. Harmondsworth: Penguin.

Beitchman, J. H., Zucker, K. L., Hood, J. E., Dacosta, S. A. & Akman, D. (1991). A review of the short-term consequences of child sexual abuse. *Child Abuse and Neglect, 15*: 537–556.

Beitchman, J. H., Zucker, K. L., Hood, J. E, Dacosta, S. A, Akman, D. & Cassavia, E. (1992). A review of the long-term effects of child sexual abuse. *Child Abuse and Neglect, 16*: 101–118.

Birksted Breen, D. (1993). *The Gender Conundrum*. The New Library of Psychoanalysis. London: Routledge.

Chasseguet-Smirgel, J. (1985). *Creativity and Perversion*. London: Free Association Books.

Cotgrove, A. & Kolvin, I. (1996). Child sexual abuse. *Hospital Update, September*: 401–406.

Freud, S. (1905e). A fragment of an analysis of a case of hysteria. *S.E. 7*. London: Hogarth.

Freud, S. (1931b). Female sexuality. *S.E. 21*. London: Hogarth.

Heimann, P. (1951). A contribution to the re-evaluation of the Oedipus complex: the early stages. In: M. Klein, P. Heimann & R. Money Kyrle (Eds.), *New Directions in Psychoanalysis*. London, Karnac, 1989.

Jukes, A. (1993). *Why Men Hate Women*. London: Free Association.

Klein, M. (1932a). The effects of early anxiety situations on the sexual development of girls. In: *The Psychoanalysis of Children* (pp. 194–239). London: Hogarth, 1975.

Klein, M. (1932b). The effects of early anxiety situations on the sexual development of the boy. In: *The Psychoanalysis of Children* (pp. 240–268). London: Hogarth, 1975.

Limentani, A. (1989). *Between Freud and Klein*. London: Free Association.

Mitchell, J. & Rose, J. (Eds.) (1982). *Feminine Sexuality: Jacques Lacan and the École Freudienne*. London: Macmillan.

Schechter, M. & Roberge, L. (1976). Sexual exploitation. In: R. Helfer & C. Kempe (Eds.), *Child Abuse and Neglect: The Family and the Community* (pp, 127–142). Cambridge, MA: Ballinger.

Trowell, J. (1997a). Child sexual abuse. In: Hon Mr Justice Wall (Ed.), *Rooted Sorrows: Psychoanalytic Perspectives on Child Protection, Assessment, Therapy and Treatment*. Bristol: Jordans.

Trowell, J. (1997b). The psychodynamics of incest. In: E. Welldon & C. Van Velsen (Eds.), *A Practical Guide to Forensic Psychotherapy*. London: Jessica Kingsley.

CHAPTER TWO

"A soul in bondage": the treatment of an abused latency-age boy

Nick Midgley

Introduction

Recent work in the field of neuroscience, when linked to psychoanalytic and developmental research, has helped us to develop a better understanding of the impact of trauma upon both the mind and the brain of the developing child. In the previous chapter, Trowell has described some of the effects that traumatic experiences in childhood can have upon development, but in this chapter, I want to focus not so much on the impact of trauma *per se*, but more specifically on the ways in which a child's traumatic experience enters the consulting room, often in a state "far beyond words" (Lanyado, 2009).

At least since Freud's *Beyond the Pleasure Principle*, psychoanalysts have understood the powerful link between trauma and the "compulsion to repeat", and the way in which victims of trauma attempt to master the overwhelming experience by actively re-playing the experience, whether in the form of dreams, flashbacks—or re-enactments in the analytic setting. In the consulting room, post-traumatic states of hyper-arousal or dissociation—both of which may be highly adaptive to an environment that is chaotic, unpredictable, and dangerous—can quickly be triggered by apparently minor stressors, leading the patient

21

to respond in a way that appears quite out of proportion to the current situation. As Parsons and Dermen (1999) have pointed out, for such traumatised children in psychoanalytic treatment, "all manner of objectively harmless or even friendly overtures are [experienced as] deadly provocations" (p. 329).

Sándor Ferenczi was one of the first clinicians to describe in detail the ways in which trauma enters the analytic relationship. In his *Clinical Diary*, which he began in the late 1920s, recording the extraordinary self-examination of his personal and professional identity as he worked with a series of severely damaged and regressed (adult) patients, Ferenczi came to understand something about the way in which his patients had coped with traumatic experiences, including sexual abuse and extreme violence, when they were young children. He describes how, if the child is not able to modify external reality, and prevent the trauma from taking place, then the only alternative is to modify *internal* reality—with a "splitting of the self into a suffering, brutally destroyed part and a part which, as it were, knows everything but feels nothing" (Ferenczi, 1931, p. 135).

Ferenczi goes on to describe how, in the immediate situation of a violent attack, "one would expect the first impulse to be that of reaction, hatred, disgust and energetic refusal ... [But because of enormous anxiety] these children feel physically and morally helpless, their personalities are not sufficiently consolidated in order to be able to protest, even only in thought" (Ferenczi, 1988, p. 201). Yet for Ferenczi, such experiences are only the first phase of what goes to produce childhood trauma. He argues that most children can get over severe shocks "if the mother is at hand with understanding and tenderness and (what is most rare) with complete sincerity" (1931, p. 138). It is only when the adult world around the child is unable to help her manage her experience—or more importantly, actively denies the reality of her experience—that the event becomes "traumatic" in the full sense of the word. This is especially true when a violent or sexual attack comes from an adult on whom the child is also dependent. This can create an almost intolerable contradiction, leaving the child with what Len Shengold describes as a "terrible and terrifying combination of helplessness and rage", feelings that must be suppressed if the victim is to survive:

> Because he or she cannot escape from the tyrant-torturer, the child
> must submit to and identify with the abuser. The result is that such

children remain in large part possessed by another, their souls in bondage to someone else. (Shengold, 1989, p. 2)

All of this has important therapeutic implications. In his *Clinical Diary*, Ferenczi describes his growing realisation that it is not enough for childhood trauma to be uncovered or remembered in the analytic setting; it must also be experienced:

> After uncovering and reconstructing the presumed trauma, an almost endless series of repetitions follows during the analytical sessions, accompanied by every imaginable kind of affective outburst ... the patient sinks into a kind of jumble of hallucinations, emotional outbursts, physical and psychical pain, into a feeling of helplessness and inability to comprehend. (Ferenczi, 1932, p. 106)

Ferenczi believed that if the analyst, when faced by the patient's trauma re-emerging in the treatment, retreated into the classical analytical stance of abstinence and neutrality, then this situation could be experienced by the patient as actually *repeating* the original trauma, in which the reality of the child's experience was not reflected accurately in the eyes—and hearts—of the adults around them. Given what was inevitably being stirred up in the analyst, such "benign neutrality" was almost certainly insincere, an avoidance of full emotional engagement.

Another way of putting this is to say that the analyst must allow the trauma to enter into the room via the countertransference, without emotionally withdrawing or "turning a blind eye" to the full horror of the situation (as may have happened at the time of the original trauma). Ferenczi concluded that analytic work with traumatised patients involves two tasks—first, to "expose the death-agony fully", and then, on the basis of the analyst's capacity to remain emotionally available, to "let the patient feel that life is nevertheless worth living if there exist people like the helpful doctor".

This is easier said than done. Therapeutic work with children who have been effected by trauma can often feel, to use Jill Hodges's phrase, like "walking on eggshells" (Hodges et al., 1994), where one false step may lead to a catastrophic collapse, often violent. For these children, the very experience of coming to recognise a need for help is likely to re-arouse extreme anxieties about helplessness and vulnerability, so that the attempt by the therapist to reach the patient "will inevitably represent a danger situation for him", often triggering a violent response (Parsons & Dermen, 1999, p. 336).

Margaret Rustin, in her wonderful paper on therapy with deeply traumatised children, describes what she calls the "child psychotherapist working with her back against the wall". She writes:

> [T]his position, with all its discomfort, is precisely the one most relevant to the child's deepest difficulties. A traumatized patient, we might say, needs to have a therapist survive what could be traumatic. The heart of the matter is that our moment of horror as therapist mirrors what the child could not cope with. It therefore encapsulates both the child's hope that someone else—the therapist—might have the resources to deal with the unmanageable, and the fear that no one will. (Rustin, 2001, p. 283)

Clinical example: Alexander

Background and social history

Ms K was an unemployed singer and a single mother in her late thirties, who lived in a small council flat on a rough estate. Her only son, Alexander, was conceived as the result of a difficult relationship that had broken down before he was born, and so Alexander had never met his father. Ms K had struggled to bring her son up on her own, with very little social or family support.

Ms K first contacted the Anna Freud Centre when Alexander was three years old. At the time, she described her child as "very demanding", and she experienced his neediness of her as unbearable, often reacting by shouting at him. The therapist who met with them felt that Ms K was quite "overwhelmed" as a mother and was "screaming to have her own space". Alexander, for his part, responded to his mother's depression with an anxious need to engage her, and—according to the therapist—did two "rather wonderful" pictures of his pet rabbits. A brief piece of work took place with the family, but Ms K proved difficult to engage, and the case was closed. Soon after, as we were to learn several years later, Ms K was involved in a serious road traffic accident, and for the next two years she was frequently bedridden and unable to fully parent Alexander, who was left to fend for himself and was often expected to care for his mother.

In the following years, Ms K's barbiturate misuse, which had been a problem for some time, became more pronounced. Especially at times when she felt overwhelmed by Alexander's demanding behaviour, she would turn to drugs, which made her withdrawn and drowsy; and as his efforts to engage her became more desperate, she could become angry and sometimes violent towards him. This resulted in a series of calls by neighbours to social services with concerns about Alexander's safety. A few times, he was briefly accommodated by social services, but with professionals all commenting on the "strong attachment" to his mother, he always returned home within a few days. And so the cycle would go on.

When Alexander was seven, an extreme incident made social services finally take action. One evening, Ms K, under the influence of drugs, verbally abused Alexander in the street, and dragged him home. She tried to put him to bed, but when he struggled to resist her, she covered his face with a pillow and tried to suffocate him. Alexander was saved by the arrival of a neighbour, who had heard a commotion. After this incident, Alexander was placed in emergency foster care and his name was put on the Child Protection Register, under the category of "physical abuse".

At this point, Ms K finally began to acknowledge her drug problem and to attend a regular treatment programme. Ms K was determined that her son should be returned to her care, and Alexander was equally clear that this was what he wanted. After four months, social services agreed that this should happen, and by the end of the year his name was removed from the Child Protection Register. Although both Ms K and her son had made considerable progress at several levels, it was felt that Alexander could benefit from individual psychotherapy.

At this point, Ms K had been off barbiturates for six months, and was working well with her own therapist within our service; but in that time, Alexander's behaviour had deteriorated. He suffered from nightmares, and at school he was not achieving academically and had poor concentration. He did not get on well with peers, and there were reports of bullying, some of which Alexander appeared to provoke. In the words of the astute referrer, Alexander was "overwhelmed by anxiety and thoughts about abandonment as well as his own potential destructiveness". Ms K agreed to the referral, and soon after Alexander turned ten, we met for the first time.

The assessment: a letter, a magic knot, and a burning house

At our first meeting, I was immediately struck by Alexander's appearance. He was tall for his age, and very thin, with bright blue eyes, open and alert. When I introduced myself, he was quiet, clearly nervous, but smiled softly and appreciatively when I voiced his anxiety.

Midway through the session, Alexander began to make an envelope. He wrote on it: "Don't open please, fine £50". I said that it sounded like the contents of this envelope were pretty secret—perhaps even dangerous—and that sometimes it might feel frightening opening things up. He quietly took another piece of paper and wrote this letter, which he showed to me:

> Dear my best mum. How are you? I love you so much. I am happy you are my mother. Do you love me? School is great. Lots of love Alexander. See you. Buy buy [sic].

I said that he wanted me to know that he loved his mum very much, but perhaps he was also worried for her, and felt he had to be good himself to make her happy. Alexander said nothing, but folded the paper and wrote on the outside of the envelope: "Dear mom and Dad were ever [sic] Dad is Ha Ha!". I added that he wished his dad could also be here, and it must be painful that he didn't know where his father is. Alexander looked quite sad, then started packing up.

The following week, we met again, and this time Alexander was more animated. He had brought some rubber bands with him, and offered to show me a magic trick, where he made a knot in the rubber band and then pulled on the knot and made it disappear. I said that problems were a bit like knots, sometimes they were difficult to get undone, but sometimes it was possible. He asked if I knew any magic, and I said maybe he was wondering if I was able to help untangle worries. He responded by tying two more knots, then he pulled one and showed that it could disappear and the other could not. I said maybe he was wondering whether his worries were so tangled up that nobody could help him get them unknotted. He nodded, then said very quietly: "This is what you do with bad worries", and he took a pair of scissors and cut the knotted rubber band into little pieces.

Alexander then got a piece of paper and started writing a story, which he called "The Burning House". In the story, a boy goes out to pick some sunflowers, and when he comes back his house has been burnt down. He saves his rabbit and calls the fire brigade, then realises that *he* left the fire on, so *he* is responsible. His house is destroyed, but he gets another house. This one is burnt down too, and the boy and his rabbit are killed.

In these first two meetings, Alexander had told me a great deal about his internal world. The envelope that mustn't be opened seems to represent Alexander's awareness of danger if he were to allow his true feelings to emerge—the neediness, perhaps, but also the rage. By keeping his feelings "under wraps", he could maintain the belief in a "best mum" who will love him—as long as he can show her how good he is going to be. But attempts to be the "good" child quickly collapse because inside he also feels himself to be so bad. His repeated efforts to make things good (getting a new house) are destroyed once again by his own "badness", and he receives the only punishment he feels that he deserves—death.

In retrospect, I felt that the disappearing knot might also reflect anxieties about loss—things that seem solid can just "disappear"— and the cutting up of the knot expressed his fear that separation could only be experienced as a traumatic loss or abandonment, not a gradual and mutual "untying". Perhaps this was also an indication of what Alexander did with his own capacity to think, when faced by over-whelming anxiety? The reference to his father's absence, of course, was also important, and was a clue about his rage towards—but also his yearning for—a father, feelings that were inevitably going to emerge in the transference.

The first year of treatment

At the end of the assessment period, our recommendation was that Alexander should have intensive treatment—starting twice a week, and gradually building up to four times per week—alongside his mother's own continuing therapy. The openness with which he had conveyed some of his internal struggles was in one respect a good indicator for analytic treatment, and I felt strongly that therapeutic work was possible with this child. Although I may not have admitted it at the time, I think there was also the beginnings of a "rescue fantasy" in my own mind, one that the professional network perhaps shared implicitly with their sense that a male psychotherapist was "just what Alexander needed".

Perhaps I was supposed to be the "missing father" that Alexander had never known—but it would not take long before it became clear that things were not going to be so straightforward as that.

Between the assessment and starting treatment, however, a further incident led to social services becoming involved with the family again, and although the assessment they undertook was kept separate from his treatment, Alexander was very conscious of social service's presence during the early period of therapy. Whereas those first meetings with me had been full of rich and powerful material, the sessions in these months were dull and repetitive, full of games of noughts and crosses or hangman, the symbolic significance of which could only be explored so many times. The need for Alexander to be in control, even at the cost of a certain deadness, was paramount. If, in our assessment meetings, it had felt dangerous to open the envelope, it now felt dangerous even to go near his box of toys. Sessions were at times interminably dull, and I struggled with my own feelings of boredom. In these first few months, I took up again and again how hard it must be to trust me when he felt under such close scrutiny.

On a few occasions, Alexander would respond to my interventions by letting me know, through his play, some of how he felt about what was happening around him. Once, he painfully expressed his own wishes and fears by speaking about his rabbit, which was about to have a litter. He described his passionate wish to see the baby rabbits "snuggled up against their mother drinking milk", while fearing that one of them might not survive, or that they would have to be given away because mother (his and the rabbits') could not cope. At times like this, I acknowledged these fears and wishes without trying to interpret their defensive quality, perhaps sensing that this period of relative calm (in the treatment) might provide a "background of safety" for the tempests that were to come.

While he carefully kept any of the "reality" of his life out of treatment, in the first few months Alexander gradually took more and more pleasure in coming to therapy and in playing simple games with me. As the frequency of sessions increased, he seemed to feel safer to express the strength of his longings, and I found that I myself was beginning to look forward to his sessions. I don't think I was fully prepared for how suddenly the emergence of Alexander's longing for a "new object" (Hurry, 1998) would flip over into its inevitable shadow—the rage at being disappointed and let down.

It was one Friday morning, about seven months into treatment, and Alexander was playing a game that he often asked to play—of throwing a foam ball into a rubbish bin in the corner and seeing how good a score he could get. On this particular morning, Alexander suddenly turned to me and asked whether I was married, and whether I had children myself? I took up his curiosity about what kind of father I would be. Alexander didn't say anything, but threw the ball into the bin once more. I wondered whether he felt that, like the foam ball, I just "threw him away" at the end of each week? Once again, Alexander said nothing.

When he returned the next Monday, however, Alexander was furious. He threw accusations at me as if he were throwing objects. Why did he have to come here anyway? What did I understand about him? Did I know what it was like to have "flashbacks" of his mother, dead on the floor? He kept referring to my wife and the "other children", and I interpreted his feeling that he couldn't believe that I cared for him when I just went off and left Alexander at the weekend. He shouted, saying that he knew I wanted to kill him, and I empathised with how terrifying this must be, and how frightened he was that if he gets angry I will retaliate and do something terrible.

Although I had some understanding of where this fury had come from, and in some ways had been expecting it, I was still totally unprepared when it actually exploded in the room. For the first time, I was given a taste of what it was like to be overwhelmed by an attack of such ferocity from this previously "gentle" child, that I felt stunned and couldn't think clearly. The traumatic experience, one might say, was now in the room with us.

Unfortunately, after this important session, Alexander's mother did not bring him back for a whole week. His mother's therapist contacted me to say that Alexander had been unmanageable after this session, and his mother had to keep him off school for three days. Ms K was apparently furious with me, and wanted me to tell Alexander that he was not allowed to behave like this, or to "take it out" on her. His mother's therapist was concerned about whether it was right to "open things up" like this for Alexander in the context of a parent who could not contain his anxieties?

A week later, Alexander did return, with his strong feelings back under wraps. He acted as if nothing had happened. After a while, I commented on this, and Alexander quietly agreed, adding that it was because he got flashbacks at school if he talked about things. Then he turned to the sink and asked "is this water safe to drink?". I remained silent, giving him space to form his own thoughts. Alexander paused, then said "yes, I think it is safe". I added that I thought a part of him believes it is safe here too, even if another part of him is very frightened of what might happen if he starts to trust me.

In the months to come, a pattern was to emerge, whereby whenever powerful feelings were expressed in the treatment, and Alexander became angry or upset, his mother would fail to bring him for several sessions, and he would return with his feelings once more "under wraps". At times, this made me feel that what I was doing was simply re-traumatising Alexander, encouraging him to "release" the demons and then failing to offer a secure space in which these feelings could be explored (see Lanyado, 1999).

Alexander continued to come, however, and gradually began speaking more about his life at home and at school. He spoke for the first time about his father and the little that he knew about him; and cautiously expressed his own wish for a father in his own life. This more trusting contact was once again punctuated by enormous explosions of rage, when Alexander would swear and physically attack the room (especially the doll's house, which he kicked ferociously), followed by attempts to "make up" with me. The way this pattern repeated itself conveyed a great deal about Alexander's fear of abandonment and anxieties about his destructiveness, which in quieter moments I tried to put into words. His behaviour was so provocative that he was constantly pushing me to retaliate—perhaps so that he would get the punishment that he felt sure he deserved; but also to "prove" to himself that I could not be trusted, that he did not need to take the risk of beginning to hope.

In the transference, the wish for a father and the rage at the abandoning father were also becoming more powerful. At the same time, the emergence of these wishes created a conflict, for Alexander's sense of psychological safety seemed to remain bound up with being part of a "team" with his mum. Any anger with his mum implied separation, and separation was deeply threatening. The introduction of a symbolic "third"—one that could offer a space for Alexander to begin a process of separation from his mother—was both a powerful attraction and a dangerous threat.

At the height of this intense period of involvement with his therapy, Ms K had a dispute with her own therapist at the clinic and suddenly withdrew Alexander from his treatment. A series of crisis meetings were called to try and address the situation, and after a number of weeks, Alexander resumed his treatment. But when he returned, things had changed. Alexander didn't want to be there. I tried to speak of how he had perhaps begun to think that I really was someone who was there for him, and that made it even worse now when he felt let down and I hadn't been able to protect our space together. Alexander told me to fuck off, and started hitting his head against the wall. Over the next few weeks, the sessions were terrible. Alexander poured out streams of accusations against me, tried to smash the things in the room, and then attacked himself, challenging me to stop him. Alexander began to miss more and more sessions, and his mother didn't contact us or offer any explanation, except to say that he didn't want to come and she couldn't make him.

With his transfer to secondary school coming up in the summer at the end of his first year of treatment, Alexander insisted that he wanted a "new start"—no more of the old school, no more of social services, and no more of me. He emphasised again how he and his mum were a "team", and no-one would come between them.

In some way, of course, he was right, for if Alexander had dealt with his absolute dependence on an abusive parent by submitting and identifying with her, then the beginnings of a trusting relationship to me threatened that identification. When the external reality of his mum's conflict with the clinic intensified the terror Alexander felt about abandoning this identification, he quickly withdrew into a more complete, utter identification with her. He appeared to repress his own feelings and resorted once more to denial, splitting, and projection of the "bad mother" to create instead the image of the "bad therapist" (Shengold, 1989, p. 65).

During the next few weeks leading up to the summer break, Alexander's attendance became even more irregular, and it seemed as if the therapy was on the verge of breaking down. His mother, too, felt it was time to move on. She said they both needed "closure", and she wasn't prepared to continue bringing him. Things were more settled at school and she was proud of Alexander's decision to say he wanted to stop. When he did come, though, it was sometimes possible to get beyond his manifest wish to stop coming to his deeper fear of loss, and to link this fear to the many losses that Alexander had already experienced in his life. Finally, as the summer break drew nearer, Alexander agreed that I should discuss with his mother about the possibility of him continuing to come to therapy once a week after the summer, and I agreed to this. The treatment had been "saved", but at a great price.

Looking back, I wonder now how much I unconsciously colluded with this decision to cut down Alexander's sessions, while at an overt level I battled ferociously to maintain the frequency of his therapy. The temptation to "turn a blind eye" (Ralph, 2001)—to think it would be better not to have to face this—was intense.

The second year of treatment

Alexander, now eleven years old, made the transition to a large secondary school far better than any of us had expected, and the school reported few concerns. At home, his mum began to earn a small income for the first time since his infancy, and they both clearly expressed their wish to "move on".

Alexander's weekly sessions took place after school at the same time as his mother saw her therapist. In the following months, his attendance continued to be erratic, and when he did come, he was relentlessly hostile. He would attack me verbally and physically, spitting his words out as if they were daggers—that he didn't want to be in therapy, that I wasn't there when he really needed somebody, and that nobody could understand what it was like to be him. He mocked my words and sarcastically mimicked what I said, or simply screamed when I tried to speak. He would pace around our small room like a caged animal, kicking at the furniture, picking up any loose objects and throwing them at my face and body, and when I tried to stop him, he said that the only thing I cared about was "my room".

As Margaret Rustin (2001) has described, in her work with equally traumatised patients, what is most significant at times like this is not the violence *per se*, but rather the sadistic intent of the violence, mocking and trying to push the therapist to break down and expose their "despicable" weakness and vulnerability. During this period, I often woke up in the morning dreading my sessions with Alexander and half-hoping he wouldn't come. In the sessions themselves, I often felt like I couldn't catch my breath, almost *as if I was suffocating*. (Only in supervision afterwards was I able to make the connection with Alexander's own terrifying experience at the hands of his mother.)

But if it was necessary for me to have some experience of being the victim of the trauma, at least in an attenuated form, there were also times when I felt like the potentially abusive adult—a role, as Ann Horne has pointed out, that "challenges our professional identity as belonging to the 'good guys'" (Horne, 1999, p. 354). Certainly, there were times, when Alexander's attacks on me were at their height, when I felt like I could have killed him, feelings that took a great deal of supervision and analysis to gradually acknowledge. And yet, as Winnicott (1949) spelled it out in his important paper "Hate in the counter-transference", such acknowledgement is vital, for the analytic patient cannot be expected to tolerate *his* feelings of hate if the analyst cannot tolerate his own hatred of the patient.

Faced by such powerful transference and countertransference enactments, it is tempting, as a therapist, either to emotionally cut off and withdraw, which may well evoke the child's anxiety about abandonment, or to respond punitively, in a way that confirms the child's inner representations of the adult world. Even if the therapist simply interprets the violent behaviour, as I sometimes tried to do by suggesting that Alexander was angry because he felt I was not always there for him, this may well be experienced by the child as being blamed for what he has done and the "understanding" is experienced only as a kind of humiliation. Monitoring my own *use* of interpretations was an important, but chastening, experience. Often, I found myself giving far more interpretations to Alexander the more lost, uncertain, and overwhelmed I was feeling myself. While the interpretation might have been "correct", its impulse—as Alexander no doubt sensed—was to defend myself, to get back some control, perhaps even to attack him back.

For Alexander, his violent attacks left him in a constant expectant state of punitive retaliation. Yet after many months of violent abuse, even though I was not consciously doing anything different from before, Alexander's violence gradually subsided. Perhaps this was due to the fact that he experienced some relief that I continued to be there for him, "undestroyed and undestroying" (Shengold, 1989, p. 313). Even now, I am not sure what it was that allowed this shift to take place, although Shengold's description of abused patients rings true. He writes:

> For these patients ... that the analyst continues to be there ... despite
> the murderous pitch of the patient's feelings, is a kind of miracle
> that has considerable ameliorative power. (1989, p. 313)

In the last two months before the summer break at the end of the second year of treatment, Alexander spoke again about his father, and his envy of those who have everything he wished he could have. He told me of his sense of having lots of different selves—his "hyper self" that acts crazy, his "pissed-off self", and his "shadow self", and how these can at times overwhelm him, making him feel utterly out of control. In conversation, we pieced together how Alexander sees his "real self" as so vulnerable and defenceless that to allow it to appear would be extremely dangerous and take considerable courage.

One day, Alexander brought a pen-knife to the session and spoke of being bullied at school and his thoughts of turning the knife against himself and wanting to die. (At that moment, I thought back to that early meeting when Alexander had cut the knot into tiny pieces with his scissors.) We spoke of this now as his "darkest shadow self", and I remembered also his "furious self", and how for so long, this was all that he had shown me, and that perhaps that had been his only way of letting me know what it felt like to be a victim of bullying. Alexander smiled weakly, and said "I'm sorry, I wasn't really angry with *you*".

Although I was extremely worried about him during this period, I was also hopeful. Perhaps for the first time, after two years of treatment, it felt as if Alexander was beginning to tolerate some insight into his intra-psychic conflict, to bear some true depressive feelings, and to use his therapist as a separate, and potentially helpful, object (Shengold, 1989, pp. 311–315). But bringing the psyche back to life out of the ashes, as Alexander was beginning to do, also carries immense risks.

The following week, Alexander arrived, eager to show me his new school bag. After a little while, I said that I'd been thinking a lot about what we'd been talking about the previous week, and I guessed that he had too. Alexander nodded his head. After a pause, he said that yesterday he'd felt like stabbing himself. I asked what had made him feel like that, and he said he thought it was probably not having a father. I took this up, and he talked again about his father not even having cared enough to stay around and know that he existed.

Then gradually, he began to unfold the events of the previous day: his mum had been using drugs, and when she does that she scares him. (This was the first we had heard that she had begun using drugs again.) He told me himself for the first time the story of when his mum tried to suffocate him with a pillow. I acknowledged how scary this must be—and that without his dad, it meant that the person he loved the most was also the person who at times had been most frightening. He told me that last night she had been "off her head" and shouted at him, and he had gone to his room and gone to bed. The tears poured down his face as he told me that she had said "I'm going to kill you". He said that at times like that, he wanted to die—he wished someone *would* kill him—why didn't she just kill him? And there was nobody he could turn to.

When Alexander said this, I wondered if that was the worst thing of all, and remembered how he had sometimes screamed at me "why weren't you there when I needed you?". I wondered whether those were the times when his mother was using drugs again and he'd wanted to tell me but couldn't? Alexander nodded, and I acknowledged how scared he must have been about telling me, and how angry that I didn't stop these awful things from happening. By this point, it was almost the end of the session. Before finishing, I asked Alexander for permission to speak to his mum's therapist about what had been happening. He agreed to this, but when I spoke of how we would also need to think about contacting social services, Alexander's face crumpled into tears again, and he sobbed.

I shared my concerns with my colleagues, and we decided to offer Ms K a review meeting with the consultant psychiatrist. At this meeting, Ms K acknowledged her drug use and began to address what she would need to do to keep Alexander safe, and we agreed to share our concerns with social services and see how they could help. The psychiatrist liaised with the school, trying to see what help the school could offer regarding bullying. And I agreed to continue to monitor the situation in Alexander's therapy.

But when Alexander returned to therapy, after missing one week, he had once again become extremely angry. He was furious that I had mentioned social services, and told me that I was trying to ruin his life and to kill his mum. I tried to take up his fear of hurting her, but Alexander worked himself up into a rage, mocking my "cowardice" and telling me I was ruining his life. Then he walked out, and did not return in the last weeks before the summer break.

Towards the end of the summer break, we heard from Ms K that she had found a new flat in another part of London, and that Alexander would not be able to continue attending his therapy, as it would be too far to travel. My colleague who worked with Ms K tried to negotiate with her about the possibility of him continuing therapy; or at least to have a planned ending. Despite numerous phone calls, letters, and offers to speak to Alexander, I was not allowed to have any direct contact with him during this period, and when it was clear that Alexander would not be returning to therapy, we tried to help facilitate a referral to local services, so that Alexander could continue to access therapy. Ms K refused. We shared our concerns about the situation with social services in the area that the family had moved to, who said that they would monitor the situation; at this stage, they felt there were no direct child protection concerns. We did not hear anything further from the family; and I was not to meet with Alexander again.

Discussion

As I hope to have shown in this chapter, the interaction between traumatic and abusive experience, violent behaviour, and therapeutic help is complex and often unpredictable. Especially when the trauma has been at the hands of the main caregiver, and in the absence of any alternative protective adults, an identification with the aggressor may become the means of maintaining a sense of psychological "safety" in the face of extreme anxieties, often related to helplessness and abandonment. Such a way of dealing with internal states and external experiences, however maladaptive it may become later in life, remains deeply ingrained and inevitably is re-enacted when such children enter therapy. Unless this can happen, the children themselves may not be able to begin to have an experience of the trauma as something that can be contained and thought about.

Yet whether bringing the trauma into the consulting room is always therapeutic is by no means certain. Ferenczi, who first began the exploration of such work, believed that the analytic setting had the potential to *re-produce* the trauma, especially when the powerful countertransference feelings were denied and a defensive "benign neutrality" took its place; but he also had great hopes if the analyst could allow himself to be "put to the test", yet could maintain "genuine interest", absolute honesty, and a real desire to help. All this, he believed, might make life worth living once again for a "soul in bondage", acting as a "counterweight to the traumatic situation" itself (Ferenczi, 1932, p. 129).

And yet the need to hold onto the promise of a good and loving parent by identifying with the abuser is perhaps the source of the greatest resistance to therapy. For Alexander, the "objective" reality was a parent who really had tried to suffocate him, a reality that even I, as his therapist, had to struggle to keep in mind. To begin to actually think about this reality, as Alexander began to do after two years of therapy, posed enormous psychic risks.

Perhaps, for Alexander, these risks were too great. In his book about "soul murder", Shengold outlines some of the achievements that therapy can offer to these traumatised and abused patients, such as the ability to see, know, and stand for the terrible truth, to lessen the use of massive isolation and other defensive mechanisms and to be more tolerant of their own characteristic rage (Shengold, 1989, p. 67). But in a discussion of the victims of the concentration camps, Shengold makes an important aside that is of central importance to my work with Alexander:

> Of course [he writes] if one is still "living in a monstrous world" such insight is not necessarily useful. In the camp, denial is needed; and this can be so with children still in their abusing parent's care. (Shengold, 1992, p. 199)

This comment sums up, perhaps, the central dilemma of my work with Alexander, the dilemma that is at the heart of therapeutic work with children such as this, work which produces such extreme countertransference responses (Hoxter, 1983; Ralph, 2001; Rustin, 2001). Children who have experienced the kinds of trauma I have been describing lose not only their own sense of subjective reality, but also their faith in the external world. When childhood has been based on so much distrust—not just because of the projection of "bad" feelings, but also based on *experienced* reality—then the ability to accept the therapist as a predominantly benevolent figure who can help the patient to see and accept both their inner and outer reality "takes years of seemingly endless repetition and testing" (Shengold, 1989, p. 313). As Margaret Rustin puts it:

> Bringing the trauma into the room, into the relationship with the therapist, is what may enable us to make a difference. [But] to do the necessary work safely we have to ensure that we have time and adequate personal and professional support for ourselves. (Rustin, 2001, p. 284)

In the case of Alexander, however, we did not have the time. When faced with what might have been the start of a process of psychological separation, the therapy with Alexander broke down. It remains to be seen what Alexander will have made of his time in therapy or how his development will proceed. But although I was not to see Alexander again, a year later he sent me this letter, with which I will end this chapter:

> To Nick—Thank you for being my friend, whom I could talk to. I will miss you when you're not there. We had good sessions and bad sessions, but I don't care, because you'll always be a friend to me. Even though I shouted at you in our sessions I new [sic] you were the right person to talk to. I will miss you. Yours truly, Alexander.

References

Ferenczi, S. (1931). Child-analysis in the analysis of adults. In: *Final Contributions to the Problems and Methods of Psycho-Analysis*, ed. M. Balint (trans. E. Mosbacher). London: Karnac, 1980.

Ferenczi, S. (1932). *The Clinical Diary of Sándor Ferenczi*, ed. J. Dupont. London: Harvard University Press, 1995.

Ferenczi, S. (1988). Confusion of tongues between adults and the child: the language of tenderness and of passion. *Contemporary Psychoanalysis, 24*: 196–206.

Hodges, J., Lanyado, M. & Andreou, C. (1994). Sexuality and violence: preliminary clinical hypotheses from psychotherapeutic assessments in a research programme on young sexual offenders. *Journal of Child Psychotherapy, 20*: 283–308.

Hopkins, J. (1986). Solving the mystery of monsters: steps towards the recovery from trauma. *Journal of Child Psychotherapy, 12(1)*: 61–71.

Hoxter, S. (1983). Some feelings aroused in working with severely deprived children. In: M. Boston & R. Szur (Eds.), *Psychotherapy with Severely Deprived Children*. London: Karnac.

Hughes, C. (1999). Deprivation and children in care: the contribution of child and adolescent psychotherapy. In: M. Lanyado & A. Horne (Eds.), *Handbook of Child and Adolescent Psychotherapy*. London: Routledge.

Lanyado, M. (1999). The treatment of traumatization in children. In: M. Lanyado & A. Horne (Eds.), *Handbook of Child and Adolescent Psychotherapy*. London: Routledge.

Lanyado, M. (2009). Psychotherapy with severely traumatised children and adolescents: "far beyond words". In: M. Lanyado & A. Horne (Eds.), *Handbook of Child and Adolescent Psychotherapy*. London: Routledge.

Parsons, M. & Dermen, S. (1999). The violent child and adolescent. In: M. Lanyado & A. Horne (Eds.), *Handbook of Child and Adolescent Psychotherapy*. London: Routledge.

Ralph, I. (2001). Countertransference, enactment and sexual abuse. *Journal of Child Psychotherapy, 27/3*.

Rustin, M. (2001). The therapist with her back up against the wall. *Journal of Child Psychotherapy, 27/3*.

Shengold, L. (1989). *Soul Murder.* Yale: Yale University Press.

Shengold, L. (1992). Child abuse and treatment examined. *Bulletin of the Anna Freud Centre, 15/3*.

Winnicott, D. W. (1949). Hate in the counter-transference. *International Journal of Psycho-Analysis, 30*: 69–74.

PART II

ADOLESCENCE

CHAPTER THREE

Nobody died! trauma in adolescence

Catalina Bronstein

I would like to start with a quote from Bion:

> The more successful the memory is in its accumulations the more nearly it approximates to resembling a saturated element saturated with saturated elements. An analyst with such a mind is one who is incapable of learning because he is satisfied. (Bion, 1967, p. 29)

He added:

> I wish to reserve the term "memory" for experience related to conscious attempts at recall. These are expressions of a fear that some element, "uncertainties, mysteries, doubts" will obtrude. Dreamlike memory is the memory of psychic reality and is the stuff of psychoanalysis. (Bion, 1967, p. 70)

The reason why I quote these passages is because they highlight the line I will be taking in trying to explore the issue of trauma in adolescence. Whilst the memories of traumatic events impose themselves as a reminder of an overwhelming experience that threatened ego integrity by exposing it to an abrupt sense of helplessness, at the same time, as already stressed by Glover, memories of traumatic events can also hold a defensive function as they can be used by the subject to singularly explain a wide range of conflicts and emotional difficulties (Glover, 1929). The danger of an analysis that *aims* at reconstructing and eluci- dating trauma is that the analysis can become saturated with meaning, thus preventing the emergence of anything new and unimagined. The effect of traumatic events cannot be considered as if they were isolated psychic phenomena that need to be addressed in a special way. They should be considered alongside all other manifestations of the patient's psychic life. And this is of particular relevance when we think of adoles- cence, a time when the individual is under the influence of great physi- cal and psychological changes.

One of Freud's early cases was that of Emma, a young woman who sought help because of a symptom: she could not go into shops alone. Freud writes that Emma gave a reason for her phobia:

> [she produced] a memory from the time when she was twelve years old (shortly after puberty). She went into a shop to buy something and saw the two shop-assistants (one of whom she can remember) laughing together, and ran away in some kind of *affect of fright*. In connection with this, she was led to recall that the two of them were laughing at her clothes and that one of them had pleased her sexually. (Freud, 1895, p. 353; italics in original)

Freud goes on to explain that these memories could not explain either the compulsion or the determination of the symptom. Further investi- gation revealed a second memory from when Emma was eight years old, one that could be thought to be a traumatic situation: she went into a shop to buy sweets and the shopkeeper had grabbed at her genitals through her clothes. In spite of the first experience, Emma returned once more to the shop. Freud says that a state of "oppressive bad conscience" could be traced back to this experience (Freud, 1895, p. 354). At this stage, Freud had not yet discovered the relevance of infantile sexuality. But his proposition was that at the time of scene two (at puberty), the memory of scene one aroused a "sexual release" (Freud, 1895, p. 354) which was transformed into anxiety. This is an example of what he later called "deferred action" (*Nachträglich*[1]), which he explored further in the case of the Wolf Man.

Freud postulated two moments in the constitution of a traumatic situation: an earlier time when there is an event that is registered by the psyche but that has no traumatic effect, and a later time when the individual is able to understand it and to be moved by it and when its effect is felt to be highly conflictive and gives origin to symptoms (Freud, 1918b). The connection between the two scenes that have traumatic significance is based on links between representations, from the workings of the association of thoughts.

We might ask ourselves why, according to Freud, the scene that would mark the constitution of a previous experience as "traumatic" occurred at the age of twelve. This is because Freud takes into account different stages of development in the individual and considers that each developmental stage provides the background within which we perceive reality, both external and internal. Following this, Rangell proposed the idea of a stratification of traumas that are phase-specific during the course of development. For example, the primal scene might not be felt to be traumatic to the neonate, but it may become an overwhelming traumatic stimulus a few years later. Rangell suggests that phase-specificity is what makes both cumulative trauma and retrospective trauma have an effect on the individual (Rangell, 1967).

Without dismissing the enormous impact that pubertal changes have on the individual and the importance that developmental stages have on the constitution of what is a traumatic experience, I think that we cannot consider the impact of developmental stages separately from other psychic processes. It seems important to me to place developmental stages within the context of the complex interplay of unconscious phantasies, anxieties, and internal object relations that constitute our psychic world from birth onwards.

What is it about puberty that can dramatically change the background that informs our perception of the world?

The thrust of adolescence imposes changes that take over mind and body. Even though this is a time of upheaval that can easily lead to disturbances, it is also a time for growth, physically and emotionally. A time when differentiation from parents and cravings for new models of identification and for a distinct identity heighten curiosity, excitement, and hope, while also triggering anxiety and a longing to go back into an often idealised pre-pubertal state. A time when even the concept of time becomes part of the revolution that sets up in the adolescent's mind. The dramatic acceleration of bodily growth, the sense of urgency and need for immediate gratification, the feeling that they have no time to lose, is mixed with a sense of endless time ahead, a sense of immortality.

Adolescence is certainly a time when the now no longer child feels at the crossroads of diverse, conflictive and convergent, feelings and anxieties that have to be negotiated. These changes were described by Freud to be "destined to give infantile sexual life its final, normal shape" (Freud, 1905d, p. 207).

It could be said that some adolescents experience pubertal changes in a traumatic way. I think, though, that it is important to clarify the difference between an adolescent's reaction to a traumatic situation that happened in his infancy, childhood, or even during adolescence itself, from an adolescent who feels that pubertal changes and other developments are intrinsically traumatic.

While a particular traumatic situation that happened in childhood or in adolescence can contribute to turning the experience of adolescence itself into a traumatic one, holding on to trauma as the main explanation for causality can sometimes ease confusion in an adolescent who is struggling with conflictive feelings under the increased pressure of drives and phantasy activity that he cannot process. In these cases, a "traumatic experience" can provide a coherent narrative that eases the adolescent's anxiety about being driven mad by "out-of-control", incoherent, and confusing thoughts and feelings, thus saturating his potential psychic space with a fixed notion of causality.

Trauma

It would be helpful to remind ourselves of the distinction made by Freud between the actual traumatic *event*—which we do not have access to—and the emotional experience or response to that event, that is felt to be the *reaction* to the trauma. We don't have access to the event, we can only have access to the individual's perception and memories of a particular event. The "trauma" itself cannot be apprehended, it does not have a psychic register. As Lacan said, trauma is "something faced with when all words cease and all categories fail" (Lacan, 1988, Seminar II, p. 164). What we are left with is with the individual's experience of a certain event, and this is what we mean by "traumatic situation". The meaning of traumatic experiences can change throughout life for many reasons and amongst them we have to take into account the impact of different developmental stages on the individual and the vicissitudes of memory itself, whether it is implicit or explicit (Target, 1998).

As I mentioned at the beginning, Freud alluded to this when he postulated the concept of *Nachträglichkeit* (deferred action), thus leaving aside a "model of mechanical causality and linear temporality for a dialectic concept of causality and a 'spiral' model of temporality where future and past condition and signify each other reciprocally in the structuring of the present" (Baranger, 1988, p. 115).

The word "trauma" implies an idea of shock, of an injury or wound to the individual, and the idea of consequences or effects of such an injury (Laplanche & Pontalis, 1973). It can be used to describe a series of phenomena from a single event to an accumulation of events and, as Kris said, it is sometimes not easy to distinguish between

> ... the effects of ... a single experience, when reality powerfully and often suddenly impinges on the child's life—the shock trauma ... and the effect of long lasting situations, which may cause traumatic effects by the accumulation of frustrating tensions—the strain trauma .... (Kris, 1956, p. 72)

If we add to this Khan's concept of cumulative trauma, we have a huge range of internal and external circumstances that can be subsumed under this concept, from individuals suffering the effects of the Holocaust or torture to the birth of a sibling or the death of a parent (Khan, 1963). We might also have to take into account earlier traumas, some of which might have been very early and not remembered (Britton, 2006; Greenacre, 1953).

Even though trauma has always occupied an important place in psychoanalytic theory, its centrality diminished after Freud's abandonment of the seduction theory in favour of the role of phantasy in psychic life. However, over the last ten years, reported "recovered memories" of sexual abuse in the USA brought the issue of trauma and its reconstruction back with renewed force (Target, 1998). We encounter now not only a renewed interest on the effect of traumatic situations on the individual but also a question as to how, if at all, should analysts address the particular memories and reactions brought by traumatic events? This is very much linked to the question of how psychic change is achieved and what place we should give in an analysis to historical factors. It is also around this subject that the issue of reconstruction becomes paramount. Should we aim specifically at reconstructing trauma? Is it helpful to have this as an "aim", or is it that traumatic experiences should be considered as any other material that comes up in the patient's discourse?

Freud's development of the concept of trauma and of "traumatic situation" underwent many changes, and this has been explored in depth by many different authors (for example, Baranger, 1988; Furst et al., 1967; Garland et al., 1998; Kris, 1956; Zepf, 2008). I would just like to highlight here the move in Freud from a description that is predominantly economic to the restructuring of his theory of trauma based on its relation to anxiety, the emphases on its internal aspect without necessarily renouncing to the "real" basis of traumatic neurosis, thus including the interaction between external and internal situations and the inter-structural nature of all traumatic situations, for example, in the fear of losing the love of the superego (Baranger, 1988). We can thus see that the concept of trauma is inextricably bound up with the theory of anxiety, of drives, and of intra-psychic conflict. It is only when the concept of trauma is tied in with the concept of anxiety that the notion of "traumatic situation" acquires its full meaning (Freud, 1926d; Stratchey, 1959).

Freud's paper "Inhibitions, symptoms and anxiety" is a landmark contribution to the understanding of the workings of the ego in its relation to anxiety. In this paper, Freud brings together the economical perspective with his theory of psychic conflict. The generation of anxiety relates to a situation of danger to the ego, basically, to an *expectation* of danger. Symptoms are needed in order to protect the ego from such potential danger. But what is the source of this danger? Freud distinguishes between real danger, as one that threatens the subject from an external object, and "neurotic" danger, as the "one that threatens him from an instinctual demand" (Freud, 1926d, p. 165). But while real danger is one that is known, neurotic danger is a danger that has to be discovered. Both sources of danger can be mingled, and even though the individual might be facing a real danger-situation, "a certain amount of instinctual anxiety is added to the realistic anxiety" (Freud, 1926d, p. 168). The "danger" is linked to the ego's "helplessness": "physical helplessness if the danger is real and psychical helplessness if it is instinctual. … Let us call a situation of helplessness of this kind that has been actually experienced a *traumatic situation*" (Freud, 1926d, p. 166). Anxiety is the reaction to helplessness of the ego and is later reproduced as a signal, a weakened version in order to direct its course (Freud, 1926d, pp. 166–167).

As Laplanche and Pontalis described it, a traumatic situation refers to:

> an event in the subject's life defined by its intensity, by the subject's incapacity to respond adequately to it, and by the upheaval and long-lasting effects that it brings about in the psychical organisation. (Laplanche & Pontalis, 1973, p. 465)

> It derives its traumatic force from psychical conflict that prevents its integration into his conscious life. Its effectiveness derives from the phantasies it activates and from the influx of instinctual excitation it provokes. (Laplanche & Pontalis, 1973, p. 468)

Freud's revision of his theory of drives and his introduction of the concept of the death drive had an impact on his theory of trauma in his suggestion that the instinctual demand whose satisfaction the "ego recoils" at, can be a masochistic one derived from "the instinct of destruction directed against the subject himself" (Freud, 1926d, p. 168). Freud proposed that the death drive is always bound by libidinal forces in what is mostly a dynamic equilibrium between the drives, that is one where life and death drives come together so that we can never find pure instinctual impulses, but instead fusions in different proportions. The trauma influences these fusions, provoking an

> *entmischung* or defusion, which in turn activates the compulsion to repeat on the one hand, and on the other, demands new libidinal cathexes and new defensive measures of the ego …. (Baranger, Baranger & Mom, 1988, p. 119)

However, as Klein stated, "… no danger-situation arising from external sources could ever be experienced by the young child as a purely external and known danger" (Klein, 1948, p. 39). We can even add, as Paul Verhaeghe suggested, that, "The drive itself, independent of any externally determined trauma, has a potentially traumatising effect, to which the psyche has to come up with an answer" (Verhaeghe, 1998).

Following this, a situation might become traumatic when it is felt to trigger an unsustainable conflict between life and death drives, conflict that threatens the ego with a potential defusion of the drives and its potential annihilation (Baranger, Baranger & Mom, 1988). The traumatic experience becomes an actualisation of the subject's worst fears and anxieties, those of the survival of the self and of its objects.

Adolescence

I made an excursion into the role of the drives in the constitution of a traumatic experience as I think this is highly relevant when thinking about trauma in adolescence. Adolescents are faced with the potential overpowering effect of their drives, both libidinal and aggressive. The pre-pubertal child's image of himself has to give way to take into account a changing body, a mature sexual body with the concomitant change in his sense of identity. Irreversible sexual development and the accompanying changes in their bodies give rise to a reworking of the Oedipus complex, to a changing image of themselves as well as a changing image of the parents. These changes trigger powerful anxieties that evoke again the intense experiences and anxieties of early infancy. But these anxieties are now reawakened in a radically different setting, that of a sexually mature body (Bronstein, 2000). In the face of this, some adolescents resort to powerful defences to try to control the threat of potential disorganisation brought about by the intensification of drive activity and by the psychic conflict generated by it, with the concomitant intensification of paranoid anxiety. These are times when the adolescent might lose the capacity for symbolic functioning and feel things in a very concrete way, he might have a heightened sensitivity to feeling attacked and might feel persecuted by a harsh superego that tortures the adolescent with guilt over his overpowering sexual and aggressive impulses and phantasies (Bronstein, 2010). Within this background, certain situations that some adolescents might find difficult though not traumatic can become highly traumatic to other adolescents.

A brief example of the above is a seventeen-year-old boy whom I will call Roy and whom I saw for therapeutic consultations at a centre for adolescents. He was referred by his GP at the age of seventeen after Roy was mugged in the street and became terrified of leaving home. He recounted how, one evening, on his way home, he was mugged by two boys. It was dark and they approached him from behind. They took away his mobile phone. Roy was aware that one of the boys was carrying a knife and he wisely gave them his mobile phone without attempting to resist. This episode triggered a breakdown of his capacity to function independently. Roy fell into a state of fear and anxiety and became totally dependent on his parents and on an older sister, who had to drive him everywhere and collect him from the Tube station. Roy felt he could not go anywhere on his own. His mother brought him to see me, and she had to wait and take him back home as he would not accept going anywhere on his own.

Roy described a situation that carried great conviction for him: he felt that until the mugging, his life was absolutely fine. He had no problems, went to college, had a girlfriend. His family life was felt to be fine. The mugging had changed everything. He felt that his anxiety was justified, and for a while he firmly held on to this explanation and repeated it each time we met. We could not move anywhere, as he found any attempts at talking and thinking about anything else to be very difficult. It was as if he needed to go over and over the mugging experience. Even though this was partly in order to try to deal with it, to bind the anxiety stirred by it as well as to make him feel less helpless and more in control, it also had a very defensive quality as it suffocated any attempt at expanding understanding.

After some meetings, he did manage to tell me that some months prior to the mugging he was found to be diabetic. He had been feeling unwell for quite a while and one day he lost consciousness and had to be taken urgently into hospital. In subsequent sessions, a number of things slowly started to emerge, which I will summarise:

- He was terrified of dying from his diabetes. Friends and family were all instructed as to what they should do should Roy lose consciousness.
- He could recall that this fear was like what he had felt when he was mugged. He remembered that one of the boys pushed him and on falling he felt terrified that he might be left to die.
- When we could make the link between his fear of being assaulted and killed by some external aggressive action and his fear of the diabetes that was experienced as a potential internal killer, he started to be able to think more freely.

What started to emerge was that the diabetes was also experienced as an internal aggression, an overwhelming experience which was out of control. The "trauma" of the mugging was now displaced to another "trauma", that of his diabetes. Roy then started to be able to think and talk about a number of things that he had previously felt in an unconnected way: his rage towards his father, mainly when he felt that his father expected him to do certain things and would not respect Roy's maturity; his rage towards his mother, whom he felt was too intrusive.

He felt he could not stand up to either his father or mother. At one point, his mother demanded that he gave her his mobile phone because she suspected he was not going to school and did not believe what Roy was telling her. She wanted to check his text messages. As he refused to give her his mobile phone, she put her hand in his pocket and took the phone by force. This provoked such rage and fear of hitting his mother that he went to his room and hit the wall with his fists until he damaged himself. I think that the self-harming behaviour was triggered by his sense of hatred and impotence about how to deal with his aggression towards his mother, who was not just attacking him but also potentially exciting him through the close physical contact. Both sexual and aggressive feelings were felt to be overwhelming and could not be contained.

We could then think together about his fear of his own libidinal and aggressive impulses. In his phantasy, this was materialised by his diabetes that was felt to confirm the potentially lethal power of his feelings and phantasies. His fear of death—meaning fear of being out of control—was matched by his anxiety about having a weapon—the insulin—that he could potentially use to attack himself, even to kill himself. Whilst the insulin could be seen as what was keeping him alive, Roy mostly felt that it was a weapon that he could use to destroy himself. We could also speculate that the syringe with insulin was unconsciously linked to his phantasy of his new masculine body (and penis), a potential life-giver that could easily turn into a lethal weapon he could not control. For Roy, the need to feel in control was therefore of paramount importance.

When we think of trauma in adolescence, we have to be aware of the potential for self-destructive behaviour and that the anxiety the adolescent feels is not just about being destroyed by external forces but also by his own sexual/aggressive drives that can be experienced as coming from the body and can also, in phantasy, be projected into the body. Roy became aware of his frequent misuse of the injections that led to great difficulties in controlling the diabetes (Fonagy & Moran, 1990). There was a compulsive element in his attack on himself, with the misuse of insulin matched by his hatred of his parents and older sister whom he felt were constantly teasing him and humiliating him. His hatred and guilt could not find another resolution. At the same time, the identification with the aggressor, that, according to Blum (1987), would be automatic in the case of trauma, was threatening even more the breakthrough of his hostility, in particular towards those members of his family whom he felt were weaker (mother and sister) and into whom he projected himself as well.

The exploration of all this allowed Roy to become freer: he started to come to see me on his own, renewed the relationship with his girl-friend, went back to riding his bicycle, and became far better able to cope with his diabetes. He managed to have a conversation with his doctor and talk to him about his fears about the diabetes and to get a more realistic picture of his illness and of how to manage it. The ses-sions were no longer saturated by the mugging incident, and we could explore a range of issues, from his worries about his studies, his sexual-ity, his relationships to his peers, to his parents, and to himself.

Given the shortness of the treatment, there were many aspects that could not be explored and, without psychoanalysis, it is difficult to know more about the unconscious meanings of his actions and of the traumatic situation in their relation to his view of himself and to his early identifications. But we can still try to understand some of the many variables that underlined Roy's experience of the mugging as a "trauma". The role of aggression seems to play a particular role in it as it confirmed his fear of the potential lethal power of his own aggression. It also had a quality akin to the "threat to the psychological self" as described by Fonagy (Fonagy, Moran & Target, 1993, p. 482).

I think that the "traumatic experience" lent meaning and signification to a series of phantasies and experiences that were linked to Roy's view of himself and of his Oedipal objects. He partly held on to the trauma because of the secondary benefits of the illness and the regression to an infantile dependency on his mother that reassured him, and perhaps her as well, that he was still a little boy, therefore validating that he was in need of protection from the aggression coming from the external world. But I think that more important than this, was that the mugging became the representative, the symptom that bound the aggression he was struggling with prior to this episode.

Mourning in adolescence

Moses Laufer underlined some of the tasks of adolescence, psychological areas in which changes must normally take place. These include:

1. a change in the relationship to parents from having been depend-ent on the parents to becoming more independent emotionally

(for example, the adolescent should be able to risk involving disapproval from the parents without feeling that he must give in to them);

2. a change in the relationship to his contemporaries; and
3. a change in his attitude to his body. This involves a change in the picture of himself from that of a child who was mainly in the care of his parents to becoming the "owner" of his own body and responsible for his sexually maturing body (Laufer, 1972).

All these processes involve mourning.

Moving away emotionally from parents involves an experience of inner freedom and trust that internalised objects will continue to be loved and loving despite the differences. This task is never uneventful and will always be somehow conflictive as the adolescent needs to feel that he can "fight the parents without feeling he is harming or destroying them" (Laufer, 1972, p. 32).

Shedding of family dependences and a certain psychic restructuring to include a different physical body that includes mature genitals, as well as the reworking of the Oedipus complex, involves a re-actualisation of mourning processes whereby the acceptance of separateness from the parental object includes having to bear the passage of time. Similarly to the way by which pubertal changes become the concrete evidence of the existence of productive sexual organs that actualise the Oedipus situation, there is also an increased awareness of time passing and age. Unconscious phantasies of immortality and a sense of triumph over ageing parents often coexist with a sense of time running too fast, an experience of fragility, fear of death, and hypochondriacal ideation. The sequential, diachronic temporality underlined by Freud in *The Three Essays* has to be put together with the structural perspective where, as Green emphasised, historical and structural axes complement each other (Green, 2007; Perelberg, 2007).

Unresolved infantile conflicts become highlighted in adolescence. When, for a number of reasons, a child deals with his pre-Oedipal and Oedipal conflicts by a retreat into a world of omnipotent phantasies and denial of reality, pubertal changes can be felt to traumatically impinge on this delicate psychic equilibrium. For example, when there is a need to deny the passage of time by holding on to a phantasy of never growing up, or if the child denies the reality of his or her gender, then the changing body can be felt to be overwhelming the already precarious sense of psychic stability. The adolescent's body now imposes a reality that is difficult to sustain and to integrate, and it can lead to the adolescent having to resort to more manic defences and to take refuge in an omnipotent defensive organisation that precludes any experiences of loss and mourning (Bronstein, 2010).

This is particularly relevant when the adolescent's aggression towards both object and self impinges on the mourning processes that are a necessary part of adolescent development. When there are unresolved infantile experiences of loss and/or when one of the parents is close to death or has died, the loss can be felt to become the "trauma" that binds all the many different conflictive phantasies and anxieties. Under analytic exploration, this traumatic experience lies at the convergence of an indefinite flow of associations. It is only through the understanding of how these complexities become manifested in the transference relationship that the "traumatic situation" can be really understood.

Daniel[2]

A nineteen-year-old boy who I will call Daniel came to analysis having suffered a breakdown. He was very anxious, could not sleep, and was dangerously reckless in his behaviour, putting himself at risk of death from self-inflicted accidents. Daniel was assailed by terrifying thoughts that his father would suddenly die. He thought his problems started when his father needed an operation for a potentially life-threatening condition when Daniel was twelve. This operation came as a great shock to him and seemed to signal his father's vulnerability. I would like to discuss him in order to show how the "trauma" in relation to his father's illness could be connected to other traumatic events in his childhood as well as having the role of communicating and giving meaning to a deadly internal landscape in which he felt imprisoned.

Daniel's mother told the analyst who referred him to me that she experienced his birth to be very traumatic. She was told that the baby had the cord wrapped around his neck, and as a result she had to undergo an emergency Caesarean section. After his birth, his mother refused to see him for ten days. Daniel was never breastfed. During this initial period, he was looked after by his father and an aunt. After the birth, when the baby was taken home, he refused to take in any food. This reached such a dangerous level that his parents feared for his life.

Daniel often got involved in risky activities that could potentially lead to death, from "off-piste" skiing under dangerous weather conditions, to consuming large doses of alcohol, collapsing in the street, driving when drunk, and so on. He suffered a number of accidents, some of which left some physical impairments. He often felt that he wanted to die, whilst at the same time, he seemed to sustain the belief that he would never die.

Daniel came to analysis after spending a large amount of money on his father's credit card. He spent it on drinks, inviting his friends to clubs and flying abroad whenever he wanted to. He could not study or do anything, other than sleeping, drinking, and being promiscuous. From the beginning of his analysis, he described terrible mental states in which he was assailed by terror at the possibility of his father's death. He described the scene that occurred at the age of twelve, and then another one he remembered from when he was younger and he was fetched from school and told that his father was very ill and he thought he could die.

For Daniel, this was the "trauma" that since its occurrence permeated his life. His father survived the operation. His father's operation occurred very close to the death of Daniel's paternal grandfather. This coincidence confirmed the potential lethal effect of the death of a father. It was also felt to be the confirmation of the potential lethal effect of a son's attitude towards his father. The terror of his father's death pervaded Daniel's entire life and was the source of frequent nightmares.

Daniel lived a bit like Peter Pan, in an illusory world, an omnipotent and mindless state of mind where he never had to meet the reality of time passing. But this Peter Pan figure was not just after simple pleasures. It was also imbued with masochistic gratification. This was enacted in his life and in the analysis in many ways. The most evident manifestation of this in the analysis was his non-attendance to his sessions. Whenever he felt touched and emotionally moved, he disappeared. For a number of years, he mostly came to two or three of his five sessions. He came and went as if we were in agreement that the analysis was timeless, that it would never end, and that we would never die.

Daniel had recurrent dreams which were mostly about death. I would like to describe two dreams from different times in his analysis. These serve to illustrate how the traumatic situation was lived out in these dreams while also reflecting a constellation of his conflictive relationships to his objects.

In the first two years of his analysis, Daniel's main feeling was one of anxiety about the possibility that his father could die. In his third year of analysis, he brought the following dream:

> His father has died. He saw himself at every stage of his father's funeral and burial and at each stage he left. He sort of "forgot" that he was attending his father's funeral and left but then he got into a panic and ran to get back there. He saw himself doing this several times. He said that then, a part of himself, "another Daniel" woke him up "knowing" that he was suffering and that he was feeling unbearable anxiety. (Bronstein, 2010)

As we know, a dream is over-determined and can lead us to numerous possible interpretations. This dream on one level refers directly to his traumatic experience. It could also be understood to refer to his Oedipal conflict in relation to his father. However, the thing that seemed most alive to me was the way in which the dream communicated his unconscious awareness of his desperate attempts to try to evade his own psychic reality. A "Daniel part of himself" woke him up, knowing that he could not bear watching the "other" Daniel, the one who suffers, the one who goes back and back to the scene of the crime.

What motivates his need to go back to the dead object, and who is this dead object? The dead father of the dream is the Oedipal father, but he is also the object who carries the projections of Daniel's own deadly activities (including his attack on his own masculinity and development) which he feels forced to face by the analysis and which fills him with dread. But there is equally a sense of dread about getting away. This dread partly derived from a deep persecuting sense of guilt. I think, though, that it was mostly a dread of being left without aspects of the self, like being left without a "mind" that remembers, a cancellation of his capacity to think—a kind of *psychic* death. The conflict is unsustainable and he needs to wake himself up. The wish to change and the resistance to change are embedded in the traumatic situation. I think that, as Bion has described, they are both experienced as potentially catastrophic (Bion, 1966). The fear for his own death came up in the following dream that was experienced in a hallucinatory way:

> It was not a dream, he felt it happening, his hair was going white! He knew it and he didn't have to look at the mirror. (Bronstein, 2010)

A year later, after a very difficult and torturing separation from his girlfriend, and after a session in which I mentioned the word "mourning", he missed the next session. On coming back, he explained that he did not come because his boiler had exploded and he was left without heating and water. It was freezing in the apartment. He added that he was also angry with me because of my use of the word "mourning". "Nobody died!" he exclaimed. He then said he had a dream:

> I dreamt about my friend Michael. He knew he was going to die. This time it was not my father but Michael. He was not dead but he was going to die the next day. I cried and cried. In the dream Michael spoke to my father who said "tell me if I can do something for you" as if it was nothing very important. Daniel said: "He did not die but I knew he was going to die."

I took up that he felt that I did not recognise the impact that my use of the word "mourning" had on him. It felt like an explosion that left him without vital resources for his survival. He felt at risk mainly about coming today.

He looked upset and moved. He then brought a memory from when he was thirteen. He collected figures of footballers. He thought that his collection was fantastic. He would have liked to be a great sportsman. The album had to be perfect and he had nearly completed it. He just missed getting one.

> I was very attached to it and one day my mother got cross with me and she tore the album up. I was so upset and cried and cried. I think that she felt guilty because she then said sorry and gave me the money and wanted me to get another album but it was never the same.

I think that in this dream, Daniel could allow himself to be emotionally closer to the experience of loss and pain, a move from a rather blind and overwhelming anxiety and panic. There is also an awareness that it is about him, as Michael is a friend whom he sees to be similar to himself. There is a less persecutory atmosphere in the dream, now replaced by a sadder one. But, following his associations, we can see that psychic pain is not just about confronting painful *feelings* of loss for the object. It was derived from the abrupt loss and brutal collapse of something that keeps him going, of his only way to gain access to a sense of masculinity, to a sense of identity. This is connected to his idealisation of the footballers that he feels his mother brutally destroys, just at the point when he felt he might really achieve it (only one picture left to make the album complete).

This was being re-lived in the analysis. My use of the word "mourning" I think was felt by him to brutally threaten his own capacity to escape from pain into the idealised world. But rather than seeing the possibility of me sharing the pain with him and trying to help him, he felt it was a sadistic attack on his fragile sense of integration. It is as if he had rebuilt his shaken identity on the basis of projecting himself into idealised paternal figures, only to be threatened by the analysis with the destruction of the mechanisms on which he based this precarious sense of inner security. The "memory" of his mother's cruelty at a point when he was becoming a man brought up the complexity of his feelings towards an internalised mother (the analyst in the transference) as somebody whom he needed but who mindlessly and cruelly destroyed his search for an omnipotent, "perfect" masculinity.

But the album might not just represent idealised masculine figures. It also represents hardworking sportsmen and a hardworking child who patiently built up his album. It was also probably unconsciously linked to his experience of a mother who rejected him. What is interesting is that the method used by this "mother" which in his identification is now part of the self, is one that "eliminates", throws into the bin, positive aspects of the self. This is a method my patient employed when he threw away what he felt might be useless sessions only to realise, albeit too late, that he attacked valuable parts of the self. To become aware that he was the one who was now attacking his own valued aspects of the self and of his objects was part of the task of analysis.

It is difficult to speak of one traumatic experience in isolation. One traumatic experience can be linked to many other ones, in this case probably an earlier one, when the rejection of the baby by his mother might have been experienced as an abrupt and brutal attack, one that might have left him facing what Bion called "nameless dread".

The presenting "trauma" and its effects can be thought of in terms of particular meanings that the individual attributes to historical events. There is abundant evidence from psychological research to support this assumption that recollection is reconstructive, unreliable, and strongly influenced by motivation.

We can then speculate that the terrible thought of "the death of his father" became a very complex, over-determined construction sustained by a different number of unconscious phantasies linked both to external and internalised objects as well as with aspects of the self that have been projected into them. It is *this complexity* that I think gets lost if we think in terms of "reconstruction of trauma".

By isolating and focusing on the traumatic experience as something that needs to be "reconstructed" in its own right, the analyst, in my view, is in danger of colluding with the defensive use it *also* serves.

References

Baranger, M., Baranger, W. & Mom, J. M. (1988). The infantile psychic trauma from Us to Freud: pure trauma, retroactivity and reconstruction. *International Journal of Psycho-Analysis, 69*: 113–128.

Bion, W. R. (1966). Attention and interpretation: container and contained transformed. In: *Seven Servants*. New York: Jason Aronson, 1977.

Bion, W. R. (1976). Seminar One: 28 June 1976. In: *Bion Seminars at the Tavistock Clinic*. London: Karnac, 2005.

Blum, H. P. (1987). The role of identification in the resolution of trauma: the Anna Freud Memorial Lecture. *Psychoanalytic Quarterly, 56*: 609–627.

Brenman, E. (1980). The value of reconstruction in adult psychoanalysis. *International Journal of Psycho-Analysis, 61*: 53–60.

Breuer, J. & Freud, S. (1893). On the psychical mechanism of hysterical phenomena: preliminary communication. *S.E. 2. Studies on Hysteria* (pp. 1–17). London: Hogarth.

Britton, R. (2006). Trauma psychoanalysis: a personal view. *Bulletin of the British Psychoanalytical Society, 42(2)*: 3–6.

Britton, R. & Steiner, J. (1994). Interpretation: selected fact or overvalued idea? *International Journal of Psycho-Analysis, 75*: 1069–1078.

Bronstein, C. (2000). Working with suicidal adolescents. In: I. Wise (Ed.), *Adolescence* (pp. 21–39). London: Karnac.

Bronstein, C. (2010). Two modalities of manic defences: their function in adolescent breakdown. *International Journal of Psycho-Analysis, 91*: 583–600.

Fonagy, P. & Moran, G. S. (1990). Severe developmental psychopathology and brittle diabetes: the motivation for self-injurious behaviour. *Bulletin of the Anna Freud Centre, 13*: 231–248.

Fonagy, P., Moran, G. & Target, M. (1993). Aggression and the psychological self. *International Journal of Psycho-Analysis, 74*: 471–485.

Freud, S. (1895a). Project for a scientific psychology. *S.E. 1*. London: Hogarth.

Freud, S. (1897). *The Complete Letters of Sigmund Freud and Wilhelm Fliess, 1887–1904*. Cambridge, MA, and London: Harvard University Press, 1985.

Freud, S. (1905d). *Three Essays on the Theory of Sexuality. S.E. 2*: 123–246. London: Hogarth.

Freud, S. (1907). Letter from Sigmund Freud to Karl Abraham, 7 July 1907. In: *The Complete Correspondence of Sigmund Freud and Karl Abraham 1907–1925* (pp. 1–4), ed. E. Falzeder, trans. C. Schwarzacher). London: Karnac, 2002.

Freud, S. (1918b). From the history of an infantile neurosis. *S.E. 17*. London: Hogarth.

Freud, S. (1920g). *Beyond the Pleasure Principle. S.E. 18*. London: Hogarth.

Freud, S. (1926d). Inhibitions, symptoms and anxiety. *S.E. 20*. London: Hogarth.

Freud, S. (1930a). *Civilization and its Discontents. S.E. 21*: 124. London: Hogarth.

Freud, S. (1937d). Constructions in analysis. *S.E. 23*: 257–269. London: Hogarth.

Furst, S. S. (1967). Psychic trauma: a survey. In: S. S. Furst (Ed.), *Psychic Trauma*. New York: Basic Books.

Garland, C. (1998). Introduction: why psychoanalysis? In: *Understanding Trauma* (pp. 3–31). London: Karnac.

Geleerd, E. R. (1961). Some aspects of ego vicissitudes in adolescence. *Journal of the American Psycho-analytic Association, 9*: 394–405.

Glover, E. (1929). The "screening" function of traumatic memories. *International Journal of Psycho-Analysis, 10*: 90–93.

Greenacre, P. (1953). *Trauma, Growth and Personality*. London: Karnac, 1987.

Joseph, B. (1997). The pursuit of insight and psychic change. Conference on Therapeutic Factors in Psychoanalysis, UCL.

Khan, M. (1963). The concept of cumulative trauma. *Psychoanalytic Studies of the Child, 18*: 286–306.

Klein, M. (1948). On the theory of anxiety and guilt. In: *Envy and Gratitude* (pp. 25–42). London: Hogarth, 1980.

Kris, E. (1956). The recovery of childhood memories in psychoanalysis. *Psychoanalytic Studies of the Child, 11*: 54–88.

Lacan, J. (1988). *The Seminars of Jacques Lacan: The Ego in Freud's Theory and in the Technique of Psychoanalysis, 1954–1955 (Seminar II)*, ed. J. -A. Miller, trans. S. Tomaselli. Cambridge: Cambridge University Press.

Laplanche, J. & Pontalis, J. B. (1973). *The Language of Psycho-Analysis*, trans. D. Nicholson-Smith. London: The International Psycho-Analytical Library, 1983.

Laufer, M. (1972). Depression in adolescence. Monograph 4, Fourth Conference on Adolescence, Brent Consultation Centre, London.

Rangell, L. (1967). The metapsychology of psychic trauma. In: S. S. Furst (Ed.), *Psychic Trauma* (pp. 51–84). New York: Basic Books.

Riesenberg-Malcolm, R. (1988). Construction as reliving history. Symposium on Construction and Reconstruction, Stockholm, March 1988. *EPF Bulletin, 31*: 3–12.

Spillius, E. (1988). Introduction. In: *Melanie Klein Today*, Vol. 2: *Mainly Practice*. London: Routledge.

Steiner, J. (1996). The aim of psychoanalysis in theory and practice. *International Journal of Psycho-Analysis, 77*: 1073–1083.

Strachey, J. (1959). Editorial Introduction to Freud's "Inhibitions, Symptoms and Anxiety". *S.E. 20*. London: Hogarth.

Target, M. (1998). The recovered memories controversy. *International Journal of Psycho-Analysis, 79*: 1015–1028.

Verhaeghe, P. (1998). Trauma and hysteria within Freud and Lacan. *The Letter: Lacanian Perspectives on Psychoanalysis, 14, Autumn*: 87–106.

Zepf, S. & Zepf, F. D. (2008). Trauma and traumatic neurosis: Freud's concepts revisited. *International Journal of Psycho-Analysis, 89*: 331–353.

Notes

1. "The [latency] child is not equipped to cope mentally with stronger sexual impressions, and hence reacts to them compulsively, as if unconsciously—that is the first deficiency in the mechanism; as a consequence of the somatic intensification of the releasing of sexuality, these impressions later exercise more powerful effects as a retrospective reaction [*nachträglich*] and as *memories* than they did when they were real impressions, and that is the second psychological deficiency, because this constellation of retrospectively strengthened *unpleasure released by memories* [*Erinnerungsunlust*] makes repression possible, which would not succeed against *perceptions*" (Freud, 1907).

2. I have discussed this case in connection to manic defences in another publication (Bronstein, 2010).

CHAPTER FOUR

What's so traumatic about adolescence?

Sara Flanders

T he trauma of adolescent sexuality lies at the very heart of Freud's earliest theory of the hysterical neurosis (Freud, 1895, 1910). He understood the hysterical patient as unable to face the reality and responsibilities of sexual adulthood. Instead, the hysteric denied her sexual thoughts and feelings, discharging their intensity in the florid symptoms that to the uninitiated seemed far removed from the sexual sphere. He hypothesised that there were historical causes to the refusal of sexuality in adulthood. These patients, he thought, had suffered a premature sexual awakening in their childhood, something too much for a child's psyche to bear, something which could not be owned, could not become a part of a personal history (Baranger, M., Baranger, W. & Mom, 1988). Each of these hysterics, he hypothesised, had been seduced, usually by an adult. The distorting, traumatising intrusion of the adult desire into the child's innocent experience was the source of his patients' intolerance and rejection of sexuality when it presented itself again, after they became adult themselves. The mental representations of psychically overwhelming emotional events which had been split off from consciousness, or repressed, were reawakened after puberty, and became linked with new, adult sexual feelings (Freud, 1895). This collision of an indigestible, unconscious past with the intrusion of present experience constituted the trauma from which the adult hysteric suffered. The psychic working over, the reappraisal of the link between past and present, the task of every adolescent, was precisely the mental work that the hysterical patient could not do, as the original experience, the intrusive seduction in childhood, had actually damaged the capacity to integrate the new sexual reality.

Later, Freud would decide that the traumatic interference with normal development need not have taken place in the form of a sexual seduction; there were too many hysterics and not enough abusive fathers, in his view, to go around (Freud, 1897). He came to another conclusion (Freud, 1938) that there is something, as Laplanche (1989) would later elaborate and confirm, essentially traumatic in human sexuality itself. It comes, Freud would later theorise, of the human condition, of the long evolution which results in adult sexuality only many years after the first sexual experiences of the human infant (Freud, 1905d, 1923, 1926d, 1938). The long evolution presented two sources of vulnerability: the prolonged experience of emotional and physical dependency, and the problematic of the two phases, infantile and pubertal, in the development of human sexuality. Beginning in the baby's sensual relationship with the adult mother, infantile sexual life crescendos at the Oedipal phase, at which time the child's yearnings meet the realities of the child's limitations, culminating in a renunciation. Desire then subsides into latency, only to burst again on the scene at puberty, when the earlier renunciation must yield to a new demand for acceptance of a new reality, sexual adulthood.

Puberty constitutes a discontinuity that "cannot be bypassed or postponed" (Gutton, 1998). It "comes as a surprise to the child", who cannot have anticipated the shock of the sexual capacities—to conceive, to impregnate, coupled with sexual feeling. Gutton, in emphasising the shock of adolescence, develops the psychoanalytic understanding so eloquently emphasised by Anna Freud (1937), who focused on the complex demands made on the mind of the adolescent, whose ego is weakened precisely as it is needed to be strong, made, temporarily, more vulnerable, more helpless, more confused by the changes taking place in the body, changes informing the relationship to the internalised parental objects, the source of emotional stability. In Gutton's words, the "pubertal" is "quite the antithesis of a movement of separation": rather, in its shocking immediacy, it is a force that fuels a "frenzy towards" the parents (1998). The pubertal scene, as he calls it, is an incestuous scene, and one from which the adolescent must retreat, into a familiar hazy adolescent withdrawal, eventually to emerge, with hopes of establishing a new, non-incestuous object choice. I would argue that this description of the "pubertal" implies a traumatic breaking through of the latency equilibrium, and the capacity to work through this trauma is the burden of each individual. Working through means mourning, bearing the loss of the child's relation to the protective adult, turning away from the parents, and towards an exogamous relationship because the newly adult sexual drives raise incestuous anxiety which must be met.

Some adolescents, like those early cases of Freud, arrive at puberty with a character structure and/or a history of previous psychological injury, or what Winnicott called an "environmental failure" or other psychological vulnerability which will make this experience of the pubertal too difficult to integrate. They will break down in adolescence, and their breakdown, as the Laufers (Laufer, M. & Laufer, E., 1984) point out, will be a developmental breakdown. The adolescent will get stuck, unable to accommodate the changes in the body, and all the changes in relation to the internal world and the external world which follow from those physical changes (Laufer, M., 1976). The Laufers have pointed out a particular difficulty for those who arrive at puberty with an idealised image of themselves. This idealised image is the product of a denial of the real condition of separateness, in particular from the mother. The aim of this idealised phantasy is understood to undermine the necessity of the painful task of separation and individuation. The idealisation contains the phanstasy of remaining fused with an idealised, omnipotent parental object, a triumph of the imaginary (Lacan, 1960) and a denial of the losses implicit in development. Puberty comes as a more traumatic shock in such cases. An idealised self, built upon an idealised body image, will not be able to sustain the incursions of the pubertal and adolescent changes (Laufer & Laufer, 1984).

Some changes, unlike puberty, happen more incrementally, allowing for information about change to penetrate the mind of the child gradually. One day, for example, the boy will be taller than his mother, this so dominant figure in his childhood will shrink, and the poignant sense of loss that is part of adolescence, the awareness of the finite nature of childhood, the responsibilities of adulthood, will impact on the child. But the boy would have been growing, slowly, year by year, information about his height is less intrusive than the more sudden intrusion of the sexual changes. The more gradual changes I am alluding to here are a reminder that there is a background to a capacity to adapt to the changes that take place in the body, to accept reality, to do the mental work of owning the relationship of past to present. In ordinary development, there are many factors that help to mitigate the trauma. Amongst such capacities are all varieties of play, which, we could say, are the child's, then the adolescent's, creative way of dreaming, imagining, thinking about a containable, bearable future (Winnicott, 1971).

Adolescence, in fact, requires creativity. This momentous adaptive task lies at the heart of much great literature. One of the most potent, ironic, and timeless metaphors of traumatic, unacceptable bodily transformation can be found in the beginning of Kafka's *Metamorphosis*. Although a narrative of a young adult rather than an adolescent, it vividly and cleverly extends a metaphor for the confusion and horror that are a part of the bodily transformation that defines the adolescent experience. At least one element of the genius of this work is that it touches forgotten aspects of our own experience, including the violent loss of whatever idealised self we held on to as we approached puberty, presenting the loss through a metaphor that fascinates but also distances us from a horror so vividly but also absurdly portrayed. The effect is uncanny: Kafka begins the story as he will continue, calmly describing a terrifying transformation, inserting it into a recognisable, everyday scene.

> As Gregor Samsa woke up one morning from uneasy dreams he found himself transformed in his bed into a gigantic insect. He was lying on his hard, as it were armour-plated, back and when he lifted his head a little he could see his dome-like brown belly divided into stiff arched segments on top of which the bed-quilt could hardly keep in position and was about to slide off completely. His numerous legs, which were pitifully thin compared to the rest of his bulk, waved helplessly before his eyes.
>
> What has happened to me? He thought. It was no dream. His room, a regular human bedroom, only rather too small, lay quiet between the four familiar walls.

Kafka will continue with the tragic-comic metaphor, treated with ironic calm, of an horrific and doomed physical transformation. Isolated in his room upstairs, no longer able to communicate through language, Gregor becomes in the frame of the narrative the object that commonly represents symbolically subjective self-hatred, a morbid loss of self-esteem. For Gregor, adaptation is absurd, he is presented with an impossible task; the actual promise of adolescence is reversed but also highlighted by this absurdity. The changes that have taken place in him make real a dread which could only be imagined or dreamed in life. And yet the hatred of the body that the story justifies is not very different from the helpless hatred with which some adolescents experience the intrusions of physical change. Kafka is cruel to his hero, placing him in a situation in which there is no reparation or potential development, and placing the reader in the position of outside observer to this appalling but affecting event. In the context of Kafka's narrative, a man becomes an insect: a psychotic absurdity is presented as real and inescapable; the hero is not psychologically stuck so much as reality has subverted any possibility of development. The hero in a theatrical adaptation at the Lyric Theatre in London exposed the sad irony of the metaphor: the dead Gregor dominates the stage at the end, a beautiful young man hanging entangled in a sheet, the youthful heroic body in absolute contrast to the insect he had become in the play.

Interestingly, Kafka offers his readers a hero who seems not to have had an adolescence. His life is shown to have grown narrow, he has become the sole economic support of a collapsed, complacent, and rather parasitical family, no life outside work, but his work supporting the preservation of the illusion of a rigidly patriarchal family life. Gregor is enslaved to this illusion, in which he appears to be the necessary economic support. The transformation into the insect suggests to me the sudden subjective awareness of the absolute loss of an idealised self, indeed, the developmental price of maintaining such an illusion, and, with it, the confrontation with a bodily change which is seen and experienced as ugly, vile, and despised. The insect is a nightmare opposite of a desexualised idealisation with which a vulnerable developing self attempts to transcend the limitations and the shame of separateness, renouncing the rewards of sexual differentiation and desire (Laufer & Laufer, 1984).

There is something of the isolation of Gregor in the life of the eighteen-year-old boy I will discuss here, who spent long hours in his bedroom, finding contact with his mother downstairs impossibly problematic. In his retreat, he struggled with dark yearnings for death as a solution to the festering hurt and shameful pain of his adolescent horror of the youthful manliness so attractively apparent to the outside observer.

As with Freud's first patients, there were elements in his childhood which help to make sense of his difficulty in owning his adulthood, finding himself at odds with his developing body, and the responsibility and pleasure of living in it.

Jimeet came for help during the year he studied for his A levels. A handsome and intelligent adolescent, he was ambitious in his studies, gifted at singing, and by the time I met him, an enthusiastic participant in the extracurricular activities offered at his private school, disclosing a surprising joy in being a part of performances. But he was a very troubled young man. He found himself often preoccupied with thoughts of suicide, consumed with self-hatred, struggling with feelings of unexpressed hatred for the mother who raised him on her own, and a less intensely felt hatred for a father who had played a small but crucial role in his childhood, before deteriorating into mental illness and alcoholism. Jimeet had struggled for several years with suicidal thoughts, had cut into his body in hatred of the feelings he could express nowhere else, feelings that despite his highly developed capacities, he could not articulate, symbolise, or think about. Instead, he inflicted wounding pain on the body which had betrayed him into adulthood.

Jimeet came for psychotherapy to a centre devoted to the application of the psychoanalytic understanding of adolescence. He came for only one year, his last year of A level study, so he was not in extended therapy, nor did he come intensively, although his once-weekly sessions were very intense, and often he worked very hard in them. There were many reasons that I and my colleagues wanted him to have more extensive and more intensive therapy, but he was adamant, he wanted to limit the dependency. He had started out seeing a counsellor who in his view left him, and he did not wish to repeat an experience of being dependent and then abandoned. Alongside his suicidal wishes, he disclosed another, life-embracing trend. He put an emphasis on his preparation to leave home, to go to university away from London, and in doing this, he protected the relationship with me from the suffocating anxiety he faced at home, the only son of his single mother. Occasionally, this claustrophobic and incestuous anxiety infiltrated the sessions, which he could acknowledge.

What had troubled Jimeet initially, and taken him to counselling when he was sixteen, were conflicted homosexual feelings for a much loved and idealised classmate. By the time I saw Jimeet, these feelings had subsided in urgency, and he had established a solid friendship with this heterosexual classmate, but he was troubled now by paedophilic fantasies, both homosexual and heterosexual, as well as a dark, almost addictive, depressive attraction to suicide, a yearning for a death that would end his struggle to find a path into adulthood. He also suffered, it was clear immediately, a profound failure to resolve the incestuous anxieties of a virtually fatherless boy living alone with his mother. From the first meeting with him, he articulated the problem and the omnipotent solution that eluded him: if he could remain small, hopeless in reality, as he was a large, slightly overweight, very handsome boy, his situation would be resolved, he could comfortably remain close to his mother, and he would not suffer the acute, skin-crawling horror of his closeness to her. When I met him, although he was eighteen years old, I had the impression that the heat of the pubertal dilemma (Gutton, 1998) had not abated for him much at all; he had not found a way around or through the discomfort of living alone with his mother. It sounded as if he hurried, or scuttled, to link his behaviour with that of Kafka's insect, into his room as often as he could when at home, avoiding his loving mother's greetings when she appeared. In his room, tormented with dark thoughts, he poured his anguish into his diary or stopped the thoughts by cutting into his arms.

Jimeet took quickly to the offer of once-weekly meetings. The initial work focused on the much lamented phantasy of attraction to children. This, he thought, was truly despicable, a feeling he judged with terrible harshness, although he seemed loath to consider the possibility of acting on what seemed to me more feelings than phantasy, though I cannot be sure about that. It emerged that the children he depicted himself as being attracted to were about ten years old. We were able to link the age he attached to them with his own memory of his estranged father making a brief, single appearance in his remembered childhood at the age of ten. This man, who had already suffered at least one of a series of mental breakdowns, returned to England from abroad, and apparently insisted that his only, very intelligent son go to private school. His father thereby instigated a severance from life as Jimeet had known it, including a relationship to a childminder, her family, other children, who had supported his life alone with his mother. She had always worked a good deal, but worked longer and harder when it became necessary to find the funds for a private school she too seems to have aspired to for him.

It was not so very difficult to follow a thread from the experience of the father's brief, traumatic, life-changing entry into and exit from his life, with the admiration Jimeet saw in or projected into the eyes of the latency-age children he worried about fancying. When I linked for him his potential yearning for and disappointment in an admired helpful father, a father whose brief appearance teased him with the possibility of intervention with both the loneliness and the gratification he faced home alone with his mother, he took it in, with adequate pain. Bowing his head in shame, I felt his emotion included some compassion for his ten-year-old self, some growing ability to be in touch with a longing that it took a number of sessions more for him to articulate for himself. Interestingly, though this moment in the treatment was very highly charged, Jimeet never was able to remember much emotion in relation to his actual experience with his father when he was ten. The meaningful emotion emerged in the present, at age eighteen, when the significance of a father gradually became a felt and articulated experience, and the reality of having a broken-down, psychotic father was more completely confronted.

The fleeting presence of a potent father in his early life appeared against a background of absence. When in his adolescence, he faced his father again, encouraged by his well-meaning mother, Jimeet met a man who had deteriorated into a drunken, messy baby of a figure, one he had to look after when he visited him in a restaurant for dinner, paying himself with the money his mother earned. He hated it. He shuddered in the telling of the encounter of his shambling father, and eventually talked of his anxiety that his emotional difficulties, the conflicts he struggled with alone in his bedroom at night, the homosexual anxiety, the allure of suicide, the rage with his all-too-loving mother, meant that he was mad like his father. Jimeet relived in the consulting room, when shuddering in horror at the messy collapse of a drunken father, or shrinking into his collar recalling his mother's intrusive kisses on his neck, a horror of his own physicality. This horror is given an ironic objective correlative in the insect of Kafka's *Metamorphosis*, the young hero having shrunk into the armoured shape of an insect, only to suffer contempt, humiliation, and death rather than adulthood and sexual fulfilment, the promise of adolescence. In Jimeet's case, the horror and disgust at his father's metamorphosis coloured his own, and at the same time, contributed to the lack of incestuous barrier in the maternal embraces that made him feel violent and self-hating.

The first sessions, then, emphasised the difficulties of not having a father who could actually function as a father in his life, protect him and his mother, get between him and her, and offer an image of a viable adult future (Freud, 1923; Green, 2005; Lacan, 1953). Rather, his father made real the regression into helplessness himself. The weekly sessions moved on to deeper exploration of the problematic of living at home with his mother, who, from his point of view, found it very difficult to help with the incestuous anxieties that in Jimeet's life had not abated much since puberty. One of the things that emerged was the extent to which he blamed himself utterly for his discomfort with his mother's intimacy, which stirred up the violent rage he could not express. He was helped to find the voice to articulate his discomfort for himself, and then to her, literally, to claim the function of the father for himself. He would carry from me and the therapeutic situation the paternal function which would help him to separate, to bear the poignance of her sadness, for which he recognised he was taking too much responsibility.

Part of his hatred for his mother was his despair of not being able to make good her loss, his growing up actually meant leaving her alone. His academic, social, extracurricular success at a boys' public school was dearly bought. She had missed out on a lot, and so had he. His sense of her being absent, being busy earning the money during his childhood, rang painfully true. He may have felt murderous, but he did not want to hurt his mother, whose tears he hated because they provoked an inordinate guilt. Eventually, he faced them. He found it possible to confront her, to tell her not to kiss him on the neck, not to run her hands in his hair, he would not go alone with her on holiday again; he was, in short, no longer standing in phantasy for the partner she did not have. His predilection for the company of intact families in which two parents meant the adolescent would not be guilty of too much destructiveness if he argued or rebelled, was driven by this anxiety of damaging his mother if he made his boundaries clearer. Over the period of his coming, he found that he became able, up to a point, to argue with her, disagree, be angry without feeling so damaging, and so be more comfortable with the loving feelings that were certainly there.

A striking evolution in the appearance of this young man took place during the period of his brief psychotherapy. His was a metamorphosis in reverse. As is often the case with adolescents who are struggling against a breakdown in their development, which usually includes an attack on their sexually developed body, the relief from self-hatred discloses itself in a more graceful, sexually attractive appearance. He no longer suffered a compulsion to attack a hated manliness that had erupted traumatically to spoil the idealised special boy of latency. He was able to do some mourning, particularly for the loss entailed in his father's deterioration, less for the absence of his father in his childhood. His mourning was limited, his capacity to feel sadness in relation to his steadily deteriorating father showed itself only once in the one-year period, and that when he was at his least anxious, most pleased with himself. For adolescents who are so sensitive and confused about what is normal and what is not, the eventual coming to terms with the abnormality of a parent marks another piece of hard mental work, specifically, the struggle to disentangle the identifications with the parent of the same sex. The fact of the extremes presented by this father, absent and idealised in childhood, or present and disintegrating in adolescence, mirror the poles of the idealised and denigrated adolescent body in the mind of the adolescent himself, and increases the difficulty in metabolising an acceptance of the changes taking place, leading to a sexually specific adulthood.

The estrangement from the body is also a feature of the heroine of Carson McCullers' *The Member of the Wedding*, a straightforward tale of a girl's alienation from the developments taking place within herself and around her. She reels first from the shock of her widowed father telling her it is time she no longer slept with him, she is too big, and then, as she struggles with her new estrangement from childhood, another shock, her older brother announces his wedding. In the passage below, Carson McCullers deftly illustrates the alienated void Gutton describes following puberty, the subjective state into which the information about the brother is inserted. The consequence of the news of the wedding is for the depressed girl to refuse the information, a rejection of the reality of the sexual world she has entered, as she faces an Oedipal task that the narrative implies had been avoided due to the fact of her mother's death in her infancy. Carson McCullers has given us an historical foundation for the particular difficulties of her young heroine.

> It happened that green and crazy summer when Frankie was twelve years old. This was the summer when for a long time she had not been a member. She belonged to no club and was a member of nothing in the world. Frankie had become an unjoined person who hung around in doorways, and she was afraid. In June the

trees were bright dizzy green, but later the leaves darkened, and the town turned black and shrunken under the glare of the sun. At first, Frankie walked around doing one thing and another. The sidewalks of the town were grey in the early morning and at night, but the noon sun put a glaze on them, so that the cement burned and glittered like glass. The sidewalks finally became too hot for Frankie's feet, and also she got herself in trouble. She was in so much secret trouble that she thought it was better to stay at home—and at home there was only Berenice Sadie Brown and John Henry West. The three of them sat at the kitchen table, saying the same things over and over, so that by August the words began to rhyme with each other and sound strange. The world seemed to die each afternoon and nothing moved any longer. At last the summer was like a green sick dream, or like a silent crazy jungle under glass. And then, on the last Friday of August, all this was changed: it was so sudden that Frankie puzzled the whole blank afternoon, and still she did not understand.

It is so very queer, she said. "The way it all just happened."

"Happened? Happened?" said Berenice.

What has happened in the novel is the announcement of the marriage between her older brother and a woman she does not know. It follows, we learn, the heroine's ejection the previous spring from her father's bed. "Who is this great big long-legged blunderbuss who still wants to sleep with her old Papa?" (p. 32) and a brief troubled period of adolescent acting out, sexual and delinquent. The heroine we meet in the novel has resigned herself to depressed withdrawal into a summer of playing cards with her beloved black housekeeper and a six-year-old cousin. Into this regressive regimen of sameness enters news of her brother's marriage. For the greater part of the short novel, we watch her manic denial of her exclusion from the honeymoon, her delusional plan to be taken along with the bride and groom, out of the town she lives in, the situation she is in, the task of adolescence facing her. The delusional reversal of reality is expressed by the heroine in a poignant and illuminating phrase she repeats as her inspiration: "They are the we of me." When the event finally takes place, the abject girl calls out to the reality of the receding couple, not any longer the assertive and manic "They are the we of me", but the more plaintiff and abject plea "Take me". They don't.

The situation of Carson McCullers' heroine, for whom the world of the couple comes as a violent shock, is not so remote from the case of Fernanda, who came to psychotherapy at the age of eighteen, with a background of pre-pubertal trauma involving the shock of a confrontation with, first, her father's leaving when she was four, but, more recently, her inclusion, as a latency child, in the honeymoon of her mother's second marriage. Carson McCullers' heroine is forced to face painful truth and constructs a wish that obviates her pain. Part of Fernanda's problem was the inability of the adults to help her with a reality that became more disturbing and confusing because it was not in any adequate way mediated by the adults around her. As is often the case, there was parental collusion in support of an idealised phantasy that she was not separate from her mother, she might now be included as a part of a couple, a member of the honeymoon. This event was a disaster all around.

Fernanda was first brought to a children's service when she was still a child. She was an angry, but also depressed, eleven-year-old child whose angry mother brought her for help. She could not tolerate her daughter's emotionality. A profoundly disturbed mother, and a seriously troubled daughter, they were helped to remain physically separate. Fernanda remained at boarding school, where she would stay until she left at eighteen, planning then to return to London, and embark on a therapy which was held out to her as a life-line, a hope that she might one day get some help to face the exigencies of her life. While at boarding school, she survived, she took exams, she made a few friends, but she was often suicidal, alarming the therapist, who had undertaken to keep in touch with her, with letters of black despair, of suicidal imaginings which, however, she claimed she would not act on—and she did not, as many despairing adolescents do. Her period at boarding school was not without movement, or some successes. At the age of sixteen, accompanying her mother on a visit to her mother's native country, she had her first sexual experience with the son of her mother's oldest friend. It all took place in a town in a country where her mother imagined they would all live together one day. It is of course significant that this was the son of the mother's oldest friend; it was an entry into sexual life in a situation which blurred the boundaries of the mother and daughter's separateness. There is in its logic, for Fernanda, and for her mother, some of the inclusion on the honeymoon, only reversed.

Here, it was Fernanda's turn to have the sexual relationship, and the mother perpetuating the illusion: *They are the we of me.*

Fernanda began bingeing when this boyfriend visited her home in England. One night, as both mother and her new boyfriend slept in separate rooms in her house, she, alone, awoke, crept into the kitchen, and began to eat in a frenzy of confusion and release, the beginning of an addiction to bingeing and vomiting that constituted her way of controlling overwhelming anxiety, and was the symptom she brought to me, at the age of eighteen. Her involvement with a boy had not brought the elusive normality, and did not for her accompany a necessary process of mourning, the pleasure of the new sexuality coupled with a relinquishment of the illusion of inseparability from an actual parent. That long and poignant process which is such an essential part of the adolescent adaptation to adulthood was not for her, and she was paying a high price for the evasion of this necessary mental work.

But the foundations for meeting adolescence were poorly formed. Fernanda's mother had divorced her father when she was small, and had divorced Fernanda from her father simultaneously. The habit of violating the reality of their separateness was firmly entrenched in the mother's mind. The father was escorted from the house by police, and Fernanda was forbidden to see him by a mother unable to hold on to a sense of her daughter's difference from her. The parental separation was an extreme event as described by Fernanda, a violent expulsion, in which her father was banished, only managing to see his daughter much later by illicitly meeting her at the school gate. Moreover, the logic of her mother's behaviour contributed to the illusion that Fernanda was a kind of Oedipal victor: she would become the mother's partner, the mother's completion, the mother's mirroring double. Here trauma is met not by its recognition and its placing into a meaningful historical context (Baranger, Baranger & Mom, 1988), but trauma, unmetabolised, driving a delusional solution, creating a bubble for puberty to break (Laufer, 1984). Later, trying to remain her mother's permanent baby, as well as her extension (Lacan, 1960; Leclaire, 1975), and at the same time trying to enter into adulthood, she was presented with a profound contradiction. She remained stuck in a psychological position in which she was constantly facing something like the rug pulled from under her feet. Reality continually undermined her false position, her endeavour to "have her cake and eat it too".

In this way, the traumatised adolescent often makes things worse for herself, leaning on magical, manic defences (Klein, 1940) which break down in the face of reality, exposing the adolescent again to the experience of being emotionally overwhelmed. Such a cycle drives the suicidal thoughts, suicide representing a way of putting to an end the destructive repetition.

When I met Fernanda as her therapist, when she was eighteen, now living with her mother, I met a young woman paralysed with fear of her own emotionality, at the same time, a girl doggedly determined to take up the therapy offered to her as a life-line, even if the reality of her encounter with me proved to be something very hard to swallow. I found her perilously stuck and exceedingly boring, bringing a flattened emotionality I have observed in other frightened adolescents, terrified and made helpless before the emotional demands of their own development. I came to understand her perfectionism, her control, her frozen emotionality, as her attempt to maintain an idealised narcissistic equilibrium, one which allowed for no change, no development, no conflict with the maternal object to whom she bound herself as an idealised extension. It was a nervous, untenable, incestuous position. She was eventually able to acknowledge this.

Relinquishing the position of the idealised, unseparated baby extension of maternal narcissism (Laufer, 1984; Leclaire, 1975) was the central task of the therapy. It meant returning to the traumatic moment when Fernanda, like Frankie in *Member of the Wedding*, confronted the fact of her exclusion from a sexual couple. But Frankie in the novel only imagines herself into the honeymoon. The adults in the novel's world do not collude with the disturbed adolescent. Fernanda experienced a far more confusing situation when she was taken, for reasons never made clear, but in my view a product of her mother's psychotic functioning, on her mother's and stepfather's honeymoon. It was an experience of terrible humiliation. She relived in the transference the humiliation when she was, in her view, brutally reminded of her place: another driver, a man, had beeped at her car to get out of the way, as she drove to a therapy session. She was reminded of the honeymoon, when she was forced to get out of the bath, where we might imagine she was soothing herself in compensation for the confusing tensions of the honeymoon. With me, she disclosed herself, still smarting from a sense of injustice and exposure, rather than wondering at the inappropriateness of it all. She reported with the hysteric's *belle indifférence* her defiant resistance to leaving her mother's bed on the occasion of her mother's honeymoon. The lived-out drama represents the action normally left to phantasy, the psychological argument with the relinquishment of childhood which is required of every child who becomes at puberty a sexually adult person whose place in the parental bed becomes actively incestuous. Of course, the paralysis in the sessions had to do with the dangerous incestuous nature of our relationship, the explosive violence that hovers just under the surface of incestuous collusion.

Fernanda is an example of the adolescent for whom pubertal development constitutes too great a shock to an already compromised and fragile mental equilibrium, an equilibrium in no way prepared for the disturbances of puberty, a rigid equilibrium that is bound to shatter traumatically before the demands, as Freud pointed out so long ago, of adulthood (Freud, 1895). This girl's traumatic sexual development was founded on a fragility created by earlier childhood trauma, the violent separation from the father mediated in a mad way by her mother, who, I wish to say, recognised her daughter's vulnerability, if not her own, and, within her limitations, supported her daughter's treatment after she returned home from boarding school. Indeed, Fernanda often reminded me of the good physical care she must have received, and continued to receive, from a mother careful and loving in her preparation of food, even in her capacity to build out of little material wealth an economic foundation for her daughter's future. But she was not able to provide the foundation for Fernanda's capacity to bear her own emotions, either emotional pain or strong passions of any kind, or to own and reflect a conflict. With so little preparation to take responsibility for her own thoughts and feelings, Fernanda showed herself in therapy reluctant to bear the difficulty of thinking or owning conflict, preferring omnipotent defences, like the control of food, or leaning on the black-and-white but also totally unreliable machinations of the mindfulness she grew up with, the paranoid world she had internalised. Fernanda would find it intensely difficult to "become a subject" (Cahn, 1988) which would necessitate giving up the identification with her mother's omnipotent and paranoid thinking.

Concluding thoughts on trauma and adolescence

Early on, Freud moved away from regarding the causes of neurotic alienation from sexual life as the product of childhood seduction, towards an understanding of neurosis as a product of development itself, in particular the long and complex historical evolution of sexuality in each individual's life (Freud, 1926d). The seductive childhood scenes reported by his patients he came to understand as more frequently than not a product of the patient's sexual phantasies. The fertile ground for trauma resides in the long period of dependency, the result of the vulnerability and the helplessness of the human infant to satisfy his own needs, to quieten the agitation of the drives. The passions are strong and the young ego weak, which leads to the primitive defences that hamper later development. But even before he had arrived at his understanding of the origins of traumatic experience and the substrate of anxiety deriving from that origin of helplessness (Freud, 1926d), he gave up his theory of overt sexual seduction in childhood as the cause of the rejection of adult sexuality in the *après coup* of the hysteric's traumatic response to pubertal development. And from the beginning, even when he hypothesised the childhood seduction as the precursor to hysterical development, he placed the notion of the adult sexual trauma in the arena of psychic life, in the joining of past to present in the mind of the adolescent or young adult. The traumatic potential resides, he would later affirm explicitly, in development itself (Freud, 1938).

Laplanche and Pontalis (1968) have developed the notion of a primary seduction, suggesting that there is in fact a traumatic intrusion of adult sexuality into each mother–child relation, the impact of the adult's unconscious on the child the universal seduction that lays the foundation for the relationship to sexuality within the individual. This would represent an original trauma of intrusion (Laplanche, 1989), one which is certainly the case when there are powerful projective mechanisms coming from a more disturbed parent (Williams, 1997), and which would in my view present particular potential for an aversive response to the adolescent experience. Of the two cases I have discussed here, we see the eating-disordered, rigid, and controlling mentation of Fernanda making it particularly difficult for her to integrate her anxieties about separateness, her terrors of emotions and passion. Her lack of the wherewithal to sustain the shocks of pubertal change, was, I felt, the product of maternal projective intrusions throughout her life.

When Freud moved to examine the deeper origins of trauma, he emphasised not the impact of the intrusion noted by Laplanche and Pontalis, later more fully developed by Laplanche, but the overwhelming nature of the needs of the human infant. For Freud, the original exposure to helplessness, ultimately to death if the primary caretaker is lost, is the original trauma to which some are exposed far more painfully and damagingly than others, but no one escapes completely. An anxiety, of annihilation, associated with an abandonment, would be more clearly a feature again of the mental functioning of Fernanda, and indeed, the suicidal mentation she displayed was ubiquitous in the first years of her therapy. She seemed to have little in her mind to help her when she met any difficulty at all, let alone the difficulties faced in relation to the intensities of sexual relationship. She reflected a maternal object who found her otherness unthinkable, a maternal object difficult to separate from because mentally she did not really acknowledge her daughter's separateness, a maternal object who had not been able to facilitate a space for thinking (Bion, 1962). She was a poor ally in the struggle to accept reality, one might say she psychologically abandoned her daughter to face reality alone. With such unpredictable paranoid functioning in the parent, the mental work required for the daughter to separate was often foreclosed. So, despite incestuous anxiety, she clung to her mother, and experienced an intolerable reawakening of the pubertal crisis (Gutton, 1998). Fernanda's way of meeting anxiety was to explode into frenzies of bingeing and vomiting.

We see in Jimeet, who I believe was not projected into with the violence so evident in Fernanda's history and personality, and who was very able to think and did not have the labile or rigid quality of a personality traumatised from early infancy, nonetheless a struggle with acute incestuous anxiety, preoccupying thoughts of suicide, fear of madness, homosexual anxiety. Puberty broke in on him with violence too, stirred him into extreme states of mind, and was met with some collusive myopia on the part of his single-parent mother. He too needed help with the incestuous anxiety that is the burden of any adolescent, but particularly for an adolescent who has not had to abandon the project of being his mother's idealised partner until the changes in the body break in upon this *modus vivendi*. For Jimeet, there was also the impact of paternal abandonment in reality, and the psychotic breakdown which totally debilitated his father's functioning as an adult. Hating him for his inadequacy, a turning point came for Jimeet when he found himself saying with an affirmation that surprised him, "I want a father", at the same time facing the broken nature of his own.

I would link the father Jimeet wanted with the father who facilitates separation from the subjective immersion in mother–child relations, the father identified with time and the sense of history (Baranger, Baranger & Mom, 1988) which eventually stretches to incorporate the traumatic intrusions and absences, the paternal function which structures the space for thinking (Green, 2005; Lacan, 1953) the working through that is a product of mourning the losses associated with growing up. The brief work with Jimeet included only a limited transference repetition of the claustrophobic incestuousness that invaded his relation to his mother. He embraced the frame of the treatment, understood implicitly its paternal significance, but did not trust it to contain more than once-weekly therapy. With Fernanda, the terror of a primitive maternal object appeared regularly in a much more prolonged and more intensive therapy. Some confrontation with the more primitive level of object relations helped her to face some of her tenacious clinging to the omnipotent solutions linked to the difficult primary object.

But no adolescent, as Anna Freud and Phillippe Gutton have noted, escapes the emotional upheaval presented by the pubertal intrusion on the safe harbour of latency. And a boy or girl can cling to an identity as the idealised completion of a parent in order to avoid the demands of development in a home with both parents present, where there is no actual paternal abandonment, no psychotic parent to collude with infantile omnipotence, and so intensify the traumatic impact of pubertal change. Yet, for the most part, and as the result of impressive and often creative mental work, never without cost and sometimes at great price, most cross the bridge to adulthood.

References

Baranger, M., Baranger, W. & Mom, J. M., (1988). The infantile psychic trauma from Us to Freud: pure trauma, retroactivity and reconstruction. *International Journal of Psycho-Analysis, 68*: 113–128.

Bion, W. R. (1962). *Learning from Experience*. London: Karnac.

Cahn, R. (1998). The process of becoming-a-subject in adolescence. In: M. Perret-Catipovic & F. Ladame (Eds.), *Adolescence and Psychoanalysis*. London: Karnac.

Freud, A. (1937). *The Ego and the Mechanisms of Defence*. London: Hogarth.

Freud, A. (1958). Adolescence. *Psychoanalytic Study of the Child, 13*: 255–278. [Reprinted in M. Perret-Catipovic & F. Ladame (Eds.), *Adolescence and Psychoanalysis*. London: Karnac, 1998.]

Freud, S. (1895d). *Studies on Hysteria. S.E. 2*. London: Hogarth.

Freud, S. (1897). Letter 69 to Fleiss. *S.E. 1*: 259–260. London: Hogarth.

Freud, S. (1905d). *Three Essays on the Theory of Sexuality*. *S.E. 7*. London: Hogarth.

Freud, S. (1905e). Fragment of an analysis of a case of hysteria. *S.E. 7*. London: Hogarth.

Freud, S. (1923b). *The Ego and the Id*. *S.E. 19*. London: Hogarth.

Freud, S. (1926d). Inhibitions, symptoms and anxiety. *S.E. 20*. London: Hogarth.

Freud, S. (1938). *An Outline of Psychoanalysis*. *S. E. 23*. London: Hogarth.

Green, A. (2005). Configurations of thirdness. Chapter 11 in *Key Ideas for a Contemporary Psychoanalysis*. London: Routledge.

Gutton, P. (1998). The pubertal, its sources and fate. In: M. Perret-Catipovic & F. Ladame (Eds.), *Adolescence and Psychoanalysis*. London: Karnac.

Kafka, F. (1915). *The Metamorphosis*. New York: Bantam Classic, 1972.

Klein, M. (1940). Mourning and its relation to manic depressive states. In: *Love, Guilt and Reparation*. London: Hogarth, 1975.

Lacan, J. (1953). The function and field of speech and language in psychoanalysis. In: *Écrits: A Selection*. London: Tavistock, 1977.

Lacan, J. (1960). The subversion of the subject and the dialectic of desire in the Freudian Unconscious. In: *Écrits: A Selection*. London: Tavistock, 1977.

Laplanche, J. (1989). *New Foundations for Psychoanalysis*. Oxford: Blackwell.

Laplanche, J. & Pontalis, J. B. (1968). Fantasy and the origins of sexuality. *International Journal of Psycho-Analysis, 49*.

Laufer, M. (1976). The central masturbation fantasy, the final sexual organization and adolescence. *Psychoanalytic Study of the Child, 31*: 297–316.

Laufer, M. & M. Eglé Laufer (1984). *Adolescence and Developmental Breakdown*. London: Yale.

Leclaire, S. (1975). *On Tue un enfant*. Paris: Éditions du Seuil.

McCullers, C. (1946). *The Member of the Wedding*. London: Penguin, 1972.

Perret-Catipvic, M. & Ladame, F. (1998). Normality and pathology in adolescence. In: *Adolescence and Psychoanalysis*. London: Karnac.

Williams, G. (1997). The "no-entry system of defences": reflections on the assessment of adolescents suffering from eating disorders. In: *Internal Landscapes and Foreign Bodies: Eating Disorders and Other Pathologies*. London: Duckworth.

Winnicott, D. W. (1971). The location of cultural experience. In: *Playing and Reality*. London: Tavistock.

PART III

ADULTHOOD

CHAPTER FIVE

External danger and internal threat

Ronald Britton

Introduction

The concept of psychic trauma is Freud's earliest analytic offspring. Even the *Oxford English Dictionary* attributes to psychoanalysis the extension in meaning of the word to include mental as well as physical trauma. Currently, it figures mainly in two different ways in our psychoanalytic discourse: in considering infantile and childhood trauma as a cause of subsequent psychopathology; and in our understanding of post-traumatic states in adult life. When we address either of these topics, we have to remind ourselves that not all who suffer severely as children develop serious psychopathology; and we know from armed conflict and civilian disasters that only a minority become seriously disabled by post-traumatic neurosis. As Freud pointed out, psychoanalysis is good at retrospectively locating significant events in the histories of individuals but not at predicting their consequences in advance. And we are always at risk of succumbing to what the philosopher Henri Bergson called "the illusions of retrospective determinism", a belief that because something happened, it necessarily happened.

It may seem anomalous that current contributions on post-traumatic neurosis in adults by a number authors, such as Caroline Garland (1998), draw on Kleinian theory, yet you will see almost no use of the term "psychic trauma" in the theoretical papers of most Kleinian and post-Kleinian writers. This is true of me personally. I have had quite substantial experience of psychiatric battle casualties; I have written on "The deprived child" (Britton, 1978) and, at the Tavistock Clinic, I was involved in a workshop devoted to studying and providing psychotherapy for severely abused or neglected children ((Boston & Szur, 1983). And yet you would look in vain in the index of any of my books on psychoanalytic theory for the word "trauma".

I believe that this absence is because the concept of psychic trauma has been incorporated into the theory of general psychic development that Melanie Klein produced and Bion extended. Pathological (traumatic) versions of the paranoid-schizoid and depressive positions are described; the early Oedipus situation and its vicissitudes; and the consequences of failure of "containment" that may result, as Bion put it, in psychological catastrophe. I also suggest that implicit in this view of traumatic experience within the positions of infantile development is the idea that it can in some cases be a consequence of internal as well as external events. As Winnicott put it, "id-excitements can be traumatic when the ego is not able to include them" (Winnicott, 1960, p. 141). In other words, that as well as exogenous there is endogenous trauma: that the unconscious can flood and traumatise the ego. When this happens, a state of psycho-phobia can develop as a consequence that may result in a fear of thinking or dreaming. For such analytic patients, true free association would seem like a suicidal act and dreaming a terrifying possibility. Therefore, they have problems with the analytic method itself and fiercely resist it, or develop defensive methods of controlling it whilst appearing to comply with it. I have discussed the technical difficulties and my approach to them in earlier papers (Britton, 1989, 1998). I think that André Green has described something very similar to what I am calling psycho-phobia in his concept of "the central phobic position" (Green, 2000, p. 436), where he describes a situation in some patients of terror when one trauma awakened begins to resonate with others, leading to feelings of being invaded by uncontrollable forces and objects.

Endogenous trauma

In 1914, Freud returned to the subject of trauma after a number of years in his paper "From the history of an infantile neurosis", commonly referred to as "the Wolf Man case" (Freud, 1918b). He wrote, "The old trauma theory of the neuroses, which was after all built upon impressions gained from psycho-analytic practice, had suddenly come to the front once more" (Freud, 1918b, p. 95). Freud attributes the onset of his patient's childhood neurosis at the age of four to a traumatic experience. "But", as he says, "the event ... was not an external trauma, but a dream from which he awoke in a state of anxiety" (ibid., p. 28). The patient said, "In great terror, evidently of being eaten up by the wolves, I screamed and woke up... it took quite a long while before I was convinced that it had only been a dream. I was three, four, or at most five years old at the time. From then until my eleventh or twelfth year I was always afraid of seeing something terrible in my dreams" (ibid., p. 29).

Freud wrote:

> We know from our experience in interpreting dreams that this sense of reality [emphasised by the patient] carries a particular significance along with it. It assures us that some part of the latent material of the dream is claiming in the dreamer's memory to possess the quality of reality, that is, that the dream relates to an occurrence that really took place and was not merely imagined ... if it was to be assumed that behind the content of the dream there lay some such unknown scene—one, ... already forgotten—then it must have taken place very early. (ibid., p. 33)

Freud, as we all know, went on to establish to his own satisfaction the date of the observation of parental intercourse that he was convinced was the "unknown scene". "Thus in the first place the child's age at the date of the observation was established as being about one and a half years." Freud added (in a footnote), "The age of six months came under consideration as a far less probable, and indeed scarcely tenable, alternative" (ibid., p. 36). By dismissing this, he leaves out of his thinking the possibility of an infantile precursor colouring or shaping the later observation made at eighteen months.

In order to explain the traumatic effect of the dream, at the age of four, Freud returns to his old theory of *Nachträglicheit*. He assumed that affective force was added to the existing memory traces of the earlier observation because of the greater development of the patient's sexuality. In his early use of this term *Nachträglicheit*, he had in mind puberty (Freud, 1895, p. 356); now in the Wolf Man case, he had in mind the Oedipal phase of the four-year-old.

The theory that has developed since that time, particularly by those influenced by the ideas of Melanie Klein, is almost the reverse of his earliest formulation of "deferred action". Namely, that extra power and disturbance comes from the resurrection of infantile phantasy evoked by later events. Thus I would take it that the added force and primitive fears of the Wolf Man's dream come from the infusion of infantile phantasy into the childhood recollections of the four-year-old that were themselves provoked, no doubt, by events of the day. Freud himself suggests that there may be primal phantasies that precede observation of all kinds of parental interchange that shape the perception of the child. In Bion's version of this theory, the unsaturated, structured expectation of an as yet unperceived event is called a "pre-conception".

Using these ideas, I can, just to illustrate my point, produce an alternative, speculative reconstruction. Let us suppose that the Wolf Man had a pre-conception of a feeding breast and a pre-conception of a primal scene. In infancy, these pre-conceptions are "realised" and given shape in a variety of phantasies based on bodily experience, perception, and desire. At six months, he observes sexual intercourse between his parents and that provokes phantasies, largely in the form of oral and anal activity. A year later, he observes a similar event, and that stimulates his curiosity and feeds into his developing sexual theories. At four, his grandfather's story of the tailor and the wolf coalesces with other stories that stir his oral, anal, and genital desires and his anxieties. These link up with his childhood recollection of the witnessed primal scene; this converges with the infantile phantasies of the primal scene that bring with them projective identification, confusion, and infantile terror. This eruption of infantile thinking into his dream becomes the endogenous trauma that at the age of four initiated his childhood neurosis. Here then is a nightmare that inflicts on the dreamer a traumatic experience: it is not a dream that reproduces a traumatic event; it is a traumatic event itself. It had the same psychic status as the events of waking life and the same power to terrorise. The trauma that induced the neurosis was endogenous and it left behind a fear of dreaming and perhaps a fear of thinking.

The difference between Freud's *Nachträglichkeit* and my post-Kleinian version of the role of deferred action in traumatic experience is that in the former the force is presumed to come from current drives applied to past memories; in the latter the force comes through the link made between the present and the terrors of infantile phantasy. (I have refrained from wider discussion of *après coup* in order to keep my account simpler.)

Clinical example: Miss A

I would like to use a clinical illustration to take this further. This was a patient who, like the "Wolf Man", was terrified of dreaming and had protracted periods of insomnia as a result. She was also very afraid of her daytime thoughts and was compelled to empty her mind of them by repeatedly flushing the lavatory. The quality the world outside acquired as a consequence of its impregnation with her thoughts was a sense of menace. She located the unknown menace at as great a distance as she could and found it impossible to travel outside a personal boundary which roughly coincided with the outskirts of London. There were also areas inside London linked by association with various traumatic experiences. One such was the Middlesex Hospital which combined an actual memory of childhood hospitalisation with a dread of its name because of her fear of confusion and horror of sexual ambiguity. This meant that she had in addition to avoiding the hospital to eliminate any risk of seeing its name in print or of thinking of it. Thus she was menaced from within by her own potential thoughts and from without by the dangers she located in the physical environment. If she remained in her own rooms, they would fill up with her thoughts; if she escaped to the outside, she faced a dangerous world.

Her situation was epitomised in a screen memory she often repeated to me of an episode that occurred during the Second World War, when she was an adolescent. It was a recollection of a traumatic situation that functioned as a screen memory. Such screen memories, with the configuration of object relationships and always exactly repeated narrative of some particular event, contain within them earlier experiences, and infantile phantasy. In analysis, they often represent some current preoccupation and they form a template for apprehensions about the future.

A traumatic narrative of this kind is a multi-faceted psychic structure of recollected past, interpreted present, and anticipated future. Though her account included the situation that produced the traumatised experience, its precise reiteration appeared to provide a rigid container within which she confined psychic elements whose liberation she dreaded. The "traumatic memory" was therefore a "pathological organisation" (Steiner, 1979), in much the same way that a perverse ritual can be. Reiteration and repetition, therefore, were her means of confining chaos. In this respect, like many other traumatised individuals, she resembled Coleridge's Ancient Mariner who had compulsively to tell and retell his tale:

> Since then at an uncertain hour,
> Now oft times and now fewer
> That anguish comes and makes me tell
> My ghastly aventure.

> (from *The Rime of The Ancyent Mariner*
> by Samuel Taylor Coleridge)

In her reiterated memory of adolescence, Miss A was in a public air-raid shelter during a bomb attack in the Second World War. She felt suffocated in the shelter with her mother, whose anxiety oppressed her. She felt very urgently that she must escape, but at the threshold of the shelter, she was terrified when she saw bombs falling and the street on fire. An air-raid warden confronted her in the entrance obstructing her departure and ordering her to stay. Her conflict between fear of the outside and dread of the inside was intense and apparently irresolvable. She collapsed in the doorway, retaining consciousness but becoming mute and entirely without bodily sensations; she remembered not being able to feel the pins which the examining doctors stuck into her. You will recognise the reversal in her story of Freud's description of the primal father obstructing the child's attempt to undo the trauma of birth by re-entry into mother, like the Cherub with the flaming sword, preventing the re-entry of Adam and Eve into Eden described in *Paradise Lost*. My patient was trying to escape from the suffocating relationship she had with her mother but was confronted in the world outside that dyadic relationship with a terrifying father. This latter version of father was based on violent images of the primal scene; some seen, some overheard, some imagined, and all populated with infantile phantasy.

It was the fear of a recurrence of the traumatic state that was used thereafter as an internal threat compelling her to perform compulsively various activities. "If you don't wash your hair", for example, "you will get the feelings": said an internal voice. The "feelings" which she so dreaded was the experience of having no feeling. Another recurrent fear was that she would be apparently dead and then buried alive. Freud's comment on this particular phantasy is very pertinent in her case. He wrote in a footnote of 1909:

> It was not for a long time that I learned to appreciate the importance of phantasies and unconscious thoughts about life in the womb. They contain an explanation of the remarkable dread that many people have of being buried alive; and they also afford the deepest unconscious basis for the belief in survival after death, which merely represents a projection into the future of this uncanny life before birth. (Freud, 1900, p. 400)

When Miss A was a toddler, her mother was taken to hospital as an emergency with a tubal pregnancy. She overheard her two aunts describing this in lurid terms as the baby that had to be killed to save the mother. Subsequently, she imagined herself to be the unborn child trapped in her mother's inner tube in a situation where only one could survive at the expense of the other. At the time of the air raids, she and her mother, prior to the oft-recounted episode, had taken shelter in a London Tube station, where she had a gross panic attack. My patient's recollected adolescent scene had many precursors in childhood traumatic events, nightmares, and night terrors, and, as analysis revealed, infantile phantasy.

Miss A spent her days attempting to leave her mind behind her. I first saw her in her late middle age, but she had been a psychiatric patient continuously since adolescence. She was always convinced that part of her mind could be cut out, and had in fact at one time narrowly escaped a proposed psychosurgery because of her even greater fear of anaesthesia.

As one could expect, she was able to use analysis to stabilise herself but not alas to completely abandon her pathological defensive organisation. Freud's comments on resistance and recovery are particularly pertinent in this case. He wrote, "The crux of the matter is that the defensive mechanisms directed against former danger recur in the treatment as resistances against recovery. It follows from this that the ego treats recovery itself as a new danger" (Freud, 1937, p. 238).

A brief history of the concept of psychic trauma

Before discussing my ideas further, I want to give a brief account of the history of the concept of psychic trauma. Freud derived his original idea from Charcot's theory of post-traumatic paralytic hysteria in adult life and his discussions with Breuer on the case of Anna O. Freud's bold addition was to extend Charcot's theory to all cases of hysteria and to propound the concept of psychic trauma. In 1893, he wrote:

> There is a complete analogy between traumatic paralysis and common, non-traumatic hysteria. The only difference is that in the former a major trauma has been operative, whereas in the latter there is seldom a single major event to be signalised, but rather a series of affective impressions.

Freud added, and I would like to emphasise this:

> even in the case of the major mechanical trauma in traumatic hysteria, what produces the result is not the mechanical factor but the effect of fright, the psychical trauma. (Freud, S., 1893, pp. 30–31)

The story of Freud's subsequent abandonment of his original theory is familiar to all of us. The theory was to receive a number of obituaries published by Freud himself, beginning in 1906, but we now know he had already mourned its loss in 1897, only four years after the first announcement of its birth. In a letter to Fliess in 1897, he wrote, "I no longer believe in my neurotica [theory of the neuroses]. Now I have no idea where I stand" (Masson, 1985). What eventually took the place of his original traumatic theory of the neuroses was one based on the sexual development of children and the anxieties of the Oedipus complex. In 1906, Freud, in reviewing the development of his ideas, was able to write:

> I over-estimated the frequency of such events [sexual seduction] though in other respects they were not open to doubt ... [this] ... also made it necessary to modify my view of the mechanism of

hysterical symptoms. They were no longer to be regarded as direct derivatives of the repressed memories of childhood experiences; but between the symptoms and the childish impressions there were inserted the patient's phantasies (or imaginary memories) ... (1906, p. 274)

In the light of this theory, Abraham, a year later, published a paper on the effects of actual childhood sexual abuse. In this, he distinguished between "sexual traumas which take the child unawares from those which it has itself provoked or which are due to temptation or seduction". He arrived at the conclusion about that segment of abused children who subsequently developed neurosis, "that their sexual development was precocious and their libido itself quantitatively abnormal, and that their imagination was prematurely occupied with sexual matters to an abnormal degree" (Abraham, 1907, p. 54).

In the following period, the concept of psychic trauma was completely overshadowed by the theory of sexual development in psychoanalytic theory. Then, in 1914, as I quoted earlier, Freud wrote in the Wolf Man case, "The old trauma theory of the neuroses which was after all built upon impressions gained from psycho-analytic practice, had suddenly come to the front once more" (Freud, 1918b). In this paper, he was determined to demonstrate how adult neuroses had childhood precursors, to emphasise infantile sexuality; to attest to the importance of specific, personal events; and to rebut what he saw as Jung's attempt to locate neurotic difficulties as originating in adult life and the mythic childhood of mankind rather than in the childhood of the individual man.

However, having, to his own satisfaction, demonstrated the importance of the particulars of the childhood history of his patient, he proposed the universality of the primal scene in psychological development. A year later, he made use of this idea in another paper:

Among the store of unconscious phantasies of all neurotics, and probably of all human beings, there is one which is seldom absent and which can be disclosed by analysis: this is the phantasy of watching sexual intercourse between the parents. I call such phantasies ... —and others—"primal phantasies". (Freud, 1915c, p. 269)

Freud based this paper on his consultations with a young woman seeking legal redress against a man she claimed had "abused her confidence by getting unseen witnesses to photograph them while they were making love" (ibid., p. 263). Freud became quite satisfied that this was a false belief and that the traumatic episode that precipitated her delusion was based on the eruption of a phantasy. The patient had willingly embarked on a love tryst with a man but interrupted their love-making and almost immediately afterwards formed a delusional belief that a concealed third person had photographed them. Freud's reconstruction of her thinking was that the third person of the Oedipal triangle had been phantasied as the intrusive watcher. He then went further and hypothesised that the girl patient had suffered the eruption into her love-making of a phantasy of the primal scene. In reaction to this, he hypothesised, she had in phantasy taken the place of her mother as participant and assigned the role of malevolent observer to an unseen voyeur.

It is a remarkably imaginative theoretical paper with several anticipations of later theory (Britton, 1999); the point I want to make for my present purpose is that Freud treats the eruption of a childhood phantasy of the primal scene as the trauma. It is an endogenous trauma. An unconscious phantasy is provoked in an otherwise non-traumatic, intense sexual situation, and it is the primal scene phantasy that is the trauma. This in turn leads to a subsequent defensive organisation formed around a delusional belief of being watched. Caroline Garland, in her discussion of post-traumatic states in adult life, draws attention to the way in which in some individuals, where a complete denial of an unacceptable trauma has led to a violent rupture of the link to reality, delusional beliefs are used as pathological repair; as Freud described in Schreber's case (Garland, 1998, p. 10).

Freud's paper on the young woman with the sexual delusion was written in 1915, a year of incredible output, and we can see the interest in trauma being submerged by the torrent of new ideas pouring forth. Ten years later, Freud, in his paper "Inhibitions, symptoms and anxiety", produced a new model of psychic trauma and its sequelae. He distinguishes between fear, fright, and anxiety. Fright (*Schreck*) is the affect of traumatic experience (I think it could be even better translated as "panic" or "terror"); fear is attached to an object or activity and circumscribed by it; anxiety is an apprehension of danger. Realistic anxiety anticipates potential danger and neurotic anxiety phantasied danger. However, the traumatic situation itself is one in which fright (panic or terror) floods the individual; it is unbounded and at its core is helplessness (Freud, 1926, p. 166).

He also in this paper adduces the notion of repetition as an attempt to "master" what is originally a passive experience of being over-whelmed. In a healthy form, this can be found in children's play; in symptomatic form, in compulsive repetition and in repetitive traumatic dreams. In addition to attempting to round up the new ideas and the accumulating contradictions of psychoanalysis, he also intended to put in its place Rank's theory of birth trauma and Ferenczi's extrapolation from it. He writes in a mood of irritation, "Rank's contention—which was originally my own—obliged me to review the problem of anxiety once more" (ibid.).

Freud himself had first suggested birth trauma in a footnote added in 1909 to *The Interpretation of Dreams*. Freud strongly repudiated, however, the re-emergence in Rank's work of the cathartic theory of his early days with Breuer which he clearly believed his subsequent work had long transcended. He also suggested that if adverse birth-ing experience was a factor in subsequent neurosis, this should be established by research. Phyllis Greenacre took Freud's hint that if the birthing experience itself was a source of anxiety, then individual natal histories should be relevant. She concluded that, "severe suffering and frustration occurring in the antenatal and early postnatal months, espe-cially in the period preceding speech development, leave a heightened organic stamp on the make-up of the child ... which heightens the anxi-ety potential and gives greater resonance to the anxieties of later life" (Greenacre, 1953, p. 50).

Freud, in the same paper, produced a theory of repetition in play in response to this early adverse experience:

> The ego which experienced the trauma passively, now repeats it actively in a weakened version, in the hope of being able itself to direct its course. It is certain that children behave in this fashion towards every distressing impression they receive, by reproducing it in their play. In thus changing from passivity to activity, they attempt to master their experiences psychically. If this is what is meant by "abreacting a trauma", we can no longer have anything to urge against the phrase. (Freud, 1926, p. 167)

This was already being exploited in the developing use of play analysis of children by Melanie Klein, "In this way", she writes of one of her early cases, "Erna enacted before me one of the first traumata in her experience ..." (Klein, 1926, p. 136).

Play as a means of mastering anxiety was really the starting point for Melanie Klein's analytic observations and theorising. She took play to be the counterpart of free association and applied to it the same sort of symbolic interpretation she would have to adult dreams. So she assumed there was an analogical link between the repetitive dreams of post-traumatic states and children's dramatisations in play. Later, this was to be further developed in the often subtle re-enactments in the transference in adult analysis.

Clinical example: Tracy

I can give an example of the immediate aftermath of a traumatic situation in the play of a little girl that illustrates vividly this repetition in play. In this example, we can see how a violent episode is transformed into a dramatised version of the event, and her position of helpless, frightened onlooker transformed into that of cool narrator. It also illustrates another point. The child segregates the immediate recollection and representation of the violent family events from representation in play of other phantasy material. I made use of an observation of Klein in understanding this material, that children usually represent family members with domestic animals and primitive phantasies with wild animals.

Tracy was a four-year-old who was part of a dysfunctional family and therefore the subject of a supervisory care order. The social services department concerned had close links with the Tavistock Clinic and had arranged for her psychotherapy. Tracy suffered from bad dreams and night terrors. The care order also meant that she was escorted to and from the clinic and the carer gave us news of family events. On this particular occasion, we were informed that the night before her regular session, she and her baby brother were together with their parents when father attacked mother, who then attempted suicide and was taken away in an ambulance.

Tracy quietly entered the therapy room, took out her personal toy box, and began to play. She took out the pig family and then built a wall of sand, on the other side of which she put the wild animals including the crocodile so that they were separated. Having done this, she took the pig family, consisting of father pig, mother pig, and two little pigs, and put them in a circle. Father pig then attacked mother pig; mother pig then threw herself down and lay injured. An ambulance arrived and took mother pig away. During this, intermittently, Tracy repeatedly built the sand wall higher and fingered the crocodile, particularly its teeth. I commented that she wanted to make sure that the wild animals, which were like her bad dreams, did not get mixed up with the farm animals who were having an upsetting time like her family: that she didn't want her bad dreams to get mixed up with anything that happened at home. She responded to this by taking a little human baby figure over the wall from the farm side to join the wild animals.

Here I think we can see that traumatic events have already been taken in play into a narrative with some symbolic representation by the pig family. They have also been segregated from dream and phantasy represented by wild animals. Tracy's response to this interpretation was to put the baby into the arena of the wild animals. The older pig child, representing her current child self, remained on the other side of the barrier. This, as I would understand it, located infantile phantasy on one side and her childhood traumatic experience on the other.

A recent experience with an adult patient illustrated for me what happens when this is not achieved. The patient, a practising psychiatrist, arrived for her analytic session one day in a state of panic and helplessness. She had just been badly frightened by a menacing psychotic patient in an interview. Interestingly, my patient was one who could have been described as psycho-phobic and had tried to get through analysis without free associating whilst ostensibly doing so. In the immediate aftermath of the current trauma, it was not difficult to link the situation, via the transference, with childhood terrors of her father, who was prone to inflict violence on her mother, and, with the help of subsequent dreams, to infantile phantasies of monstrous non-human figures. The point I wish to make about this is that the distinction between these different psychic elements, childhood memories, nightmares, infantile phantasies had collapsed into the current traumatic event, and freedom from the traumatic effects only followed the re-establishment of the different psychic identities of these components.

Discussion

My discussion of endogenous trauma is not intended to diminish the importance of trauma resulting from external events nor to create an antithesis; it is simply to add to the self-evident effects of the conspicuous wounding events of a dangerous world some traumas that may arise from internal events. As I said, very little is to be found under the heading of "psychogenic trauma" in the later writings of Klein, her immediate followers, or the contemporary post-Kleinians. I do not think, as some critics suggest, that this is because they have regarded it as unimportant, but because Melanie Klein subsumed trauma into her central theory of development. Essentially, this is a theory of anxiety in which some traumatic experience is regarded as an inevitable part of infancy. As described by Melanie Klein, the para-noid-schizoid position, the depressive position, and the early Oedipus situation include danger, a sense of helplessness, and the risk of being overwhelmed by instinctual forces. Traumatic experience is always imminent, and parental love, care, and understanding are required to keep it at bay or to counteract it. "The first external source of anxiety can be found in the experience of birth", she writes, and adds "it would appear that the pain and discomfort he has suffered, as well as the loss of the intra-uterine state, are felt by him as an attack by hostile forces" (Klein, 1952, pp. 61–62). She goes further than this, however, by suggesting that there is an innate fear from the outset. She wrote, "my analytic observations show that there is in the unconscious a fear of annihilation of life" (ibid., p. 29). This she remained adamant about, and it matches a comment she made very late in her career about young children, on "the terrifying character of some of their internal-ized objects" (Klein, 1958, p. 241). These archaic monsters "are split off ... and relegated to the deeper layers of the unconscious" (ibid.). Pre-sumably in favourable circumstances and good health, these deeper layers remained unplumbed except in fiction or occasional dreams. We feel secure in a world free from mythic monsters. However, if any of these phantasies gained access to the ego where they were given the status of belief, a traumatic experience would follow.

Klein encapsulated the clinical phenomenon she described as an innate fear of annihilation, within Freud's theory of the death instinct. She was clear that there was a fear of annihilation and that there was an innate destructive impulse, and she derived both from Freud's concept of the death instinct. However, as Roger Money-Kyrle suggested: "Freud's theory of a death instinct and Melanie Klein's view that there is also a basic fear of death are conceptually distinct" (Money-Kyrle, 1955, p. 288). I personally find it easier to think of an inborn fear of annihilation and innate hostility to the outside world as separate entities. I would not equate this primitive fear of annihilation with what an adult would call fear of death. It is a more inchoate fear with an actively fragmenting quality. It seems to correspond to nameless dread described by Bion as raw infantile experience unmodified by maternal containment (Bion, 1962).

I would agree with Money-Kyrle when he says, "that there are fears more basic than the fear of castration or loss of love ... There is for instance the terror of disintegration." He adds in a footnote, "The terror of disintegration may perhaps be equated with Freud's concept of traumatic anxiety" (Money-Kyrle, 1955, p. 288). I think he is right. We meet this terror in the analysis of borderline patients, where it appears as a fear of dissolution of the self, or a terror of the destruction of all meaning. The eruption into consciousness of such terrifying beliefs is endogenously traumatic. The threat in this case is not the loss of an object, it is loss of "sanity" and the transformation of the uncomprehended into the incomprehensible.

We derive our sense of security from benign unconscious beliefs. Whilst they prevail, as a background of overall wellbeing, we can entertain worrying possibilities without succumbing to an anxiety state. If these belief systems are disintegrated, we may be exposed to the intrusion of unintegrated phantasies that might gain the status of belief and thus arouse terror. I think we produce systems of belief as naturally as we wear clothes, and they are part of the protective shield to which Freud drew attention. A traumatic experience disrupts this steady knitting of psychic wool into acceptable patterns of belief. In the traumatic state, together with affects such as fright and helplessness, we find confusion, bewilderment, incoherence, and loss of confident expectation. For at least a moment, or perhaps forever, the pre-existing unconscious belief system that underpinned the individual's sense of safety, and his unarticulated assumption of the rightness of things, are shattered. I suggest that the disruption that can produce this can come from inside as well as outside; that trauma can be endogenous as well as exogenous.

References

Abraham, K. (1907). The experiencing of sexual traumas as a form of sexual activity. In: D. Bryan & A. Strachey (Eds.), *Selected Papers of Karl Abraham*. London: Hogarth, 1927.

Bion, W. R. (1957). On arrogance. In: *Second Thoughts* (pp. 86–92). New York: Jason Aronson, 1967.

Bion, W. R. (1962). A theory of thinking. In: *Second Thoughts* (pp. 86–92). New York: Jason Aronson, 1967.

Britton, R. S. (1978). The deprived child. *The Practitioner, September, 221*.

Britton, R. S. (1989). The missing link: parental sexuality in the Oedipus complex. In: J. Steiner (Ed.), *The Oedipus Complex Today* (pp. 83–101). London: Karnac.

Britton, R. S. (1998). *Belief and Imagination*. London: Routledge.

Coleridge, S. T. (1798). The Rime of the Ancyent Mariner. In: W. J. B. Owen (Ed.), *Wordsworth and Coleridge, Lyrical Ballads*. Oxford: Oxford University Press, 1967.

Freud, S. (1893a). On the psychical mechanism of hysterical phenomena. *S.E. 3*. London: Hogarth.

Freud, S. (1895). *Project for a Scientific Psychology. S.E. 1*. London: Hogarth.

Freud, S. (1906a). My views on the part played by sexuality in the aetiology of the neuroses. *S.E. 7*. London: Hogarth.

Freud, S. (1914d). On the history of the psycho-analytic movement. *S.E. 14*. London: Hogarth.

Freud, S. (1915b). Thoughts for the times on war and death. *S.E. 14*. London: Hogarth.

Freud, S. (1915f). A case of paranoia running counter to the psycho-analytic theory of the disease. *S.E. 14*. London: Hogarth.

Freud, S. (1918b). From the history of an infantile neurosis. *S.E. 17*. London: Hogarth.

Freud, S. (1926). Inhibitions, symptoms and anxiety. *S.E. 20*. London: Hogarth.

Freud, S. (1937c). Analysis terminable and interminable. *S.E. 23*. London: Hogarth.

Garland, C. (Ed.) (1998). *Understanding Trauma: A Psychoanalytical Approach*. London: Duckworth.

Green, A. (2000). The central phobic position: a new formulation of the free association method. *International Journal of Psychoanalysis, 81*: 429.

Greenacre, P. (1953). *Trauma, Growth and Personality*. London: Maresfield Library, Karnac, 1987.

Klein, M. (1952). Some theoretical conclusions regarding the emotional life of the infant. In: R. Money-Kyrle, B. Joseph, E. O'Shaughnessy, & H. Segal (Eds.), *The Writings of Melanie Klein*, Vol. 3 (pp. 61–93). London: Hogarth, 1975.

Klein, M. (1958). On the development of mental functioning. In: R. Money-Kyrle, B. Joseph, E. O'Shaughnessy, & H. Segal (Eds.), *The Writings of Melanie Klein*, Vol. 3 (pp. 236–246). London: Hogarth, 1975.

Masson, J. M. (Ed. and Trans.) (1985). *The Complete Letters of Sigmund Freud to Wilhelm Fliess, 1887–1904*. Cambridge, MA: Harvard University Press.

Money-Kyrle, R. (1955). An inconclusive contribution to the theory of the death instinct. In: D. Meltzer and E. O'Shaughnessy (Eds.), *The Collected Papers of Roger Money-Kyrle*. Perthshire: Clunie Press, 1978.

Paskauskas, R. A. (Ed.) (1993). *The Complete Correspondence of Sigmund Freud and Ernest Jones 1908–1939*. Cambridge, MA: Harvard University Press.

Steiner, J. (1979). The border between the paranoid-schizoid and the depressive positions in the borderline patient. *British Journal of Medical Psychology, 52*: 385–391.

Winnicott, D. W. (1960). Ego distortion in terms of true and false self. In: *The Maturational Processes and the Facilitating Environment*. London: Hogarth, 1972.

CHAPTER SIX

The Kraken awakens: the re-emergence of traumatic experiences when defences break down

Joanne Stubley

Below the thunders of the upper deep;
Far far beneath in the abysmal sea,
His ancient, dreamless, uninvaded sleep
The Kraken sleepeth: faintest sunlights flee
About his shadowy sides; above him swell
Huge sponges of millennial growth and height;
And far away into the sickly light,
From many a wondrous grot and secret cell
Unnumber'd and enormous polypi
Winnow with giant arms the slumbering green.
There hath he lain for ages, and will lie
Battening upon huge seaworms in his sleep,
Until the latter fire shall heat the deep;
Then once by man and angels to be seen,
In roaring he shall rise and on the surface dies.

—*The Kraken*, Tennyson, 1830

Written in 1830 by Alfred Lord Tennyson, the mythical creature the Kraken describes rests in a timeless slumber on the ocean bed. It is only with the apocalyptic fires that he rises, and in a fury, reaches the surface and expires. I hope to use this metaphor to describe an example of a brief psychoanalytic consultation model for survivors of external, adult trauma, originally developed by Caroline Garland in the Trauma Unit at the Tavistock Clinic.

> I close my eyes and I am in the olive grove. I can smell the dry, almost salty air and hear the breath of the wind through the branches of the trees. The birdsong is just beginning its morning chorus. There is a particular moment in growing olives that when broken apart they will bleed with a kind of milky oil, that smells intensely of heat and olives and the rich earth. There are over forty trees in the grove and in the clear, morning light they are gently swaying. There are twenty of us in that company, all young Lebanese men like me, waiting with our machine guns and our hearts pounding. Within two hours, all of the olive trees are gone and only three of us remain. This is what I see over and over again—no, not see but live again each time I sleep or at moments when a smell reminds me of the olives or the sunlight has a similar quality or I smell salt and it is the smell of blood in my nostrils.

Mr K, as I will call him, described this to me within the context of a brief psychoanalytic consultation for trauma. This scene had happened over twenty years before, and yet it was only in the last few months that he had begun to have these re-experiencing symptoms of nightmares and flashbacks, so typical of post-traumatic stress reactions. In the intervening period, the memories had, like the Kraken in Tennyson's poem, lay sleeping their timeless, dreamless sleep until woken and brought to the surface by subsequent events. In the poem, the Kraken dies in being brought up from the depths. One hopes that in the light of the working through in the consultation, the memories also lose their monstrous power.

Trauma has, from the very beginnings of psychoanalysis, always had a pivotal role in the development and elaboration of theory. I hope to use the example of Mr K to elaborate our understanding of the impact of trauma on the individual and to focus particularly on this issue of time. How do we understand what has happened in Mr K's mind that these traumatic events can apparently be contained in the mind for years, only to burst forth much later with their full ferocity and intensity, as though time has stood still? What does this tell us about the nature of time and temporality?

Freud tells us in 1909, "A thing which has not been understood inevitably reappears; like an unlaid ghost, it cannot rest until the mystery has been solved and the spell broken" (p. 122).

Mr K first presented to his GP with a number of somatic complaints. He described a numbness in his left hand that some times spread up his arm. This was intermittent and he noted that it was more likely to occur when he was upset emotionally. He had a brief altercation with a shop assistant that had appeared to precipitate one of these attacks but he also explained that it could come out of the blue. He told the GP that he felt like an old man. He had found himself talking out loud on the street, with no recollection of the words spoken but he notices others are looking at him. Sudden and violent episodes of shaking uncontrollably, when he cannot breathe and he feels his body goes numb, were also reported. Mr K had lost ten kilograms in weight in less than a year and his sleep had been disturbed by nightmares and oversleeping. Mr K described a shadow flitting across the corner of his vision, like a person, but knew this was not real. Mr K had stopped going out, answering his mail or his telephone. The GP noted that Mr K appeared very bewildered by what had been happening to him.

Indeed, there was a real sense of the mysterious in Mr K's initial presentation. He could not seem to find any kind of satisfying explanation for himself that would account for his situation. The GP decided to call this agitated depression and started Mr K on anti-depressants and sent him to the counsellor in the practice. This encounter led to Mr K being referred to the Trauma Unit in the Tavistock Clinic. The counsellor noted that Mr K was "generally a resourceful man who has coped with a history of severe trauma and losses in his country of origin. Consequently, he has little understanding of his current psychological state and finds this distressing." Mr K told her that he had separated from his girlfriend fourteen months before. He emphasised the fact that he did not feel these were sufficient triggers to explain his psychological state. He also mentioned noise intolerance and hyper-vigilance in association with other post-traumatic symptoms such as intrusive nightmares and phobic avoidance.

For his first appointment, Mr K was on time. He strode rather purposefully out of the full lift. I said my name and he introduced himself as K and offered me his hand. It was a firm, warm handshake. He was a tall, thin, middle-aged man wearing shaded glasses with a trilby hat and casual but expensive clothes. He made good eye contact and there was something personable and likeable about him. Mr K spoke with an Arabic accent, but his English is almost faultless. There are moments when this slips a little, and usually this seemed to be when he was more disturbed by our conversation.

Mr K immediately emphasised to me that he did not understand what had happened to him. It did not make sense to him. He said he was very pleased to be here and hoped I might be able to help him. He had been very excited about coming because he does need help. He came here at 10.30 am (the appointment was 1.30 pm) to have a look at the place. Then he went away and had a coffee and now had come back. But when the receptionist called his name, he felt panic inside (he puts his hand on his chest).

I begin to say something about his anxiety in coming here for help. He seemed to both agree and dismiss this at the same time, saying yes but this is not who he is. He is a strong man, or used to be, and he cannot understand what is happening now. He also made it clear that there was something about his coming early that was more in keeping with a soldier in a danger zone than an anxious patient, and this was part of what he felt he didn't understand. He spoke of how he had been OK until eighteen to twenty months ago, when he had lost his job and lost his girlfriend. But he had many losses in the past and somehow, he seemed to say, these current losses were insufficient to explain his response.

The appearance of the soldier at this time in the consultation was a clue to what appeared to be happening in Mr K's internal world. Time was, in effect, collapsing in upon itself. The soldier that I later discovered he had been in his youth was also present alongside this middle-aged man in the room. It is an instance of the repetition compulsion in action—a kind of symbolic equation in its concreteness that demonstrated the impairment in symbolic functioning in this area of his mind.

Mr K talked a little about having gone into the army at sixteen and having many terrible experiences. He said he would talk about these some time, and I made it clear that I understood he may not wish to speak of these things now. His response was to suggest that of course he was able to, he simply did not feel the time was right. There was an increasing sense of the way he would do this particular manoeuvre in the room with me. He would seem to offer me something to think about, I would then wonder about it or make some kind of comment on it, and this would lead him to move charmingly away with a suggestion that of course none of this really mattered terribly much to him, he was simply being polite with me.

He told me that he had come to the UK fourteen years ago and had managed to "put it all behind me". This was said as though it were the most understandable thing in the world, and when I questioned how he might have done this, he smiled and said by being busy. He had studied and worked very hard. He had also been very outgoing and confident and lively, with many friends and always much to do. He had found himself a good job in management and earned a decent living. He emphasised that he made over £60,000 a year and had been very good at his work. At the same time, he had also taken a degree in the Swedish language and had made use of this in his work. He had many friends and acquaintances, and spent most of his time socialising and enjoying himself. The impression he gave was of a lively, busy existence that had suddenly and dramatically come to a halt. This was linked to a particular incident that had occurred several months ago when he had lost his mobile phone, with over a hundred and twenty contacts in the address book. I commented on how this loss seemed to describe a way in which he had felt the many connections and ties he had to this busy life had been severed.

With this comment, as with a number of others, Mr K appeared touched by what I had said. Tears welled up in his eyes and one or two would even need to be wiped away. What was conveyed at these moments was an enormous sense of shame at finding himself in this vulnerable state, and it was at these times that he would repeat the idea that he did not understand what was happening to him, this did not make sense. Any further interpretation from me would then be brushed aside. For instance, I spoke to him about his shame at finding himself in this state, as though the recent losses were not felt to be sufficient to explain what he was experiencing. He would respond by turning away from his own distress, making light of what had happened to him, and adding that, compared to what he had experienced in the past, this was nothing.

I gradually heard how he had unexpectedly lost his job when the company was downgrading. He had then lost his girlfriend, but he wanted to assure me she was not someone he was serious about. He is not the marrying kind, and this was not a serious relationship. In fact, he thought this woman had really just been with him for his money—she had spent over £40,000 on his credit card. When he lost his job, she didn't stay around for long.

I thought Mr K wanted to emphasise his own perturbation and confusion about his situation. However, I also felt he presented these losses and then dismissed them in a manner that was reflected in the way in which he managed his own emotional state and his contact with me in the transference. As I began to speak to him about this, he was clearly aware of this process inside him and agreed that he had lived a great deal of his life keeping much of his external experiences and his internal states at a distance. He was also able to acknowledge that this was what he was doing in the room with me. This was said with an idea that this was a highly desirable state and reflected the strength inside him that he had indeed managed for so many years to keep himself in this virtually untouchable state where people, events, feelings, and memories could not touch him. With shame and embarrassment, he described to me how he had decided in the New Year period to kill himself. He had taken all of his antidepressant capsules, opened them up, and put the powder into a bottle of vodka. He had also been drinking beforehand. When he tried to drink it, the taste was so terrible that even with the addition of orange juice, he was unable to proceed.

In trying to think with Mr K about this experience, there was a question in his mind as to what had kept him alive. At first, this was very concretely experienced as due to the unbearable taste. There was considerable shame at this idea that he had been so weak that he had behaved in this way. However, he also described a way in which he felt himself to be back in the army, still fighting in a war zone, and that he needed to turn his attention back to the enemy. I thought this was clearly confusing and disturbing for Mr K and he was struggling to make sense of this experience. It seemed to link with what had happened in his need to scout out the Tavistock before coming to his appointment: he was living in a kind of dual reality where past and present were entwined, and at times he was not fully able to distinguish which reality he was reacting to. When I described this thought to him, Mr K turned to his dreams. He said that he had spent many years not dreaming at all. He had begun to feel something close to envy at others who were able to talk about their dreams as though they were interesting and curious phenomena that added to the richness of their lives. All this had now changed. Mr K had powerful, vivid nightmares that recreated in detail many of his experiences from the war. At this point, he told me that as well as being in the army for a number of years, he had also been in the secret service and had held a very important post at the time he had come to the UK. Again, he suggested that there was much to talk about here but he was not willing to do so at this time. I felt he wished to excite my curiosity, but I also felt there was a way in which he was attempting to titrate the contact with me, to limit what was said in this first meeting. He agreed with this interpretation.

In the subsequent meeting two weeks later, I thought Mr K looked a little more at ease, although he began by wanting to tell me that this time he had nothing to say. He had difficult experiences in the past but he felt that it was not helpful to speak of these. He had managed them for many years and this was not something he wanted to do. I acknowledged this and linked it with the shame he feels at finding himself in this state and coming to see a woman he does not know to talk about such terrible things.

At this point, Mr K turned his attention to a wall hanging in my room, an African print that is used to disguise an old viewing mirror between two rooms. He pointed to it and said he did not like this. He wondered where it was from—perhaps Afghanistan, he thought, or Turkey. He didn't like it but that was funny because he did like those colours, there was just something about it. Mr K would often return to his feelings about this print, and I was able to interpret to him that I thought he was telling me about his anxieties and uncertainties about who I am and whether he really felt able to trust me when a part of him didn't like what I represented.

Mr K then began to describe how he has been doing a lot of writing every day. He doesn't go out very much, except to go to the shops early in the morning when there are few people around. He doesn't like going out where there are too many people, particularly anywhere that he has to wait. He can't do it, his temper is too great. He never used to be like this, but it is not right to put other people at risk in this way. When I wondered what he was afraid might happen, he described how he has had considerable training and experience in the secret service and the impulse to hit out violently when he is standing in a line at the post office or the local shops is worrying in this context.

I found myself at this moment and at an number of others wondering about how much truth was contained in his description of his past, and this was highlighted as he went on to talk about having been second in command. There was a mixture of disbelief and intrigue in the way

I found myself approaching this material. This lessened as he began to speak more about his childhood. I also felt that he was somehow aware of this in the transference as he began to talk to me about how foreign his experience would be to a European who had not grown up in the midst of this violence and destruction that his country had been virtually decimated by. I felt he spoke at these times with considerable affection and melancholy for what had been lost—to him and to his people.

Mr K described an early childhood of wealth and happiness. He was the firstborn son to a well-off intellectual and cultured family. There were three maids to care for him in his early years, and he laughed as he suggested that the constant attendance made learning to walk a painless experience. He subsequently had two brothers and two sisters. This idyllic experience was shattered when the conflict broke out. Mr K was twelve when his father left the country, leaving him as the man of the house, responsible for his mother and siblings. His mother was pregnant with his youngest sister at the time. Mr K was unable to attend his school because it was in the conflict zone, and he had to move to the local school, losing many of his friends. Mr K's father, who worked for an airline company, apparently had to leave to continue his work. However, Mr K made it clear that he felt his father had escaped, with a suggestion of dereliction of duty implicit in this statement.

I commented on the way in which Mr K was telling me that everything in his life had suddenly changed from being safe, happy, and protected to uncertainty, fear, and responsibility. In response, Mr K elaborated on this by telling me about the shortages and rationing that had occurred. There were queues for everything. He used to stand in line at the baker's every morning. This could take hours and one was limited by how much one was able to get, even with the wait. He knew one man in the neighbourhood who ran a restaurant. He had three daughters and in order to be able to get a sufficient supply of bread for his customers, he would get all his children to stand in line so they could each receive the maximum ration. One day, the enemy bombed the queue. All three girls were killed. Mr K witnessed this event.

He told me the story in such a way that he seemed unsure whether I was really able to take this in. After a pause, I acknowledged this, suggesting how terrible for a young boy to have to experience this, to see these things. Mr K shrugged this off in what felt an increasingly familiar way. He told me that he, like so many, saw a great many terrible things and this was, after all, a long time ago. There was a silence and then I linked this story of the queue of children bombed with Mr K's current difficulties in being with people and waiting in line. I wondered whether this was perhaps part of his struggle to queue now and contributed to this feeling of uncontainable rage.

Mr K drew his breath in sharply, then said, "Oh, I hate you. Yes this could be so." He was silent for a moment then shook his head and repeated that this was so long ago and he had seen so many terrible things since. There were so many things he could tell me about but he doesn't want to do that, he doesn't want to speak of these things yet. There is too much and the story is too long.

In later sessions, we were able to think about this initial, surprised response of "I hate you" in terms of his repeated attempts to keep me and himself at a distance from his past and the associated affect. It was as though my interpretation had somehow managed to get past the soldier inside, guarding him against being too close to such dangerous links and emotions. In that moment, I had become the enemy.

André Green describes Freud's notion of time presented in the *Three Essays on the Theory of Sexuality* as: "the idea of layers of lava overlapping each other, causing emotions of successive temporal currents to cohabit" (Green, 2007).

Mr K returned for his next appointment to tell me immediately that the problem with waiting was now much improved. He felt this must be due to the antidepressants, although he also thought that was surprising as he had now been on them for several months. But somehow he felt calmer and was not so anxious about exploding into a rage. I thought he both wanted to tell me this to acknowledge the work we had done, but also wanted to keep me at a certain distance, held at bay by the antidepressants. I also wondered whether this reflected his anger at needing to come to talk to me as he then spoke of my wall-hanging again. When I interpreted something of this to him, his pleasure at feeling better perhaps mixed in with his unhappiness at needing to come here and speak to someone like me, he smiled in a way that felt warmer than any previous contact made.

In this session, Mr K began to tell me more about his dreams. He said that for over twenty years, he had been someone who did not dream. He would listen to others speaking about the stories and the wishes their dreams played with and he would wonder what that was like. He would sleep five or six hours in the past and awake from a dreamless slumber, ready to face another busy day. However, since everything had changed, his nights were full of faces. He asked me whether I was aware of how faces may fade with time, losing the detail of what someone looks like so that it is impossible to fully recall their features or any distinctive details. Mr K seemed to want to fully impress on me his sense that this is what should happen. He then described how in his dreams and nightmares every night, he would see the faces of friends he had not seen for over twenty years and yet they would appear as though it were yesterday.

Mr K was clearly disturbed by the timelessness of the unconscious that brought in his dreams these faces back to him from a past he had tried so hard to forget. It appeared to be, to him, a powerful representation of what he was struggling with in his life—how to begin to understand the way in which this area in his mind that had been kept so separate was now flooding into his life, intruding the past into the present.

Mr K described one recurrent dream. However, there was a way that he told this story that made it difficult to know whether it was a dream or a memory. My sense was that Mr K also had this struggle. He told me that when he was in the army, probably at about seventeen or eighteen years of age, he had a good friend who had survived a number of battles with him. Mr K would often have problems with losing his keys, to the point where his mother had made a chain to put them around his neck. One evening, he and his friend were in the mess when someone asked them to take a box to another site. Mr K couldn't find his so his friend took the company jeep instead. It wasn't until he left that Mr K remembered the keys were around his neck. His friend had to travel some distance to get to the jeep, and on the way he was hit by a bullet in the leg. His friend rang them in the mess to get help but by the time they got to him, he had died from blood loss.

When Mr K had finished telling this story, he pulled a chain out from around his neck and showed me his keys. He told me that every night he sees this friend in his dreams, his face so clear that it is as though he is still there in the mess. Mr K looked very distressed as he said this and then covered his face with his hands. We gradually began to talk about his guilt at what had happened. Mr K again suggested that there was a great deal I did not know. He spoke of so many good comrades who had been lost. At this point, he told me the story of the olive groves that I began with. I felt both of these descriptions suggested a strong sense of survivor guilt, and I began to wonder how much this had been one of the contributors to the need for his withdrawal from his past.

Freud describes in "Thoughts for the times on war and death" (1915b) that the loss of a loved one provokes a particular form of guilt that he called "survivor guilt". This is based on the notion that all love relationships contain ambivalent feelings of love and hate. Even the smallest degree of hate leads to triumph, if only unconsciously, at the death of the other, as it is experienced as though it were the death of the rival or enemy.

> There adheres to the tenderest and most intimate of our love relations a portion of hostility which can excite an unconscious death wish.

In the following session, Mr K began in an acutely anxious state. He had been sitting in the waiting room when someone had walked in. He wished to emphasise to me that he had been sitting where he could easily see who came in and out, so it was not about being surprised. He described various somatic components to this anxiety, many of which linked with the GP's original description of his presentation. The overwhelming impression was a sense of his body being out of his control. He spoke of his previous physical strength and stamina—he could swim the channel if he had to and he could lift enormous weights. He used to run regularly, and he could run for miles and miles without stopping. I felt this held both an omnipotent view of what he had been able to contain in the past within the physical confines of his body. I also thought he wanted to emphasise his sense of weakness now that he was unable to control this body of his.

Mr K moved on to talk more about his background. He told me that six years ago, his father had a car accident in which he had been injured and his own father, Mr K's grandfather, had been killed. This led to Mr K saying that he hated his father. His father had left them and since then has had four more wives, moving from one to the next after usually having one or two children. Mr K now has about six half-siblings. His father is married to a thirty-two-year-old woman and they have two young children. Mr K looked disturbed by this thought. After a pause, he then asked me if I had children. He did not want to have a family; he didn't think it was for him. He had many nieces and nephews and this was enough.

He then said that he thought there was likely to be another outbreak of war soon and that perhaps he should return. He was very well known in his country. When he was twenty, he had been a national hero—they need such things in times of war, and perhaps he should return now as many people believed he should.

We began to speak then of his guilt at being alive when so many, including his brother, had died; at being here in the UK and not there when war continued to rage. Mr K said that his country contained four million but there were twenty million of his people scattered around the world. His journey here had been a long one, and we did not have time for it today, but it needed to be told. Indeed, there was increasingly an awareness that his many stories of loss and separation did need to be told. The outcome of Mr K's brief trauma consultation was an awareness that he needed to confront time in the context of his life as a whole. This awareness shifted Mr K from being a "trauma" patient into a wish to be a patient who might make use of once-weekly work with me to understand the nature of his internal world in the context of his external reality.

Discussion

Clearly, there are many different aspects that could be addressed in Mr K's presentation and history. What I wish to pick up here is the question of time. How time is experienced is closely linked with understanding the nature of trauma, loss, memory, phantasy, and reality. Mr K had his world turned upside down when he was twelve and the conflict began. For the next decade, he had numerous severe traumatic experiences as a civilian and then in the army and secret service. On coming to the UK, Mr K appeared to make use of various defensive manoeuvres to place these experiences into some kind of temporal container—we may say with hindsight, a time bomb—where they remained for many years. With a series of losses and separations, the container broke open, flooding Mr K with these traumatic events of the past as though they were in the present. The Kraken, the monster of the deep, sleeping his timeless, ancient, dreamless sleep, awakes.

Freud suggested that the origin of the sense of time came from the discontinuous method of functioning of the perceptual conscious. He says, "It is as though the unconscious stretches out feelers, through the medium of the system Perceptual-conscious towards the external world and hastily withdraws them as soon as they have sampled the excitations coming from it" (Freud, 1925a, p. 231). Here Freud is talking about time in its chronological sense.

Perelberg describes the complexity of Freud's notions of time, which include development, fixation, regression, repression, the return of the repressed, the timelessness of the unconscious, and *après coup* as some of the axes of temporality. As she says:

> Dreams enabled Freud to discover a dismembered temporality, the rules of primary process and the timelessness of the unconscious. In the three essays of sexuality, the theory of infantile sexuality returned to a time that was ordered traditionally, that is in terms of the growth characteristic of life. (Perelberg, 2007, p. xiv)

With the Wolf Man came further elaborations on the notions of time. André Green described this as the "disposition to re-acquisition", where primal phantasies are re-actualised through individual experience (Green, 2007). In 1926, Freud suggested that most of the repression we deal with in our therapeutic work represents cases of repression by deferred action, *après coup*. By this, he meant that experiences and memory can be revised at a later date, when the individual reaches a new stage of maturation. The notion of *après coup* links up with the function of repetition. Freud suggests that memory is present several times over (Freud, 1926d).

Roger Money-Kyrle postulates that we are all born with certain facts that are part of our innate understanding and knowledge of the world. One of these facts is the recognition of the inevitability of death. This knowledge is founded on an awareness and acceptance of the reality of the passage of time, and that loss is an essential component to living (Money-Kyrle, 1968). Denying the passage of time is intrinsic to resistance to change, to mourning, and ultimately death. James Rose suggests it is also intrinsic to the denial of bodily and psychic development (Rose, 1997).

Did Mr K's years in this country before his breakdown represent a kind of psychic retreat from the intolerable pain of mourning the traumatic losses he had endured? A retreat that kept at bay the guilt, pain, and fury that he could not face? Having had his world destroyed twice—first, the sudden loss of the idyllic existence of a childhood where even the pain of learning to walk is cushioned, and then the wartime

traumatic experiences—one wonders whether further loss could simply not be tolerated. Perhaps the scene in the olive grove can be seen as
a screen memory for the earlier trauma of his childhood loss. One may
also wonder about the sense of his mother's absence in this early happy
childhood, with hints of significant problems in the marital relationship
alongside a number of younger siblings, all of which may have contributed to a sense of the loss of his mother.

Freud used the notion of screen memories to refer to a situation in
which an earlier memory is used fit a later event as well as one in which
an earlier event is screened by a later memory. Thus screen memories
may cover both past and present, holding on to an experience of time
that stresses trauma rather than history.

The Kraken lives in the timeless deep, reminiscent of the timelessness of the unconscious where these traumatic experiences had been
held, untouched by the passage of time over many years. A number
of analysts have described this kind of phenomena with various
terms, each holding a somewhat different emphasis—Rosenfeld's concept of "psychotic islands" (Rosenfeld, 1987) or Segal's "pockets of
vulnerability" (Segal, 1986). Captured by all is the idea that the mind
is capable of comprising different co-existing fields in which different
conditions prevail.

Mr K had encapsulated his traumatic experiences inside a defensive
structure of disavowal and manic omnipotence. In so doing, the experiences were not available to the passage of time, to the work of mourning. The failure to mourn instead leads to the kind of identification
described so vividly by Freud in "Mourning and melancholia" (Freud,
1917e). Mr K identified with the dead and damaged objects associated
with his traumatic experiences, leading to a kind of limbo or half-dead
state where he was unable to be fully alive, to have contact with himself
and his objects and with the passage of time. To do so would risk knowing about temporality, the potential for loss and separation, and hence
mourning.

From an object-relations perspective, one may suggest that the
appraisal of time passing is born of the ego's negotiations with its internal objects. Schafer suggests that it demands acceptance of separateness, mortality, and the fact that every moment is different and that,
once past, is lost forever (Schafer, 1976). This contrasts with the static
quality of the repetition compulsion based on fixation and repression

which implies that the past may be redone if not undone. For Mr K, it seems that the accumulation of losses—his job, his brother, his girl-friend, and the money she took from him—ushered in temporal aware-ness and, with it, the return of his appalling and overwhelming losses in the past.

When Mr K comes to the brief consultation, it is with the Kraken already at the surface, thrashing and roaring. The traumatic experiences of his childhood and early adulthood were present again, demonstrat-ing Freud's notion that "memory is present not once but several times over" (Freud, 1926). The opportunity provided through the brief con-sultation offered Mr K the possibility of the Kraken losing its immense, timeless hold on his life. Mourning the losses he has experienced may with time allow the Kraken "to rise and on the surface die".

References

Freud, S. (1909b). Analysis of a phobia in a five-year-old boy. *S.E. 10*: 122. London: Hogarth.

Freud, S. (1915b). Thoughts for the times on war and death. *S.E. 14*: 275. London: Hogarth.

Freud, S. (1917e). Mourning and melancholia. *S.E. 14*: 239. London: Hogarth.

Freud, S. (1925a). A note on the "mystic writing pad". *S.E. 19*: 227–232. London: Hogarth.

Freud, S. (1926d). Inhibitions, symptoms and anxiety. *S.E. 20*. London: Hogarth.

Garland, C. (Ed.) (1988). *Understanding Trauma: A Psychoanalytic Approach*. London: Tavistock Clinic Series.

Green, A. (2007). The construction of heterchrony. In: R. Perelberg (Ed.), *Time and Memory*. London: Karnac.

Money-Kyrle, R. (1968). Cognitive development. *International Journal of Psychoanalysis, 49*: 691–698.

Perelberg, R. J. (2007). Introduction. In: *Time and Memory: The Power of the Repetition Compulsion* (pp. xiii–xi). London: Karnac.

Rose, J. (1997). Distortions of time in the transference: some clinical and theoretical implications. *International Journal of Psychoanalysis, 78*: 453–468.

Rosenfeld, H. (1987). *Impasse and Interpretation: Therapeutic and Anti-Therapeutic Factors in the Psychoanalytic Treatment of Psychotic, Borderline, and Neurotic Patients*. London: Routledge.

Schafer, R. (1976). *A New Language for Psychoanalysis*. New Haven: Yale University Press.

Segal, H. (1986). Notes on symbol formation. In: *The Work of Hanna Segal: A Kleinian Approach to Clinical Practice*. London: Free Association.

Tennyson, A. (1830). The Kraken. In: *The Works of Alfred Lord Tennyson* (p. 46). London: Wordsworth Poetry Library.

PART IV

OLDER AGE

CHAPTER SEVEN

Trauma in old age: "passengers, next station is old age—are you ready?"

Arturo Varchevker

Ageing

As you can infer, the title of this chapter uses a metaphor which is about travelling by underground and suddenly becoming aware that the next station is your coming birthday and now your birthday means old age! The other possibility is to become aware that the next station that you are approaching could be your death. From birth to death, we are travelling through time, and death is part of life. This means that there is no life without death. It is like a marriage and both members are required. Each station represents a stage of the life cycle, and each stage highlights specific characteristics, like childhood or adolescence. It is important to become aware that there are age-dependent changes; this means developmental changes, as well as developmental disturbances and pathologies, occur throughout the individual's life, and there are specific disturbances and pathologies that acquire a particular significance in each stage of the life cycle. The experience of old age and ageing is quite variable because it is affected by multiple factors belonging to the sociocultural, medical, and psychological domains.

It is important to acknowledge that in countries where health and economic conditions are very low, adolescence and old age have a very brief span. In the Western world, approaching sixty years of age tends to activate considerable anxieties related to the noticeable changes that affect the individual. Therefore, when we are addressing the individual's entrance into the process of ageing, we are dealing with the gradual capacity to deal with final losses. This includes having to deal with the painful awareness that the "new me" is also part of the "old me". In some cases, there is a tendency to take flight into narcissistic mechanisms of delusional views of oneself. These can be mobilised by changes in appearance, such as white hair, wrinkles, and postural problems; there may be other physical disturbances such as sight problems, loss of memory, reduction of sexual libido, pains, physical vulnerability, and illnesses. There are other changes that tend to take place around this time, such as retirement and family changes, such as children becoming independent and developing their own families. All these changes, plus changes associated to loss of families and friends, usually activate anxieties and pose a significant challenge to how the individual is going to cope and deal with it all. I will add that sometimes there is also a significant challenge for those around the older individual, including their family. The process of ageing activates anxieties about losses and death, and some of these anxieties, when there are developmental difficulties or failures, can feel overwhelming. There are anxieties related to what is going on in the present, and this experience can be affected by cultural and historical factors, difficult family circumstances, and previous traumatic experiences. Some manage to blockade them in their unconscious, others develop disturbing reactions.

Often, elderly people would like to be young; sometimes, this becomes such an intense desire that it dominates a considerable part of their existence and a sense of false identity and vulnerability becomes quite noticeable. To a large extent, the main aim is to avoid confronting the limitations that are developing within the ageing process and the difficulties that these losses bring about. It is quite noticeable that physical and mental limitations that belong to the ageing process activate the above mentioned mental functioning. This handicaps the acknowledgement of the genuine positive resources of the individual. Instead, what takes over is a sense of unreality, sometimes leading to manic omnipotent functioning. All this is successfully exploited by business advertising that promises that the person will look young or be young forever.

At the same time, it is also important to acknowledge that many old people do not feel old in a negative or self-defeating way; quite different from the elderly people I just described, they feel lively and confident. They have been working for many years, and there is an attitude of independence accompanied by the wish to enjoy life. When faced with problems, they do not bring a threat to their sense of identity or personality derailment. Often, they look at the past with a mixture of nostalgia and distance. They feel they have a life to live.

In the last decades, there have been substantial changes due to many sociocultural factors, but more especially due to technological development. These developments in science and better living conditions brought an increase in longevity. In the last 25 years, the number of people who are aged 65 or over has increased by 18 per cent in the UK, and it is estimated that the population ageing will continue. By 2031, a 77 per cent increase is expected in those aged 75 and over, reaching a total of 15.8 million (BMJ 2010; 340: c3057). Life expectancy has become one of the very important challenges in this century due to the wide implications that it brings.

There are different contexts and several ways of approaching the subject of ageing. Different disciplines contribute to our understanding of this phenomenon and the multiple factors that affect and relate to old age. I want to explore one particular aspect, which is the experience of trauma and traumatic situations and how this manifests when there is a healthy development or when there are developmental disturbances in old age. My clinical experience in this particular area comes from psychoanalysis, family therapy, and individual therapy of patients who suffer trauma.

But prior to this, I want to make some useful reference to the concept of mourning or working through losses and to the development of melancholia when there is a failure to work through loss. The significant losses through the ageing process confront the individual with the reality of loss, its implications, and the inevitability of the final loss, death. In his memorable paper "Mourning and melancholia", Freud (1917e) conveys that during the process of mourning a lost loved one the individual revisits or relives in memory of the lost one, and that within the process of mourning a decathexis of the lost object gradually occurs. In contrast, the melancholic identifies with the lost object, which is perceived as hateful and invested with negative judgements and persecuting qualities. According to Freud, the world of the mourning individual becomes poor or empty when loss occurs, while it is the ego of the melancholic that becomes poor or empty. The work of mourning implies the capacity to differentiate and separate from another person, the individual is able to accommodate and accept the loss. In melancholia, the individual identifies with and is full of self-reproaches against the loved object, which is never relinquished. Freud's distinction between mourning losses and melancholic identification provides significant understanding of the possible emotional reactions to loss related to the internalisation of love–hate relationships which play such a crucial role in the development of the personality. All this is part and parcel of individual emotional development which also includes the capacity to deal with Oedipal anxieties at different stages of the life cycle.

When the individual steps into older age, a major test to his psychic equilibrium and capacity to develop takes place. Prior to this phase of the life cycle, growth and development have been an ongoing challenge. Now the big challenge is how to continue growing up and developing while physical and mental decline are hovering around like a menacing cloud. This cloud announces the losses to come; social discrimination filters through everyday life, and death becomes part of the individual's universe. My view is that a growing sense of reality enables the individual to turn to his own resources. These are partly related to how the previous phases of development have been worked through in terms of dependency, separation, losses and gains, or achievements and how these are viewed from the present perspective. The integration of the past and the present is going to be a significant supportive platform in dealing with the new scenario, which means saying goodbye to life and entering the last step, death.

During the ageing process, the individual has gone through a wealth of life experiences, positive and negative, while losses are looming around or possibly come to the fore. For example, parents could be very old, dead, or may be close to dying; friends and relatives become ill and die; children are leaving home or already have done so; retirement from work or rearranging work life is part and parcel of the various changes to come. Sudden illness can be a disturbing alarm to the individual's vulnerability associated with old age. Freud commented on the lack of elasticity of elderly people and stressed the difficulties of working through cumulative trauma. At the time of writing that, he was going through a profound grief over the loss of his beloved child, and this was also the onset of the malignant illness that later ended his life.

During old age, the notion of time acquires a different dimension, and painful emotions about lack of achievements and fantasies about the future can activate a complex emotional turmoil. When frustration and psychic pain are difficult to tolerate and there is a failure or avoidance of mourning, individuals tend to resort to all sorts of coping defensive manoeuvres. The tendency then is to find ways to rid themselves of the threatening experience through mechanisms of withdrawal and projection. Manic reactions may be another form of evasion: becoming overactive; regressing into adolescent types of behaviour; withdrawing into lonely activities as a form of retreat, becoming sexually overactive and promiscuous as a way of asserting potency; and becoming more authoritarian, powerful, and aggressive to push away any sense of weakness or fragility.

The individual's sense of identity feels under pressure, and there is a struggle to maintain it. In some cases, this can lead to different forms of passivity and depression, which often appear and reappear. When passivity takes over, it may destroy initiative, and hopelessness may be used as a form of control. There is also the possibility of a depressive breakdown, depending on the individual psychopathology. In some cases, hyperactivity or manic behaviour is another form of defence to avoid these issues, especially when narcissistic needs can be successfully fulfilled through this.

Physical and psychological deterioration are in the forefront in the ageing process and one of the tasks of old age is a readjustment of the ego, which comes into conflict with the ego ideal, on the one hand, and with the fear of losing ego boundaries, on the other. The concerns that the ageing person has about their body and mind increase in importance and contribute to reinforcing an existing identity or creating a new one. How the ageing person negotiates and works though the experience of ageing has a crucial positive or negative effect in reinforcing confidence and inner strength, or lack of it, which is so important at this stage of life. This could be a traumatic experience, and quite often an unexpected injury, illness, or mental failure may act as an unexpected intrusive trigger.

The theme of trauma

Trauma has been known throughout the history of humankind. The word "trauma" comes from the Greek word, meaning wound. Freud (1917e) referred to a stimulus that overwhelms the individual; it is too strong to cope with, and is the source of disturbances. There are significant moves in Freud's thinking in relation to trauma reflected in the development of his theories. An important one is the move from a topographical model of the mind to a structural model. Freud (1926d) referred to traumatic anxiety overwhelming the ego's capacity to function.

Donald Kalsched, in his book *The Inner World of Trauma* (1996), begins his unfolding of the theme of trauma by asking a series of questions, elucidating how the psyche responds "inwardly" to overwhelming life events. The questions he poses in the introduction are: "What happens in the inner world when life in the outer world becomes unbearable?"; "What do dreams tell us about the inner object-images of the psyche?"; "What patterns of unconscious fantasy provide an inner meaning to the trauma victim when life-shattering events destroy outer meaning altogether?" Throughout the book, he uses the word "trauma" to mean any experience that causes the child unbearable psychic pain or anxiety. For an experience to be unbearable means that it overwhelms the usual defensive measures which Freud (1920g) described as a "protective shield against stimuli".

Trauma varies in magnitude, circumstance, and type, and has been written about in the psychoanalytic literature variously depending upon degree, causation, and theoretical differences. To mention some of these contributions: Khan (1963) wrote about "cumulative trauma" resulting from unmet dependency needs that mount up to devastating effect; Winnicott (1965) talks about "primitive agonies"; and Kohut (1971) talks about "disintegrative anxiety"—an unnameable dread associated with the threatened dissolution of a coherent self. Caroline Garland, in her book entitled *Understanding Trauma* (2002), describes trauma "as a kind of wound". She says, "When we call an event traumatic, we are borrowing from the Greek where it refers to a piercing of the skin, a breaking of the bodily envelope. In physical medicine, it denotes damage to tissue." Like Kalsched, she quotes Freud's metaphorical description of the way in which the mind can be thought of as being enveloped by a kind of skin, or protective shield.

For Freud, the mind's capacity to shut out excessive amounts and kinds of stimulation is even more important, in terms of maintaining a workable equilibrium, than is the capacity to receive or let in stimuli. In infancy, the mother mediates and filters both internal emotional experience and environmental. Garland argues that, for adults: "some have built up inside themselves, partly as the outcome of good parental provision, a capacity to take care of themselves in the best meaning of that phrase. Others will have been unable to achieve this degree of autonomy." "When traumatic events unfold they extend far beyond the visible, into the depths of the individual's identity, which is constituted by the nature of his internal objects—the figures that inhabit his internal world, and his unconscious beliefs about them and their ways of relating to each other."

We consider that trauma is an unexpected massive intrusive experience that emotionally overwhelms the individual and activates a series of psychological and physical symptoms. It is important to outline that trauma is different from the range of common stressors, even if common stressors can activate very distressing reactions according to the individual's containing capacity and developmental structure. Trauma can occur as the individual is alone or within the family or within a small or large group.

The traumatic experience manifests by an immediate reaction of fear and intense anxiety that threatens the ego's capacity to contain it. Other symptoms that can be provoked by trauma are a series of overwhelming emotions like horror and losing total personal or situational control; in general, the individual is taken by surprise and the intense fear and pain feels overwhelming. This can disturb thoughts and emotions about oneself and the way the world is perceived. The normal functioning of the individual can be greatly disturbed at work or relationship level. Also symbolisation can be affected, and this manifests in an impaired capacity to describe what is being experienced. Feeling low and a reduced ability to concentrate is another common feature. In general, everything around trauma provokes a sense of lack of safety that activates a series of defence mechanisms, the most common of which is avoidance. There are also different levels of dissociation. On some occasions, the trauma can be put aside and repressed and may be awoken later on by a connecting experience.

For example, a patient unexpectedly fell on the street while she was trying to catch a bus and suffered serious injury to her ankle, shoulder, and arm. She had to cancel several sessions and could not go to work for more than a week. As soon as we resumed work, it was clear that what had happened to her put her in touch with an earlier trauma when her husband had died in a car accident. Apparently at that time everybody around her had been very impressed by how well she coped with this tragedy. The overwhelming emotional state triggered by her fall and physical injuries felt like an intrusive explosion in her mind;

her reaction was: "I can't carry on with this ongoing torture. I'm ready to leave this world! I have had enough!" This was also connected in her mind with much earlier experiences: her mother was always busy looking after her business and her father was usually abroad due to his work. There were many references to several carers, nannies, babysitters, and aunts, but there was an absence of a steady, stable, containing figure in her early development. My impression is that she had started to feel vulnerable about her ageing process and this added a significant meaning to her reaction.

Post-traumatic stress disorder (PTSD) is defined as an acute stress disorder characterised by feelings of dread accompanied by somatic reactions provoked by a major life stress. The experience is re-lived in an intrusive way through various forms: nightmares, waking thoughts, hallucinations, dissociations, flashbacks, phobias, compulsive avoidance of situations that are associated to the event; sometimes there is an inability to recall partial aspects of the traumatic event. Other symptoms include phobias related to the event that can manifest an avoidance of situations that may relate to the trauma, and also lack of sleep, change of mood, and difficulty in concentration.

The symptoms may be present for several days, weeks, or become chronic. How the person reacts and copes with what has happened and what is happening is extremely important. It is already well documented that some individuals who are affected by horrific traumas do not develop PTSD, and some individuals who suffer small traumas develop PTSD. If there is sound early emotional development and an adequate supportive environment after the trauma, the recovery is likely to take place. This means that the individual has been able to internalise a good containing object relationship or sound mentalisation and possibly has a reliable or sound supporting environment in the present.

The historical origins of psychoanalysis to some extent are linked to the exploration of trauma. Influenced by Breuer's view that hysterical symptoms were originated in the past and were forgotten, Freud's therapeutic approach was to help the patient to remember under the effect of hypnosis. This cathartic method was the precursor of the notion of regression and the importance of the past in relation to the present. This led later to the notion of sexual trauma and then to the notion of fictitious reality; and from there to the notion of unconscious fantasy and psychic reality. However, the distinction between trauma and other disturbing situations and reactions is quite important as there is a tendency to blur trauma with any stressing, uncontained experience; this tends to happen within the psychoanalytic field. For instance, Gerzi (2005) quotes Winnicott in relation to this issue, "There is a normal aspect of trauma. The mother is always 'traumatising' within a framework of adaptation" (1965, p. 146).

It is more accepted now, and this is also my view, that "trauma" is different from "losses". Sometimes these experiences become confused because trauma can incorporate the experience of loss. It is important to stress that there are situations in which trauma is overcome and this can lead to a new opening which could be a positive development, and there are other situations when the opposite occurs. In relation to the positive outcome, I would like to mention a colleague of mine who was in her mid-sixties. She was struggling at that time to cope with the death of her husband. She lived in a beautiful old house full of old furniture and precious objects that belonged to her late husband and her family. Her house was broken into by robbers and ransacked. Initially, she was shaken. It felt a real trauma, and it lasted several days, but then I was impressed by her quick recovery. She told me that she was amazed by how well insured she was and, to her surprise, the insurance was going to cover all the losses. She would not have been able to move from her house or give away the family belongings. Some went back to several generations. It felt such a responsibility, she would have felt very guilty if she would have tried to sell them or give them away. She had dreamt since her twenties of living in a modern house with modern furniture. It had seemed an impossible dream; she could not let her husband or her family of origin down. The following year, she was able to do it, and I was amazed at her new energy and creative side.

There is another aspect of trauma that has been mentioned by Dana Birksted-Breen (2003) and this is unconscious trauma. She quotes Botella and Botella (2001) referring to basic infantile trauma; it resides in the experience of not being represented in the mother's mind, or losing the internal representation of the object when the object is no longer present in external reality. Bion's (1962) reference to an emotional state of nameless dread when projections cannot be contained and can lead to a catastrophic state of mind, and Green's notion of the dead mother (1965), make a valuable contribution to the understanding of this phenomenon. In the chapter dedicated to trauma in adulthood, Ron Britton draws attention to the fact that in the psychoanalytic literature of

Kleinian and post-Kleinian analysts, the word "trauma" is hardly used. He suggests that the notion of trauma is incorporated in the theoretical description of pathological versions of the paranoid-schizoid and depressive positions and the lack of containment that may lead to a catastrophic state of mind described by Bion.

This brings to mind a patient whose mother suffered post-natal depression when his sister was borne and had a couple of psychiatric admissions. He dreamt that thieves managed to break in and took his computer and mobile. All the work he had done was in his computer. After some associations that felt more like an avoidance than true associations, I reminded him that I had suggested in the previous session that he was so frightened to acknowledge that he had anything of value because he was convinced that either it would be robbed or disappear. There was also a moment when he became very emotional and the analysis became alive but then went flat, dead, and empty. He said that he did not know what I was referring to. After a pause, he said that he remembered that in the dream the insurance had sent an inspector who questioned him and he felt persecuted by it. I said that now he feels persecuted by our exploration. He said that he rented a room when he was student at the university; the landlady was abroad when the house was broken into by burglars. He did not suffer any loss but he had recurrent nightmares after that, and he is often frightened that someone is going to come in when he is asleep. Soon after, he had to move because the landlady sold the house. Probably she is dead now because she was quite old at the time. He said that he knew he had a positive feeling when he left the previous day's session and can't understand why he did not want to come today. Then he had to rush because he was totally unaware of the time. In this case, it is possible to see how frightening it is to acknowledge anything positive in himself, the analyst, or analysis.

When the older person had difficulties in coping with the stressors that accompany the process of ageing, a trauma may lead from PTSD, but it is also important to be aware that on certain occasions trauma as well as illness can be used to avoid present stressors. In those cases, passivity, negative attitude, and depression become a familiar development.

In relation to this comes to mind a person whom I saw as an NHS patient using an interpreter because he could not speak English in spite of living in England for several years. This patient was in his early fifties, had been an army man in Iraq, and during the war had been taken prisoner and suffered torture. He managed to come with his family to the UK as refugees. His wife was now fluent in English and one of his sons was in full employment, the other was going to start university, and his daughter was in a secondary school. He was suffering PTSD and was quite depressed. He had been on medication for quite some time but was not able to leave his flat on his own and was spending most of his time sitting in the dark or in front of the television. It was clear that he kept his experiences of been in prison and torture at a distance; he made some superficial descriptions and references to it, but asserted he did not want to talk about it, it was too difficult for him to talk about it. He had already refused other types of treatments. I had assumed that the difficulties were related to his need to keep such frightening experiences at a distance, the fear of reliving them, and the fear of exposure. When some time later he disclosed that he was able for the first time to go down stairs, crossed the road, and bought cigarettes, I felt that there was a real sense of a possible improvement and change. However, gradually, I realised that his conscious fantasies continued having the upper hand; he had an ongoing day-dream in which he was able to regain his job as an army man or policeman here. At one level, he knew that this was not possible but carried on day-dreaming about it. To some extent, he was familiar with his old symptoms and survived the torture, but new anxieties were aroused by the migration to such a different environment that activated overwhelming paranoid anxieties. He did not know how to swim in these waters, and his traumatic experiences and lack of inner resources activated paranoid anxieties about adjusting to the new habitat and new life.

Conclusion

The transition in each stage of development brings about changes and losses; they are like normal crisis points. The passage from one stage of development to the next one is a progressive move. Some of these transitions are experienced or perceived by the patient as traumatic, or catastrophic in Bion's terminology (1965), and like in major catastrophic events it is important to consider the pre-catastrophic, pre-transition internal state and the post-catastrophic, post-transitional state. Crucially important is to take notice of how these two views manifest in the present and affect the view of the future. This takes into account previous developments in terms of the person's capacity for mourning losses and coping with new developments. Constitutional factors and interactive contexts exert an influence and play a part.

The theoretical and technical psychoanalytic frame does not change when working with older patients. It is important for the analyst not to lose his psychoanalytic balance when the pressure to do so can be considerable, especially when one is dealing with trauma and the pressure to act out or be sympathetic instead of analyse is considerable. These difficulties are more apparent in the later years, when the individual is physically and mentally losing ground or deteriorating. At this stage, proper understanding and adequate stimulation can make a significant difference. Otherwise, when older people are ignored, the emotional effect on them is quite intense, and their passivity or self-destructiveness can take over and their lives easily drift away. In some cases, it is quite surprising to see the significant, quality changes that can be achieved.

Of course, real psychic change emerges through the patient's inner strength to take responsibility for the changes that take place in their body and mind. This manifests itself in the patient's capacity to say goodbye to what is gone and to bear what has not been achieved in order to be able to make the most of what there is. It is a way of fuelling liveliness and therefore supporting life when death is close by. Ultimately, much courage is needed to face those tragic circumstances when the basic quality of life is no longer there, if it is gone forever through mental or physical impairments, and when the end of life is near.

References

Baranger, M., Baranger, W. & Mom, J. (1983). Process and non-process in analytic work. *International Journal of Psycho-Analysis, 64(1)*.

Baranger, W. & Baranger, M. (1969a). *Problemas del Campo Psicoanalitico*. Buenos Aires: Kargieman.

Baranger, W. & Baranger, M. (1969b). Proceso En Espiral Y Campo Dinamico. *Revista Uruguaya de Psicoanalisis, 59*.

Bell, D. (2006). Existence in time: development or catastrophe? *Psychoanalytic Quarterly, 75(3)*: 783–805.

Bion, W. R. (1962). *Learning from Experience*. London: Heinemann. [Reprinted, London: Karnac, 1985.]

Bion, W. R. (1965). Transformations. In: *Seven Servants*. New York: Jason Aronson, 1977.

Bion, W. R. (1970). Attention and interpretation. In: *Seven Servants*. New York: Jason Aronson, 1977.

Birksted-Breen, D. (2003). Time and the après coup. *International Journal of Psycho-Analysis, 84*: 1501–1515.

Botella, C. & Botella, S. (2004). *The Work of Psychic Figurability: Mental States without Representation*. London: Routledge, The New Library of Psychoanalysis.

Britton, R. (1998). Subjectivity, objectivity and triangular space. In: *Belief and Imagination*. London: Routledge.

Britton, R. (2003a). *Sex, Death, and the Superego*. London: Karnac.

Britton, R. (2003b). Narcissism, Part III. In: *Sex, Death and the Superego*. London: Karnac.

Dario, R. (2005). *Selected Writings*. London: Penguin.

Davenhill, R. (Ed.) (2007). *Looking into Later Life*. London: Karnac, The Tavistock Clinic Series.

Ferro, A. (2005). *Seeds of Illness, Seeds of Recovery*. London: Routledge, The New Library of Psychoanalysis.

Fonagy, P. & Target, M. (2003). *Psychoanalytic Theories*. London: Whurr.

Freud, S. (1914c). On narcissism: an introduction. *S.E. Vol. 14:*. 67–102. London: Hogarth.

Freud, S. (1915b). Thoughts for the times on war and death. *S.E. 14*. London: Hogarth.

Freud, S. (1917e). Mourning and melancholia. *S.E. 14*. London: Hogarth.

Freud, S. (1920g). *Beyond the Pleasure Principle. S.E. 18*. London: Hogarth.

Freud, S. (1926d). Inhibitions, symptoms and anxieties. *S.E. 20*. London: Hogarth.

Garland, C. (Ed.) (2002). *Understanding Trauma*. London: Karnac.

Gerzi, S. (2005). Trauma, narcissism and the two attractors in trauma. *International Journal of Psychoanalysis, 86*: 1033–1050.

Green, A. (1965). The dead mother. In: *On Private Madness*. London: Hogarth.

Gringberg, L., Sor, D. & Taback de Bianchedi, E. (1993). *New Introduction to the Work of Bion*. New York: Jason Aronson.

Heath, I. (2010). Life and death. *British Medical Journal, 340*: 2970.

Jacques, E. (1965). Death and the midlife crisis. *International Journal of Psycho-Analysis, 46*: 502–514.

Joseph, B. (1985). Transference: the total situation. *International Journal of Psycho-Analysis, 66*: 447–454. [Reprinted in M. Feldman & E. Bott Spillius (Eds.), *Psychic Equilibrium and Psychic Change: Selected Papers of Betty Joseph*. London: Routledge, 1989.]

Joseph, B. (1989a). On passivity and aggression: their relationship. In: M. Feldman & E. Bott Spillius (Eds.), *Psychic Equilibrium and Psychic Change: Selected Papers of Betty Joseph*. London: Routledge.

Joseph, B. (1989b). Psychic change and the psychoanalytic process. In: M. Feldman & E. Bott Spillius (Eds.), *Psychic Equilibrium and Psychic Change: Selected Papers of Betty Joseph*. London: Routledge.

Kalsched, D. (1996). *The Inner World of Trauma*. London: Routledge.

Khan, M. (1963). The concept of cumulative trauma. In: *The Privacy of the Self*. London: Maresfield Library, Karnac.

King, P. (1980). The life cycle as indicated by the nature of the transference in the psychoanalysis of the middle-aged and elderly. *International Journal of Psycho-Analysis. 61(2)*: 153–160.

Kohon, G. (1999a). The Aztecs, Masada and the compulsion to repeat. In: *No Lost Certainties To Be Recovered*. London: Karnac.

Kohon, G. (1999b). The dead mother. In: *The Work of André Green*. London: Routledge.

Kohut, H. (1971). *A Systematic Approach to the Psychoanalytic Treatment of Narcissistic Personality Disorders*. New York: International University Press.

Plotkin, F. (2000). Treatment of the older adult: the impact on the psychoanalyst. *Journal of the American Psychoanalytical Association, 48(4)*: 1591–1616.

Puget, J. (2006). The use of the past in the present in the clinical setting. *International Journal of Psychoanalysis, 87(Part 6)*: 1691–1707.

Quinodoz, J. M. (1993). *The Taming of Solitude*. London: Routledge, The New Library of Psychoanalysis.

Riesenberg-Malcom, R. (1999). *On Bearing Unbearable States of Mind.* London: Routledge.

Schafer, R. (2003). *Bad Feelings*. London: Karnac.

Segal, H. (1958). Fear of death: notes on analysis of an old man. *International Journal of Psycho-Analysis, 39*: 178–181.

Valenstein, A. F. (2000). The older patient in psychoanalysis. *Journal of the American Psychoanalytical Association, 48(4)*: 1563–1589.

Waddell, M. (2002). *Inside Lives*. London: Karnac.

Winnicott, D. W. (1965). *The Maturational Process and the Facilitating Environment: Studies in the Theory of Emotional Development*. London: Karnac.

CHAPTER EIGHT

Immortality versus mortality: why are the elderly different?

Isky Gordon

My background is neither in psychoanalysis or psychotherapy, rather my experience comes from a combination of being close to friends, parents, and parents-in-law who have died, as well as being a senior doctor doing weekly ward rounds in the intensive care unit at Great Ormond Street Hospital for Children for over thirty years. During that period, not a week went by without at least one infant or child having died. I now lead seminars with medical students at University College London Hospitals on euthanasia—quite a challenge as this is a young, multi-ethnic group, many of whom are religious. Relevant to end-of-life decisions is the Mental Capacity Act and the accompanying advance decision (formerly living will) that came into force in October 2007. I have also spoken to groups from Help the Aged and Age Concern, as well as group GP practices, on the importance of this Act.

Trauma

Comprehensive descriptions of trauma are given in other chapters of this book; what can appear as a minor incident may be felt as a major traumatic event to the individual. In addition, one traumatic event may awaken previous traumatic events that are lying dormant in one's memory. On reaching older age, almost everyone will have suffered physical or psychological trauma during their life's journey. For a parent, the death of a child, at any stage, is a major traumatic event.

The denial of death exists in everyone from an early age. José Saramago puts it rather well in his novel *Death at Intervals* (2008) when talking about a court martial of soldiers: "… the ingenious desire for eternal life that has always inhabited the human heart". Our own death is indeed unimaginable; every one of us is convinced of his own immortality.

However, there are specific events that drive home the passing of years and that society recognises the individual as "old". These events are perceived by many as traumatic: they include becoming eligible for a heating allowance, a freedom pass for transport, cheaper tickets at the cinema or theatre. I have a close friend who will not apply for a freedom pass as he says that will mark him as old. This is his defence mechanism, or rather his denial of getting older and being closer to death. Also, society forces retirement at sixty to sixty-five years of age on a great number of people, and for many this marks the crossing of a Rubicon and that one's professional life has drawn to a close to a great degree. The question often posed at this stage is: What shall I do with my life? My life has little meaning now. Further, the body becomes weaker, and one is unable to continue to do the physical activities that have been part of routine life. One's body is letting one down, and one can not rely on oneself. This leads to a loss of confidence and eventually a dependence on others. The death of friends becomes increasingly frequent. Some years ago, when my father was eighty-five years old, he said to me on leaving the cemetery following the burial of one of his friends, that he had more friends in the cemetery than alive. The possibility of a spouse dying is a reality, and this may mean that a relationship and mutual dependence over many decades is broken, so that the survivor feels grief and the mourning may be prolonged.

Perhaps the poem by Percy Bysshe Shelley entitled "Death" (1824), and published after his death, is more relevant to the elderly:

> Death is here and death is there,
> Death is busy everywhere,
> All around, within, beneath,
> Above is death and we are death.

So old age has little to recommend it. These traumatic events will happen to each and every one of us—and having looked after my ninety-year-old parents in the last years of their lives, I can assure you that it is nothing to look forward to. However, the truth is that there is no alternative to old age.

One's beliefs or assumptions

Our security is based on the assumption that nothing untoward will happen in our daily lives. Other chapters in this book give graphic examples of the importance of such beliefs or assumptions. Political refugees coming to the UK have a belief that the UK will provide them with a safe haven. A patient was described who, for nine months, could make no progress in therapy. However, when he received the Home Office letter granting him the right to stay, then rapid progress was made. The converse is also true. The political refugee who has the belief that he will be safe in the UK but is treated badly or imprisoned here can experience this as more traumatic than what they suffered in their home country.

There is almost an innate belief in every person that he or she is immortal. This is reflected throughout life and is most obvious in the omnipotent attitude of adolescents doing dangerous acts or in the often-heard expression: "This will never happen to me". The minority of the population in the UK have a will. Many others are unable to contemplate their children, their relatives, and friends without them, and so end up unable to make a will. I have good friends who know the consequences of not having a will, recognise the need to have a will, but are somehow unable to get themselves to think of their own death. However, in old age, when one suffers the trauma of the death of one's spouse and many friends, then the belief in immortality is hard to sustain. Further, the ability of one's body to perform is reduced, and this bodily weakness is a daily reminder of one's mortality. With the erosion of the belief in immortality, there is loss of security, with the fear of dying and death. So the older person has to face the fact that their life is close to the end, which for many is a very distressing thought and not easily accepted. Here is an excerpt from the poem "The Ship of Death", by D. H. Lawrence (1941). It starts:

> Now it is the autumn of the falling fruit
> And the long journey towards oblivion.

> The apples falling like great drops of dew
> to bruise themselves an exit from themselves.
>
> And it is time to go, to bid farewell
> to one's own self and find an exit
> from the fallen self

The fear of dying is different from the fear of death, yet the two are inseparable. To explore these two aspects, we need to review the attitude of our society to death. I maintain that currently our society denies death.

In traditional societies, death was seen as a threat to the community, so rituals for both death and "burial" developed to strengthen the community; death as part of life was acknowledged. However, for the nobility, the finality of death (loss of power and influence) was not accepted. Death became the afterlife, burials required tombs to include troops, sacrifices, and gifts for the afterlife, looking for eternity. The fear of simply not-existing, that is, death, is too difficult to bear, so virtually every society developed the concept of afterlife, to give meaning to life and so avoid facing death as an end. Religion is a man-made construct, so over the last five millennia the ideas of heaven and hell and reincarnation have been developed. Has man, through religion, with the creation of heaven and hell or reincarnation, tried to convince himself that he is immortal? In Christianity, death is an extended sleep while waiting for the Last Judgement, preserving the concept of eternity. Geoffrey Gorer (1965) maintains that the media were and are obsessed with covering violent death, yet when reporting on the death of an important person, they use euphemisms such as "peacefully passed on". Gorer speaks of death as a taboo subject, while Phillippe Aries also proposed that society had "developed a silence around death" (Aries, 1988).

In 2006, at a regular Friday night dinner at our home, I was speaking to a friend who is a consultant in palliative care medicine about the debate in the House of Lords on "assisted dying", when one of the other guests interrupted, asking, "Why do we have to have such morbid discussion around the dinner table?" One explanation for this remark is well described by José Saramago in his book *Death at Intervals*: "Why not even the fact of having lived deserves mention in the book of death. And the reason is that the other name for the book of death, as it behoves us to know, is the book of nothingness."

Over the past one hundred and fifty years, society has seen an increase in life expectancy; we have seen technological advances and greater scientific understanding of many aspects of life. All these have affected the attitude and approach to death. Aries develops the idea that death became hidden away and relates this to the rise of individualism and society's adoption of science almost as the new religion. The idea is that with such advances in science and the fact that medicine now keeps people alive who would have died some time ago (doctors can do miracles?), so death should no longer exist, death has become a failure. Perhaps the most pervasive expression of the lexicon of death is the general notion that death is a disease rather than a natural and expected limitation of life. Death is to be fought against and resisted. This has resulted in some health-care professionals finding dying difficult to handle and remaining emotionally detached from the dying person and his family. Furthermore, death and burial rituals are now private affairs, with grief taken out of public society and into the secluded sphere of the home and family. Armstrong's argument that the change in language, "dead bodies rather than dying people", "the corpse rather than a dead person", reflected the new scientific approach (Armstrong, 1995). This was coupled with new legal requirements for registration of death and release of corpses for burial.

This supports Aries' argument that changes in society were driving death and burial away from being a social and community event into becoming a private individual event. Death now occurs in hospitals, hospices, and institutions, and the ritual of burial has been professionalised. Norbert Elias (1985) adds further weight to the argument that there has been a loss of cultural ritual about death, being replaced by the degree of informality that has developed in hospitals that are devoid of feeling. Anderson sums this up: "Our western culture has lost its fundamental connection to death itself ... death has become institutionalised and professionalized" (Anderson, 1949). There has also been a change in demographics whereby it is the very elderly who constitute a much bigger group in society, and thus death is more frequent in this group; a group often considered "of little social significance". As most elderly people die in hospital or institutions, people have little first-hand knowledge of death.

To summarise, there has been a change from death as an emotional and community event marked at home, to a situation in which dying more commonly takes place in an institution. The dead body is of scientific interest, and there are legal requirements for the registration of the death and the burial process involving coroners for the release of the corpse, or should I rather say, dead person. Dying and burial have become professionalised and private, and so not community events.

Let us look briefly at a different community where death has been and remains incorporated within society. The Mexican poet and Nobel Prize winner Octavio Paz observes that, undaunted by death, the Mexican has no qualms about getting up close and personal with death, he chases after it, mocks it, courts it, hugs it, sleeps with it; it is his favourite plaything and his most lasting love. Walking at night in a small village in Mexico on the eve of the Day of the Dead, I followed the music which led me to a house where a death had occurred in the past year and where the family and neighbours were celebrating the life and death of their deceased relative. Even though we were total strangers, my son and I were welcomed in and offered food and drink, as were all who entered the home. They talked freely about the dead person and the middle-aged daughter was delighted to tell me the joys and the difficulties of her late mother. In another house, seven brothers were all falling over each other to tell stories of their late father and his various exploits and indiscretions.

After sitting and talking for some time, I asked if I may take some photographs, and much to my delight, the family were keen for me to take whatever photos I wanted. Photography has acquired a significance that needs to be recognised, especially as virtually everyone now owns a digital camera. Susan Sontag wrote: "Through photographs, each family constructs a portrait of itself—a portable kit of images that bears witness to its connectedness" (Sontag, 1977). As that claustrophobic unit, the nuclear family, was being carved out of a much larger family aggregate, photography came along to restate symbolically the imperilled continuity and vanishing extendedness of family life. After the photographic event has ended, the picture still exists, conferring on the event a kind of immortality: the image world bids to outlast us all. When we are nostalgic, we take pictures.

All photographs are *memento mori* (I found three translations of this phrase: remember that you are mortal; remember you will die; and, probably most relevant to today, remember that you must die, or remember your death). To take a photograph is to participate in another person's mortality and vulnerability.

The UK has become a secular society, but little is known about how this has affected the attitude to dying or death. There are small groups who consider death as part of life, with a recognition that death is the end. For such groups, there is no denial of death, and there is a strong movement for control over the dying process, as many as eighty per cent of the population are in favour of legalising medically assisted dying. I am part of this secular group, and poetry has been of great help to me in trying to understand life and the inevitability of death. The poem "Dust is the only Secret" (1855) by the American poet Emily Dickinson is quite revealing:

> Dust is the only Secret—
> Death, the only One
> You cannot find out all about
> In his native town.

Is this attitude of denial of death true for the older person? My experience is limited to my parents, who both died in their ninetieth year, as well as my parents-in-law, who died in their late eighties. All four of them were well until twelve to eighteen months before their deaths. My parents-in-law had become members of what was the Voluntary Euthanasia Society and talked openly about death; they both planned their own funerals and spoke freely about the inevitability of death. My father survived my mother by only six months to the day; when the family went to lay the tombstone five months after her death, my father said that all he wanted now was to lie down beside her. All, except my mother, had embraced death. However, they were all clear that they did not wish to lose their dignity nor suffer pain in the process of dying; they had a fear of dying but not of death. The above recollections are not universally true. In the description of the final illness of Susan Sontag, her son, the American author David Rieff, writes:

> My mother had been ill for so much of her life, from crippling childhood asthma to her three cancers and death was no stranger to her having seen many die in the cancer wards. But no amount of familiarity could lessen the degree to which the idea of death was unbearable to her. In her eyes, mortality seemed as unjust as murder. My mother knew perfectly well that she was going to die. (Reiff, 2008)

When Susan Sontag opts for a bone-marrow transplant, that itself has major life-threatening complications and almost no chance of success, her son goes on to say, "Instead of dying in physical agony, I thought my mother would have died in psychological terror, abject and inconsolable had she not accepted this treatment."

The dying process is simply terrifying; there is a fear of a loss of dignity, loss of self-reliance, and that dying will be a painful experience. This is all critically associated with a loss of control whereby the locus of control has shifted from the dying person to those who will be caring for him or her. However, there have been remarkable advances in technology and medical science, with the result that not only do people live longer, but also some diseases that were formally fatal are now curable in a large percentage of cases, such as childhood leukaemia. Drug development allows the health-care team to virtually eliminate pain. A better understanding of the dying process has resulted in the creation of the hospice movement and palliative care physicians. The hospice movement is expanding, the speciality of palliative care is growing; both focus on the whole person/family, and the pain and suffering of the dying are catered for on an individual level. This is important good news and improves the process of dying, so removing some of the fear and loneliness. However, these positive changes are mainly directed towards patients with cancer, who in fact only represent about fifteen per cent of all deaths in the UK. In addition, these advances enhance the institutionalisation, professionalisation, and regulation of dying and death.

With greater openness in society through the media, the majority of the general population wish to have assistance to end their lives when they are close to death. This is a desire to maintain or take back control of their own fate. The Bill in the House of Lords, Assisted Dying for the Terminally Ill, was rejected by the Lords in 2006. A major campaign was launched by the bishops and religious groups in the House of Lords to defeat this bill, with the argument that life is sacred and that no doctor has the right to give the terminally ill patient medication that will allow them to end their own life at a time of their own choosing. Yet is this the compassion in keeping with the Hippocratic Oath? Dr Louis Lasagna in 1964 wrote:

> Most especially must I tread with care in matters of life and death. If it is given me to save a life, all thanks. But it may also be within my power to take a life; this awesome responsibility must be faced with great humbleness and awareness of my own frailty. Above all, I must not play at God. (ref)

This raises serious issues as to what is more important: the quality of life or the sanctity of life? In an interview on the *Today* programme, BBC Radio 4, a middle-aged daughter who nursed her dying mother made the point that there comes a time when simply existing is not living. Mary Riddel wrote about Jane Tomlinson, a woman who struggled against breast cancer:

> At a time when people dream of immortality but cannot rely on doctors to supply it, or God to underwrite it, the notion that the mind can triumph over the body has become more potent. Throw in some carrot juice, de-stressing techniques and human will and you, too, can be a miracle of survival. That is the message conveyed by pseudo-science and nurtured by raw hope. Even as Jane Tomlinson valiantly sought to prolong her life, many others are being denied the chance to end their lives as they choose. Stressing the need for legalisation of medically assisted dying for the terminally ill. (Riddell, 2007)

We all have difficulty in contemplating our own death and mortality. We can all relate to what Simon Hoggart wrote in the *Guardian* in 2006:

> I thought how lovely it would be if, after our deaths, we were allowed by whoever was in charge to return to earth, only for the memorial services of friends we admired. It would make the thought of death almost tolerable. (Hoggart, 2006)

And as so many consider discussions of death a difficult topic, so let me end on a lighter note. We must remember that life is a fatal condition and, what is more, that it is sexually transmitted.

References

Anderson, C. (1949). Aspects of pathological grief and mourning. *International Journal of Psycho-Analysis, 30*: 48–55.

Aries, P. (1988). *The Hour of Our Death: The Classic History of Western Attitudes Towards Death over the Last One Thousand Years* (trans Helen Weaver, 2nd edn). New York: Vintage Books.

Armstrong, E. M. (1995). We must not let science blind us. *BMA News Reviews*, March.

Dickinson, E. (1855). Dust is the only secret. In: *The Complete Poems of Emily Dickinson*. Boston: Little, Brown, 1924.

Elias, N. (1985). *The Loneliness of Dying*. Oxford: Blackwell.

Gorer, G. (1965). *Death, Grief and Mourning in Contemporary Britain*. New York: Arno Press.

Hoggart, S. (2006). In praise of merriment. *Guardian*, London, 26 August.

Lasagna, L. (1964). Hippocratic Oath, in ethics.ucsd.edu/journal/2006.

Lawrence, D. H. (1941). The ship of death. In: *Selected Poems D. H. Lawrence* (p. 128). London: Penguin, 1950.

Paz, O. *Selected Poems of Octavio Paz* ISBN 9780811217446.

Reiff, D. (2008). Why I had to lie to my dying mother. *Observer*, London, 18 May.

Riddel, M. (2007). Better a dignified than a brave exit. *Observer*, London, 9 September.

Saramago, J. (2008). *Death at Intervals (Death with Interruptions.)* [Trans Margaret Jull Costa, from *As intermitencias da morte*]. London, Harvill Secker/Random House.

Shelley P. B. (1824). Death is here and death is there. In: *Poems of Percy Bysshe Shelley*. London: G. Bell & Sons, 1907.

Sontag, S. (1977). On photography. In: *Image Technologies and the Emergence of Mass Society* (Part V, p. 174). London: Penguin.

PART V

TRAUMA AND THE COUPLE

The hidden traumas of the young boarding school child as seen through the lens of adult couple therapy

Francis Grier

In 1941, the Scottish psychoanalyst Ronald Fairbairn wrote:

> ... the greatest need of a child is to obtain conclusive assurance (a) that he is genuinely loved as a person by his parents, and (b) that his parents genuinely accept his love. It is only in so far as such assurance is forthcoming in a form sufficiently convincing to enable him to depend safely upon his real objects that he is able gradually to renounce infantile dependence without misgiving.
>
> —Fairbairn, 1941, p. 39

In this chapter, I would like to explore some of the seemingly intractable dilemmas experienced by certain patients of mine in their adult couple relationships. In their intimate relationships, this group of patients appear unable to commit themselves with any deep conviction of trust and security. They also share a history of separation from their parents when they were young children, when they were sent abroad to boarding school. I intend to investigate hidden dimensions of the trauma in which most of these children have been involved, which often manifest on the surface of a couple's relationship as fairly ordinary problems. It is only the intransigence of the difficulties, and a quality of underlying rage and misery, which often emerges only slowly and is quite at odds with a veneer of humour and charm, that indicate the ongoing effect of the traumatic separations these adults endured as children.

I begin with a general description of some of the principal psychologically troubling aspects of the boarding school experience. I then set out and discuss one couple case in detail, showing the particular issues by which both partners were affected, and the diversity of the problems within the relationship which partly emanated from each of their involvement as children, his directly and hers indirectly, in the boarding school system.

The boarding school system

Various authors have written about the effects of being sent away to boarding school on the development of the child. Nick Duffell, in particular, has written *The Making of Them* (Duffell, 2000), as well as numerous articles, in addition to running groups with Helena Løvendal-Sørensen for "Boarding School Survivors". (http://www.boardingschoolsurvivors.co.uk). Some significant and very perceptive papers have also been written by Joy Schaverien (2004, 2011).

George Orwell's autobiographical *Such, Such Were the Joys* (1953) and Rudyard Kipling's semi-autobiographical *Baa, Baa, Black Sheep* (1888) are enormously valuable documents, both deeply insightful and imaginatively sympathetic to the plight of very small children sent away from home to board. Kipling's work has the added merit of depicting many of the appalling dilemmas that faced many of the British parents living abroad, wishing to give their children a good education and a British identity. Though Orwell's and Kipling's accounts refer to pre-First World War experiences, many of their underlying points remained valid with regard to the boarding school culture well into the second half of the twentieth century. The ensuing description of the plight of young children in the boarding school system is partly informed by these written sources, but comes mainly from many conversations inside and outside of psychotherapy and psychoanalysis with men and women who have been directly or indirectly involved with or affected by boarding school education.

The traumatic aspect of the separation was double-faceted. The first aspect, the acute phase, consisted of the first few days or hours of the child being sent to another country, separated from parents and family. Mother might accompany the child to school at the start, but she would have to bid her child farewell immediately after delivering him. (I will write about the typical boarding-school child as male, but many girls were also sent away.) He would probably never have been parted from her for more than a few hours previously, and even then would have remained in the care of a known and trusted adult. Boarding schools used to impose severe restrictions on visits by parents, relatives, and friends. Typically, only three visits per term were allowed—in some schools, fewer—of only a few hours' duration. In the case of children from overseas, since it would seem fairly pointless for a mother to stay in the UK when she would only be granted access to her child for a few hours after a gap of several weeks, mothers would usually return to their husbands immediately after dropping their child off to school. Nor was any other form of communication (such as phone calls) encouraged.

The first few hours at the boarding school, therefore, were highly likely to prove traumatic for any child, particularly from overseas, suddenly abandoned and isolated amidst strangers in an atmosphere literally alien. No child could be adequately prepared for this experi- ence, which for many proved devastating. Children may have been told about school, they may have had siblings or friends at the school, they may even have visited the school (though this would be unlikely in the case of children from abroad), but no verbal information could contain with any degree of security, let alone tenderness, the child of six or eight, suddenly catapulted into this Spartan society. Suddenly, there were only other boys, mostly bigger, and a few men, all strangers, and a very small number of women, perhaps four in a school of about a hundred boys, typically consisting of the matron and her assistant, the headmaster's wife, and perhaps one of the teaching staff.

The second aspect of the trauma is its unremitting nature (which brings it into Khan's (1963) category of "cumulative trauma"). Almost universally, these children expected relief: their parents loved them, there must be a mistake. If they cried out in anguish, surely the par- ents or other trusted adults—often loved servants in the case of children brought up in countries which used to be part of the British Empire— would come to the rescue, as they always had in the past. Children from this background were particularly liable to be shocked. At home, they may have been accustomed to being attended to by more adults than many of their peers from the UK, since the servants would often particularly cherish the young children of the household. For many such children, the servants' native language was their first tongue; English was reserved for formal conversation with their parents and was often spoken with more difficulty. This underlines the severity of the loss the children now had to endure, in which they were separated not only from their parents and other blood relatives, but also from their servants, with whom they often had a closer emotional bond. They also lost whichever country they came from, separated from the sensual world in which they had been unconsciously immersed: sounds, sights, light, and smells. From their point of view, a grimly Spartan boarding school in a rainy, grey northern European country often formed a brutal, unthinkable contrast. The cry for help brought no rescue. There were only strangers, and even well-meaning, affectionate, and concerned adults would still be the "wrong" ones, from the child's perspective. Inevitably, the available adults were part of the system, committed to the boarding school ethos, which required them to toughen up the new arrival from the first day.

Moreover, the child was surrounded by other children, partly by other new arrivals as discombobulated as himself and in no position to be able to offer any comfort, partly by older boys, who for the most part were allergic to being reminded of their own first, often overwhelming anxieties. For them, the new arrival was a source of intense, persecutory anxiety, to be somehow defended against, perhaps by denial, distancing and rejection, or perhaps by cruelty. As with concerned adults, a genuinely concerned older boy would still be "the wrong boy", so his efforts at succour would typically be rebuffed. Moreover, since the older boy would himself probably be no more than nine or ten at most, in his immaturity he would be likely to back off when his first comforting efforts were met with rejection.

The chronic aspect of the trauma consisted, then, in its continuing, long-term nature. Children from abroad frequently did not see their parents for another year, sometimes more. Holidays might be spent with relatives or friends of the parents, whom the child had never met before. Another loss for children from abroad, ironically enough, was the loss of school at the end of term, as they were plunged for their holidays into yet another completely new situation. The ordinary way of life at home with the family was lost for ever. One patient put it succinctly thus: for him, being at home thenceforwards was always unusual, a special event, while being away at school was ordinary. There is no rhetorical exaggeration in this statement. A whole swathe of British society considered this normal and desirable for themselves and their children.

There was no opportunity for proper mourning of the crucial attachments these children had lost. There was no possibility of their mourning the rupture of their link with their own families or other significant attachments, since the school and the parents themselves colluded powerfully to deny and belittle the emotional significance of the rupture. This led to further emotional repression and shutting off within the child's mind, and to the probability of greater emotional restrictions in subsequent adult couple relationships.

As Duffell (2000) and Schaverien (2004, 2011) discuss, the child needed to survive and adapt, which required him to accept and participate in the brutally new world in which he now found himself. This entailed living in a paranoid-schizoid universe (Klein, 1946) in which the defences of denial, splitting, omnipotence, and mania were predominant, and indeed crucial for survival. The child was caught in a double bind: even though he was too young to understand fully, he would nevertheless intuit how important his schooling was to his parents—the sacrifices *they* were making (financially; *their* loss of their child); their emotional investment in the system (regarding class and status as well as educational standards); their aspirations to better themselves via their child; the weight of the tradition that valued such schooling;—so how could he complain? Letter-writing itself was formalised. The school staff scrutinised and censored all letters home. Bullying, emotional abuse, sexual abuse, the formation of mafia-like protection groups, scapegoating and being the scapegoat, were all regular aspects of the daily lives of such children. Whilst these unpleasant situations may be part of any school culture, for these children, they were unmediated by a pattern of return to the reassuring lap of the family either daily or in the holidays. They constituted the constant social and emotional environment. When the year-long separation came to an end (and not infrequently, the separation lasted longer than one year), it is hardly surprising that beneath a surface etiquette of good breeding, many children found themselves emotionally estranged from their parents—sometimes not even recognising them.

The fundamental maturational task of continuing to work towards the depressive position (Klein, 1940)—in which the loved and hated aspects of the parents are brought together in the child's mind—was a virtual impossibility. For a child to be able to risk knowing—albeit at an unconscious level—that he not only loves but also hates his mother, he needs to be contained within a relationship to the mother in which love predominates and reassures. Working through this developmental task was usually far too risky for a child from abroad, sent to boarding school. To survive, he needed to keep his parents, particularly his mother, "good". This was quite some feat in his circumstances, given that, from his point of view, his mother had rejected him, suddenly and without real warning, when he was still so young, in favour usually of staying with the husband. The child was thus in the position of the infant Oedipus, whose mother, Jocasta, colluded willingly enough with her husband, Laius, to put the small child out into the wilderness to die, apparently intent only on enjoying sexual gratification with her husband. This was no ordinary shutting of the bedroom door for a few hours, or nightly. However hateful this can be to a child in an ordinary family situation, it is nevertheless normally tolerable, because it is predictably followed by involvement in reassuring family pairings, this time of child and mother, or child and father, or with both as the loving, inclusive parents (for example, at the family breakfast). Such ordinary oscillations of familial pairings and exclusions, which provide the building blocks for working through the depressive position and the Oedipus situation, were unavailable. These children are denied the all-important experience of fluctuations between envy, jealousy, triumph, greed, happiness, sadness, contentment, depending on who's got together with whom within a well-enough functioning group of siblings and parents; instead, they are left unconsciously at the mercy of the phantasy articulated by Klein (1928) of the combined parents utterly engrossed in frightening and dangerous perpetual intercourse.

It would be logical for such a child to feel that his parents must hate him to have inflicted such an ordeal on him. However, thinking such a thought, let alone dwelling on it and letting it take hold, could lead to breakdown. Holding the complementary position of hating his parents for their momentous betrayal was equally terrible in its consequences. The child's need to survive and maintain equilibrium forced him to deny any such natural thoughts and feelings. Instead, he must idealise his mother, his father, and the parental couple as all-loving and all-wise. He must buy into the system as being the best possible. He, too, must idealise its Spartan qualities and hold them up as virtues, denigrating ordinary children kept at home and sent to day-schools. He must engage his defences of omnipotence, denial, and mania to overcome his underlying depression and misery. He must also expend much mental energy keeping all of this unconscious. On the more developmental side, he must search out interests and hobbies (for example, sports, arts, intellectual studies) in which he can emotionally invest and which he can pursue, thus providing all-important constructive and creative outlets.

However, given his situation, he may need to over-invest any such activities, highly prizing excitement and the experience of becoming completely immersed in his interests, as a means of blotting out awareness of his missing family situation, and confusing this outcome with happiness. The school system powerfully supported such psychological manoeuvres: after all, it was in no one's interests that the boy's fundamental unhappiness be known and experienced. What I am naming "the system" consisted of a large and formidable group of persons including the child, his fellow pupils, the school staff, his parents, his social class, powerful interest groups such as the military, political parties, and the state (the schools are legal charities). Its power is still strong; in previous generations, it was overwhelming. (Many parents, troubled by misgivings about sending their children away to boarding school, tended to have their doubts crushed by the power of "the system". Virtually everybody within the upper and upper-middle classes supported this form of education, most of the less affluent middle classes aspired to it, and opting out of the system was perilous, socially and professionally, particularly if living overseas in a British colony.) Indeed, one could speculate that Orwell's two masterpieces, *Animal Farm* (1946) and *Nineteen Eighty-Four* (1949), consciously representing potential Communist take-over, may unconsciously consist in part of an artistic projection of what we know to have been Orwell's personal horror (Orwell, 1953) of the totalitarian power of the boarding-school system, magnified to a national, governmental level.

The depression, loss of hope, misery, fear, hatred, jealousy, and envy that the children were forced to deny had to find homes, via unconscious projection, somewhere. Inevitably, the principal targets were the more obviously unhappy children within the school itself. Those less able to deny and hide their wretchedness automatically became the unwittingly compliant receptacles for the projection of the disowned, feared, and hated aspects of the "stronger" boys, for whom denial and projection constituted a crucial bulwark, buttressing their apparent toughness. The softer and more vulnerable side of the boy, wishing to love and be loved (Fairbairn, 1941), obviously constituted a perilous danger within this system, in which the other ordinary givers and receivers of that love, the parents, had extracted themselves from the environment. Whilst what Rosenfeld called "the sane, dependent self" (Rosenfeld, 1971) gives rise to some degree of anxiety in many, the "strong" boys' unconscious assessment that this side of themselves was to be feared, hated, therefore denied and projected, can only be deemed natural and even accurate. The fact that so often it was then taunted and attacked in those who received the projections, as scape-goats, suggests how terribly anxious these "strong" boys were about their own dependent vulnerability. Their "solution", of denying, eject-ing, and brutalising it in the spirit of tough, male camaraderie, set up psychological habits which carried the risk of becoming firmed up and addictive through the inevitable arousal of sadism and masochism and their ensuing gratifications. Moreover, even if the immediate uncon-scious aim was to render the unbearable situation of primary emotional deprivation tolerable, such habits would prove difficult to jettison or even alter once it was over, given that it endured throughout childhood from the age of eight (sometimes six, or even younger) onwards.

In many children, this seems to have led quite organically to fear and hatred of women, hidden beneath idealisation of them. The mother's betrayal probably hurt most, giving rise to intense hate and anxiety that had to be kept unconscious. It could be split off into a suitable female target, such as the matron or a female teacher, who could be hated venomously. It was arguably an impressive achieve-ment if a child was able to retain awareness of his unhappiness and to express it, an achievement shared by Orwell and Kipling (op cit.). However, even their accounts illustrate the crucial importance of ide-alising their mothers, and their need to find some other female to denigrate, in Orwell's case the headmaster's wife, and in Kipling's, his foster mother. These women may very well have been genuinely sadistic towards little boys: after all, they were operating in an envi-ronment that implicitly condoned or even invited emotional withhold-ing bordering on the cruel, not only towards farmed-out children but also towards their own affectionate natures. The system encouraged women to back up their menfolk in producing tough, independent, emotionally invulnerable boys, who could then grow up to be the men who would run the Empire. Women were therefore discouraged from being too affectionate to these motherless boys—tenderness would be seen as spoiling, pampering, producing effeminacy, and undermining a proper male attitude—so these authors' portrayals of these dreadful, all-powerful women may not be too wild. They certainly seem to have offered themselves unwittingly as hooks for the projections of the split-off, feared, and loathed aspects of the internal mothers of young Kipling and Orwell, as well as a subsequent yearning for revenge, all of which these authors were able to sublimate into their searing artistic descriptions of their female tormentors.

A man with such a background may develop serious inhibitions in loving and trusting a woman, intimately and sexually. What one finds repeatedly is an idealisation of women, accompanied by a distancing or avoidance of them in practice, usually unconscious, usually denied. This includes those men who get married and have children, but whose avoidance of sexual and familial intimacy seems to proclaim their undying fear, resentment, and grievance against any tender expression of love. Another group consists of men who flit from idealised woman to idealised woman in a series of intensely invested erotic encounters, but who flee each woman when the first sign of any ambivalence emerges.

Certain homosexual men with this kind of background will, again, typically idealise women, and can form affectionate, long-lasting, loving relationships with women, since their sexual orientation defends them against any repetition of the most intimate betrayal. A split-off hatred of women may also be characteristic of such individuals. Many men in this homosexual group cannot form stable sexual relationships with men either. Instead, they seek brief and often brutal erotic exchanges with other men, often effectively strangers. Such men may sometimes movingly speak of their uncertainty about whether they are "truly" homosexual, explaining that they have a dream of forming a lasting, secure, sexual relationship with a woman and having a family, which, unlike their own, would stay together during their children's childhoods. However, whenever they have contemplated putting this into practice, the realistic prospect makes them seize up with anxiety, driving them back into the defensive practice of often dangerous, exciting, sadomasochistic homosexual sex, with its obvious references back to the only physical love available at boarding school. Homosexuality, let alone homosexual love, was, of course, against school regulations, though the prohibition may have been honoured more in the breach than the observance; so another group is made up of men who, internalising this prohibition (usually backed up by religious sanction), maximally restrict their emotional, affective, and sexual lives, typically camouflaging this behind a charming exterior. They may find what seems the only possible outlet for their passions in pursuing an interest, which can be counted on not to betray and destabilise them.

Therapy with a couple who had direct and indirect experience of the boarding school system

I will now present the case of a couple. Although this couple were deeply affected by the boarding school background of both partners in complex, interweaving ways, nevertheless there also existed quite independent sources of difficulty.

When they presented for couple psychotherapy, Gregory and Louise had been married for fifteen years. I found them intelligent and likeable. Louise wanted them to have an active sexual relationship. Gregory stated that he regularly experienced sexual desire towards women; but not towards Louise. He was aware that Louise was "attractive"; he had been told so on numerous occasions by various friends, female and male, who had even congratulated him on catching such a desirable partner. He could even see it himself, but he could not experience sexual desire towards her.

They had got together when they were in their early twenties. They had little sex even then, but Louise fell pregnant, and they had decided to keep the child. Their conscious motives for staying together had been, to a large extent, dictated by guilt. Gregory had felt potentially very guilty about the prospect of leaving Louise with a young baby daughter; Louise had clung to him rather than be abandoned. Gregory had also felt unconfident about making a life with another woman. Anyway, he now had a child, so it seemed better to stay with Louise; and soon he felt a growing, loving commitment to the child.

Gregory found Louise excessively critical and controlling. She was always telling him what to do, always finding fault with his actions or his omissions, as well as with his character: he felt she found nothing but imperfections and blemishes in him. Louise did find Gregory sexually fairly attractive; and, after the birth of their daughter, she felt definitely that it was better to stay together. However, she acknowledged that she found much to criticise about Gregory. In particular, she felt he was not

THE HIDDEN TRAUMAS OF THE YOUNG BOARDING SCHOOL   157

ambitious enough in his work, and this apparent lack of professional drive provoked her scorn.

Her central complaint was that Gregory was incapable of showing her ordinary affection. Sex now only occurred to conceive a child: after a couple of years, they had decided on a second child, another daughter, and two years later, they had a son. She never accused Gregory of being *openly* hostile. He was civil—but never anything more. He seemed to have no romantic interest in her. If things went well for either of them, he never became more loving, his demeanour remaining eternally and distantly polite. She noticed that his sporadic professional trips abroad brought out a degree of excitement and interest that he never showed towards her and the family. She was hurt that he never seemed to experience any ambivalence about leaving her and the children behind for these trips. This changed as the children got older: he evidently minded leaving them—but not her.

The couple took their parental responsibilities very seriously. I was never in any doubt about their love for their children; and their other difficulties and mutual hostility did not prevent them from co-operating regarding the children with a marked degree of success, whether it was a question of their education, their activities, their social lives, or their health, particularly when any serious illness threatened.

Gregory had undergone a series of separations while still very young. He was the third of three brothers, seven and six years older than him, and had been born in the country where his father was working, very far from the UK. His parents divorced when he was three, after which he lived with his mother. His two brothers were already in the UK, at boarding school. When he was five, his mother formed a new, serious relationship. At six, she agreed to his father's wish that Gregory be sent to boarding school in the UK. He remained a boarder, changing school at the ages of eight and thirteen, until he went to university at eighteen. His parents never returned to the UK.

Gregory had suffered his first major post-weaning separation at the age of three, when he lost his father and his parental couple. If this loss was partially offset by his gaining his mother for himself alone, any Oedipal triumph was then shattered by his mother's sexual engagement with a new man, with whom she then formed a new, stable couple. Gregory only remembered this new constellation being presented to him in an unambiguously positive light, including the "happy" prospect of siblings. It seems likely that nobody supported him empathically in his negative experiences of losing his father and being forced to tolerate, even welcome, a new man, who he felt never really liked him. However accurate this perception was, it probably also reflected his own dislike of the interloper, a dislike that was never sanctioned. Up to this point, the young Gregory's problematic experiences, which would already be playing a significant part in shaping his character, were unconnected to boarding school issues. However, his father then ordained that Gregory should leave his mother (and her new partner), and go to boarding school, that is, go away to live alone in a foreign country, ironically enough referred to as "home". He was not even to join his brothers. The age gap meant that he would not have overlapped with them in the same school in any case; and as it happened, his parents for various reasons decided to send him to a different one. This was rejection and exile indeed. As a youngster of six, he now had to make a life for himself, quite suddenly separated from his mother.

He had been sent to a pre-preparatory school at six; after accompanying him there his mother had immediately returned to her home abroad. He spent holidays with unknown relatives and his brothers, whom he also hardly knew and who, at that age, wanted little to do with him. At eight, he returned to his country of birth one last time for a summer holiday and to his mother. Then he went to his preparatory school, another entirely new start, when he gave an outward sign of his inner disturbance: he broke down and cried almost unceasingly for three days. However, he then "sorted himself out"—his words, delivered casually in the session but aptly describing his need for what we came to call "DIY defences", since in his trauma he was emotionally contained by no empathic adult. He had never spoken of these matters, particularly of his breakdown, to anyone, including Louise, until this moment in the therapy. He virtually never saw his father again until his twenties, when his father retired to the UK. His mother would visit the UK every couple of years and he would then spend one of his holidays with her, the others (by far the majority) with relatives or with school friends. His outwardly intelligent and cheerful demeanour seems to have convinced everyone—and often himself—that he was "fine". His school experience had then continued along the lines I set out at the start of this chapter.

Louise had not herself been sent to boarding school: however, her four brothers (there were no sisters) had been sent away. Her internal situation contained the paradox of being the child who became seriously unhappy on account of *not* being sent away, thus further illustrating the extraordinary emotional pressure sometimes exerted by the boarding school ethos even in its apparent absence. Louise was excluded from the privileged position of the brothers, a position vigorously and unambivalently maintained as superior (illustrating the frequently encountered insinuation that a life without the "privilege" of boarding school will never be as successful as one possessing that advantage). Her parents were unhappy together. Her father, with whom she had the better relationship, was often absent. Her mother openly regretted having a daughter, wishing she could have had another son (whom, ironically, she would then also have sent away). As a mere female, Louise had not warranted the financial investment of the boys. Her mother had made her feelings clear about being tied domestically to a boring young girl. As soon as she decently could, she reinstated herself in her exciting full-time work (in a man's world) and arranged for her daughter to be looked after by a succession of nannies, themselves despised in the family hierarchy.

Louise's patronising attitude towards Gregory's lack of ambition was balanced by Gregory's contempt for her flightiness. He caricatured the way she would often allow her judgements to be over-balanced by her feelings. Many sessions started with Louise firing off angry volleys at Gregory for being emotionally out of touch and, as she claimed, for being very angry with her and the children—this anger was what she experienced underneath Gregory's cool veneer. She would implicitly make a strong emotional connection with me as she spoke, as if I would be bound to react sympathetically, understanding how wronged she was not to be granted a warm, sexual, and affectionate relationship, and how right she was to be infuriated by Gregory's overall meanness of character and smallness of ambition, not only professionally but as a man generally—particularly sexually.

After sitting impassively through this barrage, Gregory would then infuriate Louise further by asking politely whether she felt she had her say. Turning to me, he would then engage non-verbally with me just as strongly as Louise had done a few minutes earlier, apparently enlisting me as a fellow male who could be trusted to see through Louise's typically feminine exaggerated emotionality which, yet again, was overriding and distorting her capacity to make rational judgements. I might implicitly be invited either to have my sadism and my presumed prejudices gratified by this display of female stupidity, or to join him in patronisingly explaining to Louise how, in each of the situations she had outlined, she was, naturally, mistaken. Each incident would be parsed into its component constituents to show that he had, in each case, thought and acted reasonably. He might have suffered mild irritation with the children, but they merited a rebuke, and—here one could detect some emotional intensity—he certainly never went too far. He would also clarify his professional situation and demonstrate how Louise had totally misunderstood it. He was lucky to have his job. He enjoyed it, and it brought in a good-enough income by any ordinary standards. He also felt adequately respected at work, so in no way did he agree with Louise's criticism of his lack of ambition.

Thus the couple would typically reach stalemate. They had each delivered themselves of denunciations—in their different but equally withering rhetorical styles—of each other's character, though by now whatever sadomasochistic dividends they had previously derived from such exchanges had diminished to the point of zero, through the tedium of the repetitions and the complete lack of anything creative evolving from them. The only grounds for hope lay in their rising impatience and hatred for the static, monotonous quality of their all too frequently rehearsed grievances. I, too, felt oppressed by the numbing, dull, resentful atmosphere, pervaded by a distant threat of violence. I felt confused by the couple's competing complaints: I found it easy to identify with Gregory's polite exasperation with what could feel like his wife's hyper-emotional and illogical tantrums; yet I often felt identified with Louise's sense of being maddened by Gregory's self-satisfied, withholding coolness.

Some fluctuations in these fixed styles of relating began to appear. Through relating to me as a third party—a witness; a listener; someone who sympathetically responded to their aggrieved feelings, yet tried to assess the merits of their claims; someone who each could thoughtfully observe relating to his or her partner; someone with whom each began to identify; someone through whom each could even begin to empathise with their spouse's predicament—each started to gain a "third-position" (Morgan, 2005; Ruszczynszky, 2005) perspective on their couple interactions and their own part in them. Louise began to consider that her mocking disdain for Gregory might be excessive. I had to confront her with the irrationality of simultaneously mocking him for his lack of ambition, whilst vengefully castigating him for valuing his work above herself and the children when he did get excited about it. When

I suggested it, she could own that a principal source of her constant nagging was her sexual frustration, and that her own rage, sense of inadequacy, and unsatisfied yearning surfaced not only through her direct expressions of sexual exasperation, but also indirectly through her constant attacks on Gregory's perceived faults. I interpreted that the "great anger" she so confidently attributed to him might also emanate in part from an unconscious projection and disavowal of her own rage at her sexual unfulfilment. She could also see that, since she constantly berated Gregory, his hostile, non-sexual response was not so surprising. In general, Louise became more reflective about her own part in the couple interaction.

Gregory also began to shift. He could begin to own how, beneath his civil manner, he had been continuously and cruelly dismissive of Louise. I showed him how accurately he would intuit, take aim, and demolish aspects of her personality she either particularly prized or felt insecure about, disguising his onslaught and disarming her retaliation through understatement and wit, trying to inveigle me into enjoying the sadistic fun. I spelled out the implication behind his polite façade that the quantity and quality of her criticisms were so outrageous that he need take none of them seriously; so he would seldom answer her charges but leave her suspended, as it were, finding amusement in the spectacle.

Both spouses, therefore, began to face their own part in their daily reciprocal cruelty. Each felt depressed. Gregory gradually revealed a more powerful set of anxieties. When I pointed out how he depicted Louise as an extraordinarily powerful woman, exceedingly controlling, he confessed to Louise for the first time that he had been harbouring a harrowing dread of her throwing him out and keeping the children, thereby severing him from the people he loved most in the world. His defensive civility expressed an anxious need to assuage and calm her dangerous aggression (though, ironically, it often achieved the opposite effect). However, his fear of the greed for narcissistic dominion that he attributed to her meant he absolutely could not consent to having sex with her, because this would give her the complete power over him that he felt she craved. He was utterly convinced that she would abuse this power to bring about his downfall. Having sex with her would be tantamount to an abject submission. He would have no further leverage over her. She would be able to do exactly what she wanted, and, ultimately, she would expel him. My own feeling was that the therapeutic process was beginning to develop: Gregory was starting to express more frightening, more primitive phantasies, and I felt sure that these were the real drivers of his emotional and sexual restrictions. I strongly felt the impact from his communication of his underlying terror.

Gregory's "logic" made only the most threadbare sense to Louise. She could recognise that Gregory exerted some power over her by withholding sexual intimacy. However, far from this frustration assuring the survival of their relationship, she increasingly felt that the lack of sex was pushing her inexorably towards opting out of it. She did not concur that, if he were to consent to sex, she would consequently ask him to leave. She felt the opposite. Her conviction grew that it was crucial for them to have a more intimate and sexual relationship; she had enough not only of an undesired, celibate life but also, on a deeper level, of living with someone who constantly rejected her. She no longer felt compelled to endure the constant battering of her basic self-esteem. Having initially resembled a rather scatty and over-emotional adolescent, Louise was developing into a thoughtful woman of more serious emotional substance, and this also made a strong impression on me.

Gregory's stance began to look increasingly flimsy and unreal. Louise had made major changes in how she related to him. By now, she was no longer condescending regarding his work, instead respecting his professional record. She was also trying quite effectively to be more affectionate to him, partly because she was more aware of his good qualities, partly responding to his assertion that he would be sexual if only she were nicer to him: she was calling his bluff. Gregory told me that he could see these developments; he would initiate sessions with his observations of the changes Louise had made, all in directions that he desired. Yet he felt impelled to come out with the same old complaints, which even to his own ears sounded like a stuck record. Though increasingly unconvinced of the legitimacy of his own grievances, he could not stop himself from remaining at an emotional and sexual distance from her. He toyed with the possibility that Louise was just not the right match for him sexually, but quickly admitted that this was not the problem. He had a strong intuition that, even with another woman, his predicament would recur.

Gradually, it became apparent that, on a fundamental level, Gregory was hardly relating to Louise, as such, at all, but instead to an extraordinarily powerful internal maternal figure, a mother with the power of life and death. She was able to excommunicate him from herself and all those he loved. He felt absolutely compelled to cleave to her, and to try to ingratiate himself by rendering himself indispensable in many practical ways. But chief amongst his responses to this virtually god-like mother were fear and hate. He feared her dominion; he feared her abuse of it; he dreaded and hated her constant, castrating criticism; he loathed her emotionality; he utterly distrusted her affection, needing constantly to defend himself against her wiles, her warmth and her powerfully attractive sexuality, which would draw him into her net. Since he could not alter her attractiveness, he needed to transform his response. When his erectile response to Louise—as the personification of this cruel, tantalising Kali-like figure—registered zero, he triumphed. It was even more satisfying to be able to tell her so, flaunting his non-responsive penis before her, attempting (often with a large degree of success) to dent her self-confidence as an attractive female. I interpreted that he was required, internally, to put her down as powerfully as he believed that she intended to squash him. She must be punished, and her torment and torture must be very long drawn-out, over years. I showed him that his actions and attitudes to her conveyed that Louise needed to be tantalised by the implication that she might be loved if only she improved herself, if only she became "a nice person", followed by his cruelly impressing on her that any efforts in this direction would be futile, since he would regard them as no more than pretence. Anyway, any attempts on her part at improving things ("behaving better") was bound to prove too weak to alter his underlying distrust and aversion. Making her cruelly aware of the inexorability of his intention formed part of her apparently deserved torment. Gregory switched from brief expressions of guilt and remorse about the pain and frustration with which he was tormenting Louise, to much longer periods of no concern at all.

However hurt and resentful she felt, Louise could now see that his aversion to her emanated from some profound source of chronic anxiety within himself. She felt more concern for him, and became softer and more loving, whilst feeling that she nevertheless could not simply promise to go on giving her life to a man who constantly rejected her when it came to the more intimate expressions of love.

Gregory saw this too. He was finally convinced that his highly anxious and defended attitude to Louise was driven by powerful internal forces, which were seriously distorting the reality of his current relationship, threatening to spoil any chances he might have of future happiness with Louise, or any other woman, in the arena of intimate, especially sexual, relating.

Gregory exhibited many of the personality and relationship issues that are typical of the ex-boarding school boy. For example, he was married, had children, and avoided intimacy with his wife, though to a lesser extent with his children. It emerged that he had a number of very short-lived, exciting but also, for him, frightening affairs over the years, before and after getting together with Louise. He had homosexual relations at school, about which he had felt excruciating guilt, but could also confide that, in the present, he sometimes longed desperately for a rough, homosexual encounter. And there were many prolonged periods when he simply wanted nothing to do with any kind of sexual life.

Nevertheless, in many ways, he was thoughtful and concerned for others—at a certain distance. Interestingly, his work took him to parts of the world where people had been caught up in catastrophes, natural or man-made. During his therapy, he gained recognition for the excellence of his penetrating analyses of the plights of families and, above all, children in such circumstances.

Gregory became aware that his ongoing relationship with me in the therapy as an older man who took a regular interest in all aspects of his life over a sustained period of time had a profound effect on him, mostly positive. He realised that he often wanted to tell me how his life was progressing in areas that did not directly impinge on the couple. Behind me as a reincarnation of a sympathetic boarding school teacher lay the longing for an involved father. More negatively, I interpreted that he unconsciously experienced me as part of the ubiquitous "system", like his father and teachers, however friendly, intent on manipulating him to comply, to drop his antagonism to Louise, the embodiment for him of his betraying mother, in order to promote a false version of a happy family and thus to uphold "the system". A major complication, however, was caused by his unceasing attempt to idealise his parents. This drove him to continue to invert past and present relationships defensively. He wished to keep Louise installed as the embodiment of the feared and hated maternal figure, whilst retaining his own, actual mother as idealised, and thus to continue living in an unreal, defensively ideal version of the past, immune to the requirements of development and the passage of time (Grier, 2012). As the analyst of these manoeuvres, I became palpably a figure of distrust and fear, the bringer of bad news, and the driver of fundamental and far-reaching change in his inner world which he feared might prove catastrophic (Bion, 1965; Grier, 2005).

In the course of the therapy, Louise's history also came alive dynamically. Some of the roots of Louise's very low opinion of herself as a woman were to be found in the denigration of the female, which seemed such a hallmark of her family of origin. Her family experience was also a source for her over-emotional, irrational actions, which simultaneously expressed her enduring rage at the belittlement of her femininity whilst inevitably attracting censure for behaving like a typically crazy woman from Gregory, who unconsciously stood for her internal mother and brothers. I interpreted that her combination of continual criticism of Gregory for his weak masculinity whilst nevertheless finding him attractive constituted—amongst other meanings—a new edition of the contradictory feelings inspired by her father. Ultimately, she had felt betrayed by her father, and had resolved to get on in life without him: internally, she was set up to repeat this attitude to Gregory. Moreover, her mother provided her with a model of a strong woman as one who showed her love for her menfolk, certainly her sons, by sending them away, who despised and mocked her husband, and who set a much higher value on professional and social ambition than family intimacy.

It was all too easy for the internal constellations of Louise's and Gregory's inner worlds to dovetail dynamically. For Louise, marriage to Gregory symbolised admission to the privileged male sanctum from which she had always felt rejected as inferior: unfortunately, within the marriage, her primary experience was a cruel repetition of this denial, condescension, and exclusion. For Gregory, marriage to Louise symbolised admission and acceptance into the feminine, sensual world of warm emotions and love: but instead, he primarily felt that he re-encountered a woman who criticised and denigrated him, finally preferring to eject him from her embrace, just as his mother had done before.

For many years, they had endlessly repeated these dynamics in a stale, stalemated, loveless relationship. The addictive intertwining of their psychopathologies made it tremendously difficult for them to begin the arduous process of separating from each other and taking a fresh look at each other and at their interaction—an indispensable precondition for any serious attempt to reconfigure their relationship predominantly along creative and loving, rather than fearing and hating, lines. Nevertheless, the hope for better things had always been there.

It had been symbolised and enacted in their bringing new life into the world three times, and in their serious attempts to cooperate constructively in the upbringing of their children—particularly impressive at the start of their therapy, when their personal relationship seemed marked by incessant hatred. This contrasted with my experiences of many warring couples who do not hesitate to exploit their children in order to hurt each other as much as possible. It gave me hope that somehow this strong current of love and creativity, at present so carefully separated off and channelled into just one focus, might expand to take in each other as well as the children. Hope had also been an essential ingredient in their path to therapy, and they had each shown themselves capable of engaging and connecting with me thoughtfully and with deep feeling. It was this above all which convinced me of the potential for a deeper and more loving engagement within their marriage, if only we could succeed in breaking—via insight—their cycles of fear, suspicion, hostility, and retribution for emotional hurts of which, in truth, neither was at bottom guilty. At least, not originally: the long first anti-libidinal period of their marriage had, of course, inflicted real harm.

Louise led the way in a more reparative direction. This involved a radical reassessment of herself and her character, through which she began to come to terms with a much less idealised self-image. Although working through this with me caused her pain and depression, it also involved relief (to her surprise), since, through my acceptance of her as less than ideal, she could now begin to accept herself as a more ordinary, fallible, and hence real, woman, with currents of prejudice, jealousy, rivalry, and contempt within her personality, all of which she had been freely expressing towards Gregory, but which previously she had denied or justified through rationalisations. When these character traits could be acknowledged, they became less fixed and less toxic; concurrently, psychological space and energy became available for the emergence of more loving, tolerant, and constructive aspects of herself. This process led her to appreciate Gregory in much greater depth, as well as realising that his problems were of a different order of gravity from the faults she had been attributing to him. His emotional difficulties now gained her sympathy and concern. She had never ceased to find Gregory attractive, and she now made a sincere appeal to him to try to join her in an intimate and sexual relationship from a position of real desire and vulnerability, quite different from her previously taunting and condescending stance.

Her perseverance paid off—and I interpreted that it was not just hers. Her more overt hopefulness conveyed Gregory's more hidden, but not quite invisible, hope for change, just as his more stubborn, agitated, mistrustful, and depressed conglomeration of feelings also expressed Louise's continuing ambivalence. Before he could avail himself of a happier experience, I had to get Gregory to see how he was unconsciously acting in identification with his sadistic internal mother, inflicting emotional damage on Louise by cruelly withholding himself from her pleas for his love, as he felt his mother had done to him. He hated me for bringing this out into the open. He could not deny it, but for a while it depressed him seriously to have to confront his own active aggression and cruelty. But, finally, his pessimistic resistance to the possibility of a deeper happiness began to recede. He could begin to allow himself to be touched emotionally and sensually by Louise. At first, he experienced this as traumatic, and was deeply ashamed of his phobic anxieties. Louise found it difficult to accept his violent emotional oscillations towards and against her at this time. The couple needed the regular, firm containment and understanding of their therapy, as never before. There was often a palpable drive to regress defensively to their archaic, anti-libidinal relationship. My job was to keep following and commenting as insightfully and non-judgementally as I could on their emotional oscillations, to remember actively the journey they had been on, and to remind them of their hopes, without actually directing them to persevere. I found it a struggle not to feel demoralised myself when they lost momentum and appeared menaced by depression: it was all too easy to lose contact with all that had been gained and worked through, and with hope. When I interpreted these feelings, I think the couple felt their difficulties were being authentically recognised, my words coming as they did from my own emotional experience rather than from any distanced observation. They appeared to feel contained, and more able then to reconnect with and harness a more determined and optimistic outlook.

Fittingly, one of the strongest motivators for change were the children. In contrast to their own childhoods, Louise and Gregory eventually had to recognise that their children had a fundamental need to experience parents who not only loved them, the children, but also each other, affectionately and sexually. If, therefore, they continued to keep withholding themselves from each other, they were also withholding a fundamental building block (as they put it) from their children.

For each, the rewards were very great, indivisible though they were from pain. Gregory was able to have an experience of loving and being loved by a woman for an ongoing, prolonged period of time in a directly physical way, for the first time since the age of six. His wife had also become attentive, concerned, and empathic to his pain in a way that was quite new to him, and for which the child in him had been crying out for most of his lifetime. He could also be with his children and with his wife in an ordinarily familial, flexible, predominantly oscillating series of affectionate pairings, naturally involving someone being left out, but not for too long, nor involving excessive pain. He could identify with his children, and through them to some extent imaginatively experience family life as a child. Louise was at last able to enjoy an ongoing stable sexual relationship with a man she liked and admired, as well as loved, and she, too, could enjoy a family life in which all members were present, all interacting with each other, predominantly affectionately. But there were real losses, and old character traits never quite disappeared. An element of mistrust towards each other never vanished, and each felt the defensive pull towards an attitude of contempt to the other. Each had serious losses to mourn: not only their unhappy childhoods, so centrally marked by traumatic separations, but also the first, long period of their relationship, in which love—with all its perils—had successfully been kept at bay, the only gratifications being the excitements afforded by their sadomasochistic, mutual ill-treatment.

Conclusions

It would be a distortion to claim that this couple's problems rose purely from the evils of boarding school. Each of their childhoods had also been fundamentally affected by their parents' unhappy relationships, as is the case with many who have no link with boarding schools, as well as by many other matters. Nor did their problems simply derive from what had been done to them by others: their characters contained their own particular constellations of the universal psychological ingredients that make relating problematic: jealousy, envy, hatred, competitiveness, aggression, scornfulness, sadism, masochism, to name but a few. However, going to boarding school at a young age, particularly from a foreign country, particularly in the schools of the past, was highly likely to bring about a traumatic situation for a child. There is the ineradicable fact of the serious, long-term breach between the child and his parents. Gregory's story is meant to illustrate how a child's problems are exacerbated by this separation, which also introduces wholly new, psychologically grave difficulties, the total experience being so radical and chronic that, inexorably, the remainder of the person's life will be fundamentally affected.

There is not space in this chapter to debate the contentions often made in support of boarding schools: that they helped children from unhappy homes, that they helped British families living abroad to give their children a good education and a core British identity, that this style of schooling was second to none in promoting the qualities of independence, resilience, and leadership. The reader is invited to consider these, and other related claims, in the light of the case material; but of course they deserve full investigation and discussion. Above all, my purpose has been to show how problematic it is for adults who were members of this group of children to engage in intimate, stable, and loving relationships with an adult sexual partner and within the family, even when they long for happiness in these spheres. Through Louise's story, I have also tried to illustrate how hard it is for a woman to relate successfully to a man from this background, particularly if her own childhood has been marked by it.

This particular case has a relatively happy ending, which itself demonstrates the remarkable resilience of the drive for reparation and love in the face of such difficulties. It shows that, for some, at least, such a negative childhood experience does not automatically foreclose the possibility of loving a partner and children. However, this optimism should by no means be taken to be representative of the group as a whole. Children cannot be separated from their families for so long without real and lasting emotional damage, and it would be the work of another chapter to chart the sometimes tragic long-term consequences of this damage.

Finally, I wish to recognise that private boarding schools are now more aware of the importance of children's need for regular contact with their families, enabling this particularly through telephone and email communication, as well as permitting more direct, less rigidly rule-bound contact. Whether this is enough to make up for the loss of actually living at home would need psychoanalytic investigation. Fewer children are now sent to board at such a young age. However, there will always be circumstances that enforce long-term separation of some children from their families. It may be that some of the issues I have raised in this chapter concerning the boarding school child's experience may unexpectedly also prove relevant in other contexts.

References

Bion, W. R. (1965). *Transformations*. London: Heinemann.
Duffell, N. (2000). *The Making of Them*. London: Lone Arrow Press.
Fairbairn, W. R. D. (1941). A revised psychopathology of the psychoses and psychoneuroses. *International Journal of Psycho-Analysis, 22*: 250–279.
Grier, F. (2005). No sex couples, catastrophic change, and the primal scene. In: F. Grier (Ed.), *Oedipus and the Couple*. London: Karnac.
Grier, F. (2012). Psychotic and depressive processes in couple functioning. In: D. Bell & A. Novakovich (Eds.), *Living on the Border*. London: Karnac.
Khan, M. (1963). The concept of cumulative trauma. *Psychoanalytic Study of the Child, 18*: 288–306.
Kipling, R. (1888). *Baa, Baa, Black Sheep*. London: Penguin, 1995.
Klein, M. (1928). Early stages of the Oedipus complex. *International Journal of Psycho-Analysis, 9*: 167–180.
Klein, M. (1940). Mourning and its relation to manic-depressive states. *International Journal of Psycho-Analysis, 21*: 125–153.
Klein, M. (1946). Notes on some schizoid mechanisms. *International Journal of Psycho-Analysis, 27*: 99–110.
Morgan, M. (2005). On being able to be a couple: the importance of a "creative couple" in psychic life. In: F. Grier (Ed.), *Oedipus and the Couple*. London: Karnac.
Orwell, G. (1946). *Animal Farm: A Fairy Story*. London: Penguin Modern Classics, 2000.
Orwell, G. (1949). *Nineteen Eighty-Four*. London: Penguin Modern Classics, 2000.
Orwell, G. (1953). Such, such were the joys. In: *Essays*. London: Everyman's Library Classics, 2000.
Rosenfeld, H. (1971). A clinical approach to the psychoanalytic theory of the life and death instincts: an investigation into the aggressive aspects of narcissism. *International Journal of Psychoanalysis, 52*: 169–178.
Ruszczynszky, S. (2005). Reflective space in the intimate couple relationship: the "marital triangle". In: F. Grier (Ed.), *Oedipus and the Couple*. London: Karnac.
Schaverien, J. (2004). Boarding school: the trauma of the "privileged" child. *Journal of Analytical Psychology, 49*: 683–705.
Schaverien, J. (2011). Boarding school syndrome: broken attachments and hidden trauma. *British Journal of Psychotherapy, 27*: 138–155.

PART VI

TRAUMA AND SOCIETY

CHAPTER TEN

A German trauma?: the experience of the Second World War in Germany

Nicholas Stargardt

On Friday, 26 November 1943, Marie Vassiltchikov[a]—or "Missie", as she was universally known—walked through the foreign embassy quarter in Berlin, just to the south of the Tiergarten:

> We crossed over to Kurfürstenstrasse, where friends lived in almost every house; most of them had been hit too. The Oyarzabals' huge granite apartment building was a heap of stones. The corner of Nettelbeckstrasse (including our favourite little restaurant, the "Taverna") had been literally pulverised, only small piles of rubble remaining. Wherever we looked, firemen and prisoners-of-war, most of them … Italians', were busy pumping air into the ruins, which meant that some people were still alive in the collapsed cellars.
>
> In front of another wrecked building a crowd was watching a young girl aged about sixteen. She was standing atop a pile of rubble, picking up bricks one by one, dusting them carefully and throwing them away again. Apparently her entire family was dead, buried underneath, and she had gone mad.

—Vassiltchikov, 1988, p 118

In all wars, children are victims. The Second World War differed only in the unprecedented extent to which this was true. At least one million Jewish children perished in the "final solution", and we still do not know how many of the 216,000 victims of medical killing were children. Children were shot by German soldiers and militia men in droves in occupied Poland and the Soviet Union. Starvation and disease killed the elderly and the very young throughout occupied Europe, but especially in the east. And children were incinerated with their mothers in the fire-storms of Hamburg, Dresden, Hildesheim, Darmstadt, and a host of German cities, and were killed or froze to death in the mass flight of German civilians along the snow-bound roads from Silesia and East Prussia in 1945. And still greater numbers of children suffered in the war, losing their homes and belongings, their parents or older siblings. Some were undoubtedly traumatised to the point where they were incapable of communicating with others, like the girl that "Missie" Vassiltchikova saw dusting bricks above the place where her family lay buried, or the Polish girl who had to be taught to speak again after she was liberated from a concentration camp (Sosnowski, 1962, p. 167).

For many others, trauma manifested itself later or less overwhelmingly, leaving them sufficiently unimpaired to study, enter professions, marry, raise children, and love others. As many psychoanalysts and therapists have observed, it was often only decades later that they began the task of trying to express their buried memories, fears, and, in the case of the women survivors of the concentration camps whom Dinora Pines worked with , their suppressed rage. What interested me when I wrote about the war and the Holocaust in *Witnesses of War* was what we could learn about children's immediate experience at the time (Stargardt, 2005c). But I think a project such as that only makes sense if we are also aware of the weight of our contemporary baggage, of cultural assumptions and the shapes that experiences have taken on in later memory. Nor do I think we can ever completely escape into the historic past, unmediated by subsequent moments of recall, memory, or cultural fashioning.

I am very sceptical of a term that first entered mass circulation in the 1980s: "*collective* trauma". It promises to explain too much. It overwhelms its source material. With the best of empathetic intentions, our culture turns to notions like victimhood and social or collective trauma with an ease which creates enormous obstacles to understanding the past. Such terms are neither apolitical nor neutral. They give suffering a particular emotional colouring, highlighting innocence and recovery, what we might call the redemptive sides of pain, whilst casting destructive ones, such as hatred, rage and envy, into deep shadow. Recognition as a victim can also have a curiously disempowering effect, as historical subjects who were trying to make difficult calculations in terrible predicaments are turned into the passive objects of history.

National and personal redemption in the wake of defeat is not a new idea. In the 1920s, the political Right in Germany unanimously endorsed militant claims about the power of the "blood sacrifice" made by those who had "fallen" on the battlefields of the First World War, and the 1950s articulated a more pacific vision of national rebirth—in European countries on both sides of the Iron Curtain—through economic and social reconstruction. In Germany, such ideas went out of fashion in the 1960s and then came under attack in the 1980s, as Germans increasingly came to see the Holocaust as the central event of the Second World War. At just this time, "collective trauma" entered mass circulation to give a sense of overall meaning to the stories of Holocaust survivors—and to underline society's duty to listen to them, to help them to "break their silence" (Kushner, 1994; Novick, 1999). In the decades since then, "collective trauma" has become the first term journalists reach for when they cover ethnic cleansing, wars, and earthquakes, and it has also become the cultural gold standard of claims for recognition as victims. There is a limit to the number of occasions a whole society can stop and engage in rituals of commemoration and soul-searching.

In Norway, the collective term "war children" has been used to refer rather specifically to the children born of German fathers and Norwegian mothers during and after the occupation: for them, as Kjersti Ericsson and Eva Simonsen showed, the "trauma" that has to be overcome stems from post-war stigma and, in gaining a voice, they were also calling for social recognition and financial compensation. Fabrice Virgili has done similar work in France, and what these painful stories of individual discrimmination by neighbours, the education and welfare system, even other relatives, shows is that much of what constitutes "trauma" has a post-war political and cultural history. And it may have as much to do with societies that were not ready to listen, rather than with victims who were intrinsically unable to speak (Ericsson & Simonsen, 2005; Virgili, 2009; Warring, 1994).

In Germany, the subject of "war children" has been amplified most loudly in the run-up to the commemorations of 8 May 1945 during the last few years. When Germans gathered to commemorate the sixtieth anniversary of the end of the Second World War in May 2005, the talk everywhere turned to the suffering of German civilians. In many respects, this is a present-centred preoccupation, focussing on those aged seventy to eighty-five and upwards, who report sleep deprivation, anxiety attacks, recurring nightmares, and the resurgence of buried memories (Bode, 2004; Lorenz, 2003; Schulz, Radebold & Reulecke, 2004). But classifying these individual stories as part of a general "collective trauma" endured by a whole generation of German children obviously also advances a claim to symbolic recognition. As an analytical term, "collective trauma" tends to generate stronger moral responses than intellectual insight. It is not clear whether, or indeed, why all children should respond in the same ways: not all children emerged from the concentration camps or other sites of violence speechless. Nor, as it turns out on closer investigation, did all children undergo the same "collective" experiences in the first place.

In 1948, the directors of international children's villages gathered at Trogen in Switzerland to discuss their experience of working with war orphans. There was no consensus on what harm the children had suffered. Some considered that the violence they had witnessed was crucial, while others thought this had made little impression compared to their loss of family, concluding that their plight was similar to that of children who suffered such separations during peacetime. Some thought their memories needed to be repressed successfully for them to move on; others that they needed to express them through play therapy (Brosse, 1950a, pp. 22, 27, 43–44). Over the next decade, Ernst Kris and Anna Freud, both editors of the new journal *The Psychoanalytic Study of the Child*, pursued the subject further, Anna Freud's reflections informed by what she had seen in the Hampstead war nurseries and from working with child survivors of the Theresienstadt camp. Returning to the familiar terrain of her long-running argument with Melanie Klein about the role of cognition and the Oedipal conflict in developing a sense of self, she concluded that it was the loss of parental figures, rather than children's experience of violence which was central. This may seem a rather distant discussion now, but her work seems to have had a special reception in Germany, perhaps because her scattered essays on childhood and war were gathered together published as a single volume in German translation (Bowlby, 1965, p. 42; Freud, 1967a, 1974b; Freud & Burlingham, 1982; Kris, 1956). In any event, German analysts like Hartmut Radebold who have pioneered the current discussion of "war children" there, in fact lay great emphasis on the loss of fathers through the war. For him, absent fathers disproportionately affected the development of sons. There is of course a gender element to this, and the oral historian Dorothee Wierling has noted that protagonists of this self-styled "war child generation" are predominantly men, who pursued successful careers in West Germany in the 1960s to 1990s (Radebold, 2004; Wierling, 2009).

What interested me when I wrote about the war and the Holocaust from the point of view of children was to try to find ways back into the kinds of subjectivity they had developed at the time. There are major difficulties in recovering children's subjectivity even of such a relatively recent past. Surviving contemporary sources—such as children's letters, drawings, diaries, school-work, or adult observations, whether of children's games or of child psychiatric patients—are fragmentary and discontinuous. And there is a danger that such complicated and fragile source material would be crushed to fit a simple, over-arching interpretation, and, in the process, lose everything that was most striking and individual about it. Not surprisingly, I was very reluctant to use the term "trauma" as an interpretative category, both because of the risks of this kind of "force-fit" and because of its moral-political baggage. At the same time, I am very interested in a situation which is often to be found in cases of trauma, but is not exhausted by them: what I would call moments of "emotional rupture".

In June 1943, fourteen-year-old Alfred Völkel wrote a short memoir of his childood. He explained how he had grown up in foster care, at his grandmother's and then, from the age of ten—and the outbreak of the war—in a Bavarian children's home. He had finished school and hoped to become a clerk or a teacher, but had to accept an apprenticeship to a book-binder instead, almost certainly, a disappointment to his ambitions to join the white-collar lower middle class. Written on a single sheet of paper divided into two columns, Völkel's "Lebenslauf" is one of those deceptively "complete" documents, whose real significance—and incompleteness—only became apparent thanks to his subsequent testimony. He wrote it soon after being sent to the psychiatric asylum at Hadamar (LWV, 5031: Alfred Völkel, "Lebenslauf" and "Not just because I was a 'bastard'", MS, 1 August 1998).

The asylum, perched picturesquely on the hillside above the little town, overlooked the forgotten winding valley carved out by the

River Lahn between Marburg and Frankfurt, an area of small tin mines, Catholic observance, and rural poverty. And in January 1941, it became one of the centres for the T-4 programme of killing psychiatric patients. By the time Alfred Völkel arrived at Hadamar, the T-4 personnel had been redeployed and the small gas chamber in the basement was not being used. Psychiatric patients were now being killed in ways which it was easier to disguise. Many adult patients were put on a diet of stinging nettle soup until they died of hunger-related disease. Killing children had been disguised from the start for fear of public outcry, with doctors and nursing staff using different cocktails of drugs: powdered luminal was mixed into the evening meals, children were injected with morphium-scopolamin, or given tablets of luminal and trional. With symptoms of acute pneumonia or bronchitis, death was often painful, dragged out over several days. Alfred Völkel was given the task of sorting the children's clothes in one of the attics. On his way there, he had to walk through the closed ward, where he heard the "death rattles" of the twenty to thirty hungry and exhausted children as they battled for breath against the fluid flooding their lungs.

Völkel was not mentally disabled. He was, though he did not know it, half-Jewish, in Nazi-speak a "first degree *Mischling*". He had been sent to Hadamar alongside forty-one other half-Jewish children in a nationwide sweep of German children's homes. As the original group gradually dwindled to four boys and two girls, Alfred Völkel soon realised that each day that he was not called to the "office" was "a gift of life" (LWV, 5031: Alfred Völkel, "Lebenslauf" and "Not just because I was a 'bastard'", MS, 1 August 1998).

Thanks to the help of his immediate supervisor, Alfred managed to smuggle a letter to his uncle, Corporal Georg Völkel, who immediately wrote to the director of the asylum. Using whatever leaverage he had, he questioned whether Alfred was in fact a first- or only a second-degree *Mischling*, and pointed out that he, not the child's mother, had supported Alfred and was his legal guardian. Georg Völkel's commanding officer also wrote in support, vouchsafing him as 'a conscientious, dutiful and keen soldier'. But the *Oberleutnant* also confirmed that Völkel had mentioned disturbing rumours about the "fate of asylum inmates" which were clearly causing him grave concern, and the officer suggested that the asylum should tighten its own security and prevent letters being smuggled out. In the end, it was the authority which had sent Alfred to Hadamar in the first place whose intervention proved decisive: the Nuremberg Youth Welfare department confirmed that they were indeed not his legal guardian, and so, although he had been in a Bavarian children's home, they had no right to send him to Hadamar with the other *Mischling* children in state care. By the time this ruling arrived, four months had passed, and, of the forty-two children, only Völkel and one other terrified boy were left (LWV, 5031, Alfred Völkel; Winter, 136; Scholz and Singer).

Alfred Völkel was able to go home—as we shall see a recurring dream for children in war. There he rejoined the Hitler Youth, going on to serve in the German Army and be taken prisoner by the Allies. In 1996, fifty-three years after being sent there, he dared to visit Hadamar—still a functioning psychiatric asylum—again. Only after that did he contact the local archives and read a copy of his medical file. This was the first time that he realised that his father—a man he had never met—was Jewish and that this was the reason why he had been sent to Hadamar in the first place. If his Bavarian, Catholic maternal relatives had been careful to shield him from this knowledge and the social stigma it carried, it was his own mother's rejection he had always felt most keenly. As he wrote, he had been the "bastard" child, "scolded, punished, directed and shuttled from one orphanage to another". He had seen almost nothing of her, even when he had lived in his grandmother's house. "All I could see", Alfred wrote, "was that my mother chose others over me—a stepfather and later two half siblings". Alfred may have owed his life to the persistence of his mother's brother, but even a life-saving miracle could not undo the deep rejection he had experienced. For him, Nazi racism was etched into the most personal of all relationships, of mother and child. After the war, Alfred Völkel emigrated to the United States.

Völkel's case is significant in a number of ways, most obviously because he is one of a handful of children to be released from a killing centre like Hadamar; but it is also revealing for what it tells us about subjectivity. The complete document, the short contemporary autobiography, turns out to be a fragment, embedded in a process whose purpose was probably still obscured from Völkel at the point he wrote it. By contrast, his medical case file can explain the context and the process, retaining all the letters written by his uncle, his superior officer and the Nuremberg Youth Welfare Board, but even Völkel's later testimony almost certainly recaptures only sparse elements of how he experienced these events at the time. It is this broken mosaic, with its many lost and few retained fragments which accentuates a problem which itself is embedded in children's memories and ways of experiencing—namely a sense of the moments illuminating subjective experience being discrete, unintegrated into the kind of over-arching, connected narrative that adults can, and indeed often feel the need to, give. The fragmentary source and the isolated moment accentuate something which we are all probably already looking for when we study children and war, a sense of rupture.

Rupture is of course critical to memories of war and the Holocaust, and one of the things which is striking about it is the clarity and stability over a subsequent lifetime with which particular events are invested with this significance. One of the most revealing sets of sources are a collection of essays from the mid-1950s by West German teenagers who would have been aged four to six or seven when the events actually occurred. If their accounts are inevitably infused with later memory—one even wrote about what his mother told him later on—and bear the imprint of a broadly pacifist post-war outlook, they nonetheless evoke their younger selves at a point when they had still not yet left school or home to begin their adult lives. As a sixteen-year-old boy at the Burg Gymnasium in Essen wrote in February 1956:

> I was born just at the outbreak of war so that I cannot remember the first [war] years. But from my fifth year on, much is ineradicably etched in my memory. I sat through long nights of bombing in the cellar or bunker between shaking adults. (RA: Burg-Gymnasium Essen, UII/516, 1)

Or as a boy at the working-class vocational school put it at the same time, "Then it started in the bunker where people crouched in every corner and angle. With every bomb that fell the 'Our Fathers' sounded louder" (RA: Berufschule M2/6, 1). Having to endure months of twice- or thrice-nightly alarms under the entire flight path of the bomber fleets took its toll on sleep and nerves, but these young children also had to learn fear from the adults around them, however much their mothers thought that they were protecting them by involving them in the purposeful routines of giving them small suitcases to pack and going to bed in their tracksuits so that they would be prepared for the alarms. These were lessons which had already been learned in Warsaw and London.

One Essen boy, born in 1940, traced his first memory back to the sound of the air-raid sirens as his parents roused him from his sleep

(RA: Burg-Gymnasium Essen, UII/522). Older children recalled in early 1946 how, during the raids on Berlin, they had quickly learned to listen for the different sounds, recognising the high-explosive bombs from their "Crash bang!!!" and the "muffled crack" of the incendiaries, whose "Clack, clack clack" reminded one child of "when someone got a juicy slap" (Prenzlauer Berg, 1996, p. 35).

In other respects, however, extreme experiences such as air raids seem to have widened the divide between younger and older children. Whilst younger ones played games, fell asleep, and even waited for St Nikolaus in the air-raid cellars, they also lacked a sense what it all meant and why it was happening. By contrast, a fifteen-year-old Berlin girl, Liselotte G, had increasing difficulties reconciling the events of the nights with her rather uneventful daily routine of a school-girl living in the quiet eastern suburbs of the capital. On 29 December 1943, she noted, "It was another terrifying attack", and she had struggled to keep the composure she thought befitting for her ideal of "the German woman", silently repeating to herself the prayer she had learned for her own confirmation nine months before (Hammer and Nieden, 1992, p. 288). By 3 January 1944, she worried whether her religious faith would see her through and whether she could pass this test of "self-sacrifice" which she felt was being demanded of her. Things were not helped by the fact that, instead of receiving positive confirmation of the retaliation Hitler had promised against England back in November, she instead had a long conversation with her defeatist Social Democratic father who explained to her, in early January 1944, that Germany would be defeated and occupied by the Allies. Confused by the conflicting perspectives and moral demands, she insisted on seeing the patriotic as personal—asking herself if she was too weak to do what every German soldier at the front could do? "No & I repeat no", she declaimed silently to her diary. "I can & can sacrifice myself." And taking refuge in the Gothic mythology so beloved by Nazi propagandists:

> If victory is no longer to be had, then there is still honour", shouted Teja the Ostgoth, still fighting as he fell. Can one not shout to Germany's enemies: "you can murder me, but you cannot kill me, for I am eternal! (Hammer & Nieden, 1992, pp. 289–290)

Liselotte dramatised her need to understand war in adult moral and political terms—though one might note too the extent to which the

Nazi regime was thrusting the adult world into a particularly teenage one, with its willingness for self-sacrifice and to make boundless commitments for a cause. This was not, of course, a uniquely German experience, though in its mixture of Nazi, religious, and even oppositional ideas her variant on it clearly was. As the diaries and letters of teenage boys reveal too, this emphasis on cool composure under fire and patriotic self-sacrifice was sacralised by exchanging their Hitler Youth uniforms for those of anti-aircraft auxiliaries and later the *Volkssturm* and remained potent parts of their sense of duty into the final weeks of the war.

Younger children, by contrast, marvelled at the bombing of their cities, thrilled by the vividness of the colours and wild beauty of the sights. One five-year-old girl watching from her home outside Berlin as the planes flew in to bomb the city in 1943 remembered that "the sight of the threatening and growling aeroplanes was such that I thought I was dreaming and in a magical world" (RA, Goetheschule Essen, OII, 1). Adults commented on this side of the air war more rarely: almost certainly, they were not immune to this aesthetic sense—soldiers, for example, wrote often about the beauty of burning and destruction; but a sense of propriety held such responses in check when the victims were one's own neighbours, only for them to pop out in popular slang: the coloured, marker flares which slowly fell on their miniature parachutes were universally known as "Christmas trees".

The bombing gave rise to new children's games. Collecting *Flak* splinters was particularly prized by boys, who traded them in their school yards just as their older brothers had once swapped cigarette cards. But some other games no longer made any sense at all: one six-year-old girl found no fun anymore in one of her favourite games, jumping off the roof of the chicken hutch screaming "Stucka!" as loudly as she could. She stopped playing the game after Essen was bombed in March 1943. The make-believe had all become too real (Harald H., 1; RA, UI/no no., 2–3).

As they watched their houses burn and collapse in front of them, older children and adults had words for expressing their disbelief and their pain. They could find meaning in competing explanations—from "Jewish retaliation" to a "burden" sent by God to purify society from sin. Younger children did not have such meanings. Instead, it was the moment when their house was hit which was the meaning. Small children consoled themselves with the shoes, books and dolls which were rescued from the rubble, much as their mothers often counted the plates and glasses which had miraculously survived, as if they stood for all that they had lost. But loss also divided small children from adults. What children did do was to construct their own chronologies of the war through key events; the moment when *their* war became real. When exactly their secure world collapsed became a defining moment, dividing the war from a previous "golden age". And this remained remarkably constant against all subsequent reworkings of later experience.

For Jewish children in Germany, Austria, and the Czech lands, that moment of chronological rupture came before the war, often with their emigration, especially if it involved family separations. For Poles, this often happened in 1939–1940, with the mass shootings, deportations, and—for Polish Jews—ghettoisation which followed the German invasion. For German children in the cities of the Rhineland and Ruhr, it came with the onset of heavy bombing in 1942 and 1943. For children in the eastern German provinces, that moment was usually the mass flights of 1945. But for many other German and Austrian children growing up in the backwaters of the countryside, their intact and safe world did not end until occupation and the collapse of the Third Reich: for them, the events shaping their inner sense of time were more likely to be the capitulation of 8 May 1945 and the hunger years that followed than the Nazi period itself. There never was a homogeneous experience of this war. Any "generational" experience always has to face the extreme inequalities of experience.

Fritz Wandel and Karin Isolde Lehmann both lived in parts of Germany spared Allied air raids, and where children's first and last experiences of the war often followed one another in rapid succession, leaving behind drastic inequalities of experience. The flight of Wandel's family from the Soviet Army, the movement of their "trek" from right to left across the page following the east-west direction of maps, confronts the idyllic Lehmann home, protected until the very last, when French and German soldiers fought for control of their village in the Black Forest. For Zuzana Winterová, the loss of home is more complex, her ideal world—where children sit at table, the mother cleans and father reads his paper in the armchair—is simultaneously preserved and, as she adds the banner of the newspaper, torn apart again. Instead of *"Tageszeitung"*, daily paper, she put *"Tagesbefehl"*, order of the day, a slip with which her evocation of the safe pre-Nazi world abruptly vanished and she found herself back in the Jewish transit camp and "ghetto" of Theresienstadt (Stargardt, 1998a).

There is a different way of looking at moments of rupture. During and immediately after the war, across Europe adults were rattled and offended by the confidence and activity of children. From looking after younger siblings while their effectively single mothers went out to work, children took on ever greater responsibilities. They became beggars and smugglers to feed their families. At some point—as their parents broke down in the starving Jewish ghettos, or as they fled before the Red Army in the snows of 1945, or while they hid in their cellars during bombing raids—many children shouldered premature responsibilities, often for the whole family (Paulsson, 2002, pp. 26 and 61–66; Stargardt, 2005c; Szarota, 1985, pp. 101–130).

During wartime and post-war occupations, and in the Jewish ghettos, children had asserted themselves on the streets and market. They had fewer norms to unlearn than adults and often more drive and energy to adapt. In these moments when the war became "real", the integrity of their family worlds broke apart and children felt that they needed to patch them up again. But the same development also undermined their trust in the adult world and increased their sense of having to take responsibility for themselves. In 1945, the Polish State Institute of Mental Hygiene studied the war's moral and psychological harm through a large-scale questionnaire. Many children claimed to have learned the patriotic virtues from their parents, teachers and the Resistance. But just as many children admitted that they had learned to lie, steal and deceive, hate, treat authority with contempt, feel indifferent to all ideals, and even to have lost faith in the sanctity of human life. Set against the evidence of teenage drinking, sex, absenteeism from work, theft and black marketeering which welfare workers, juvenile courts and psychologists were reporting across the European continent, such surveys confirmed their belief that the war had destroyed children's innocence (Brosse, 1950b, pp. 19–20 and 77–100; Sosnowski, 1962, pp. 165–171). It had also taught these children how to survive. By 1946, German children were plying the black market too (Macardle, 1949, p. 287; Meyer & Schulze, 1985, pp. 100–101). In this premature and "wild" activity of children lay their capacity for treating the most extreme conditions as *normal*.

These specific moments shaped children's overall chronology of the war, establishing when the "safe" or "intact" world of childhood was destroyed. Critical to how this chronology ran was its *future* trajectory: if the family itself survived, as most German ones did, that became the central element of the tale; where the family itself was destroyed, as was often the case for the handful of Jewish children who survived the Holocaust, that shaped the tale.

There is one final way of exploring these moments of rupture, which is not dependent on future events and the survival of the children themselves. This is to consider how the war impacted on children's games. Whereas diaries and memories reveal moments of solitary introspection, play takes back into the immediacy of children's group activities. With the rise of the black market came new games like "coal thief and engine driver", which were played in Poland in 1940 and in Germany in 1946 (Kempowski-Archiv, 4622, 34). Children's games have a limited and historically repetitive repertoire, and for exactly this reason dramatic changes in the character and allocation of roles may be highly revealing. Throughout the Second World War, children played war games. In Southern Westphalia in October 1939, Detlef was able to convey some of the excitement of his battles to his enlisted father, as the ten-year-old described how his side had retaken their position under "murderous fire". His side had used sticks as hand grenades, but the enemy had thrown stones. Then Detlef had led the charge, his "sabre" raised, putting the enemy temporarily to flight. As battle resumed, Detlef's side attacked once more and withstood a fierce counter-attack: "None of us cried out and we won", he wrote triumphantly to his father (Lange, 2000, pp. 97–98).

There was nothing very new about this. Only the roles which the children competed for altered over time. Children in 1757 in Aachen or in Cologne in 1810 wanted to be the "king" or the "robber captain". By the interwar period, German and Austrian children were playing *Räuber und Gendarmes*, cops and robbers (Lessing & Liebel, 1981; Rosenhaft, 1983; Schlumbohm, 1983, p. 222; Stargardt, 1999b). Anything that is historically specific about children's games in central Europe during the Second World War is only evident against the backdrop of these more general characteristics of children's playing (David, 1964, pp. 111–114; Kempowski-Archiv, 3024, pp. 59–60).

Defeat, occupation, and imprisonment had an immediate impact upon children's games too. In Bromberg—or Bydgoszcz—four- and six-year-olds soon began re-enacting the mass executions the Germans carried out on the town square in the first weeks of the occupation, acclaiming

186 ENDURING TRAUMA THROUGH THE LIFE CYCLE

most those who cried, "Poland has not yet perished!" In Warsaw, boys played at liberating prisoners, but they were also observed pretending to carry out Gestapo interrogations, slapping each others' faces in this "wild" game. As reality invaded the make-believe, children were torn between models of heroic resistance and the allure of their conquerors (Flatsztejn-Gruda, 2004, pp. 37–38; Szarota, 1985, p. 100).

German children played at fighting the French, the English (never the British), and the Russians, but as in the older games of cops and robbers, the Germans always won. For the conquered, bringing the old games up to date often meant playing with real humiliations and immediate threats. In the Jewish ghetto in Vilna, children also began to play with a daily reality. There was only one main gate in and out of the ghetto, and each evening the Jewish police searched the Jewish workers as they returned from the workshops on the Lithuanian side of town for smuggled food, and although they risked being beaten for it, children often lingered near the gate in the hope of getting something. They also played at what they saw. As children enacted "Going through the gate", Tzvia Kuretzka recalled:

> Two main characters were selected; Levas, the hated head of the Jewish gate guards, and Franz Murer, one of the most murderous Gestapo men. The rest of the children played the Jewish workers who tried to smuggle some food into the starving ghetto and the guards who attempted to find the contraband. While the Jewish gate guards search everyone "Murer" comes, which propels the Jewish police to intensify its brutality and, at the same time, precipitates a tumult and panic among the "workers". They try desperately to toss away the small food packages, but "Murer" finds some with the incriminating evidence and the "workers" are put aside and later are whipped by the police. (Eisen, 1988, p. 77)

The two biggest boys got to play Franz Murer and Meir Levas, leaving it to the smaller ones to take the role of the adult Jewish workers, who, in reality, would often have included their own older brothers, sisters, aunts, uncles, and parents (Arad, 1982, pp. 304–305; Rudashevski, 1973, pp. 113 and 115–116). Like the adults they were playing, they were powerless to protect themselves from the blows rained upon them, in this case by the bigger, stronger children. As in the triumphant war games German children were playing at this time, power resided in the uniform. But the choice of role models was a stark one, as fear and detestation mingled with envy and longing. Where Detlef wanted to be just like his uncle and father in France, for these children being like their elders promised only fear and suffering.

For ten months, from September 1943 till July 1944, several thousand Jews from the Theresienstadt ghetto were kept in a special section of Auschwitz-Birkenau known as the "family camp", just in case the SS were to open the camp to inspection by the International Red Cross. To the great envy of inmates in other sections of Birkenau, this so-called "family camp" had special blocks for children and the inmates were allowed to keep their hair and the clothes they had come in. The children played organised games and sang, even performing a full-length musical loosely based on Walt Disney's *Snow White*. One of the Czech kindergarten teachers in the family camp also noticed the games the younger children played when they thought no one was watching. They played "Camp elder and Block elder", "roll call", and "hats off". They played the sick who were beaten for fainting during roll call, and they played the doctor who took their food away and refused to help them if they had nothing to give him in return (Otto Dov Kulka and Hoffmann-Fischel in Deutschkron, 80 and 54; Dokumentation des österreichischen Widerstandes, 13243, pp. 47–48).

Games in concentration camps did not protect children from the reality around them by preserving an ideal world of make-believe. On the contrary, they reshaped their games to incorporate that reality. In so doing, they drew the most extreme conclusion from the key lessons defeat and occupation taught all children. The first thing that defeated children witnessed was the sudden impotence of the adults they had grown up thinking were all-powerful. Power and success, the strivings of ambition and envy, were suddenly incorporated in their enemies. In some cases, children could imagine themselves as partisan fighters or members of one of the underground armies of the Resistance. But complete defeat and capitulation left few positive role models.

As the Third Reich crumbled in the rubble of Berlin during the last days of April and the first days of May 1945, German children began to express the dilemmas of their new predicament in their games. Before they had even emerged from their Berlin cellars, children started playing at being Russian soldiers. Waving make-believe pistols, they relieved each other of imaginary watches, crying, "*Uhri, uhri*" to mimick Red Army looters. As they assimilated the real and terrifying power of their

enemies and masters into their games, these Berlin children were also
enacting their own impotence and envy (Anneliese H.'s diary, in Kuby,
1968, p. 226).

Yet, the very fact of children's *play* leaves a degree of openness and
ambiguity about the meaning of their games: what does it mean for
children to consciously enact such scenarios? When, in May 1940,
Emmanuel Ringelblum over-heard an eight year-old Jewish boy in
the Warsaw ghetto screaming, "I want to steal, I want to rob, I want to
eat, I want to be a German", he was hearing the voice of pure despera-
tion and rage (Sloan, 39: 9 May 1940). But to *play* at robbing, stealing,
and being German was somehow different from this starving child's
scream. Children knew it was a game, that one scenario that they could
truly control, however powerless they might be in other respects. And
then there were things they did not play at altogether—German children
might enact Russian plunder, but not rape. Indeed, this pattern persisted
later on: as German and Austrian children wrote about the end of the
war over the next fifty years in school essays or unpublished memoirs,
they might mention the ubiquity of rape but veered away from the
subject again as soon as it touched on their own mothers (Bandhauer
Schöffmann & Hornung, 1994, pp. 232–233; Baumgartner, 1993, p. 80;
Petö, 2003, pp. 133–134 and 138; Stargardt, 2005c, pp. 321–323).

The "family camp" in Birkenau was a rectangular barbed-wire enclo-
sure situated within sight of three crematoria. Their chimneys belched
out three- and four-metre-high flames when in constant use. Whereas
the adults attempted to ignore their proximity to the gas chambers, the
children drew them directly into the fabric of their daily lives. The older
ones played games with death, daring each other to run up to the elec-
tric fence and touch it with their finger tips, knowing the high volt-
age current was usually—but not always—switched off during the day
time. One day, one of their teachers came upon the younger children
playing "gas chamber" outside their block. They had dug a hole and
were throwing in one stone after the other. These were to be the people
who were going into the crematorium and the children mimicked their
cries. In one way, their game broke down here. Whereas in their normal
games of "roll call", the little children may have had to submit to
beatings for "fainting", here no one jumped into the hole which was the
gas chamber. They had to use stones instead (Deutschkron, 1995, p. 54).
Even the smaller children, who were routinely dragooned into playing roles that entailed being punished or beaten, could not be those

people: we may surmise that to do so would, like playing at rape, have been too psychologically self-destructive. In any event, these unspoken limits to children's games suggest that, however much they may have envied their enemies, their primary drive was to adapt in order to survive.

The war was not just something that had happened to children. As they strove to survive in it and to parent their parents, it also tore apart their inner emotional world. Through their games, children simultaneously protected themselves from and adapted to a reality in which they recognised their enemies as the image of victorious strength and their parents as impotent failure. Children's games as much, as their other precocious activities, demonstrated that they were not just the mute and traumatised witnesses to this war. By its end, almost all European children had experienced military defeat and occupation. Once secure social structures became fluid, including that "safe" realm of "childhood" which so many pedagogues and social reformers had sought to create in the previous one hundred and twenty years, in order to insulate children from violence. The level of violence and the policies of the German and Allied occupations could not have been more different, but everywhere adults and children alike became acquainted with hunger, cold, and the powerlessness of adults. The "time before" might seem like a lost "golden age", but children found new roles for themselves and adapted with a speed and practicality that shocked many adults. In the process of adapting, they demonstrated just how profound were the social transformations wrought by Nazism and war: children found these things *normal*.

References

Archives:

Author's collection: Harald H., MS.

Dokumentation des österreichischen Widerstandes, Vienna: 13243, Yehuda Bacon, interview with Ben-David Gershon, Jerusalem, 17 November 1964.

Kempowski-Archiv, Archiv der Akademie der Künste, Berlin:

4622, Peter Laudan, b. 1935, "Gefährdete Spiele".

3024, Otto P., b. 1926, "Himmel und Hölle: Eine Kreuzberger Kindheit".

Landeswohlfahrtsverband-Archiv Hessen, Kassel (LWV), 5031: Alfred Völkel, "Lebenslauf" and "Not just because I was a 'bastard'", MS, 1 August 1998.

Wilhelm Roessler-Archiv, Institut für Geschichte und Biographie der Fernuniversität Hagen (RA):
Burg-Gymnasium Essen, UII/516, anon., 16 years, 14 February 1956.
RA, Berufschule M2/6, 16 years, 21 January 1956.
RA, Burg-Gymnasium Essen, UII/522, anon., b. 1940, 24 February 1956.
RA, Goetheschule Essen, OII, anon., b. 1938.
RA, UI/no no., anon. 19 years., 16 January 1956.

Published works:

Arad, Y. (1982). *Ghetto in Flames: The Struggle and Destruction of the Jews in Vilna in the Holocaust.* New York: KTAV Publishing House.

Bode, S. (2004). *Die vergessene Generation: Die Kriegskinder brechen ihr Schweigen.* Stuttgart: Klett-Cotta.

Bandhauer Schöffmann, I. & Hornung, E. (1994). Vom "Dritten Reich" zur Zweiten Republik. In: D. F. Good, M. Grandner & M. J. Maynes (Eds.), *Frauen in Österreich: Beiträge zu ihrer Situation im 19. und 20. Jahrhundert* (pp. 225–246), Vienna: Bohlau.

Baumgartner, M. (1993). Zwischen Mythos und Realität: Die Nachkriegsvergewaltigungen im sowjetisch besetzten Mostviertel. *Unsere Heimat: Zeitschrift für Landeskunde von Niederösterreich, 64(2)*: 73–108.

Bowlby, J. (1965). *Child Care and the Growth of Love.* London: Penguin.

Brosse, T. (1950a). *Homeless Children: Report of the Proceedings of the Conference of Directors of the Childrens Communities, Trogen, Switzerland* (pp. 22, 27, 43–44). Paris: UNESCO.

Brosse, T. (1950b). *War-Handicapped Children: Report on the European Situation.* Paris: UNESCO.

David, J. (1964). *A Square of Sky: The Recollections of a Childhood.* London: W. W. Norton.

Deutschkron, I. (Ed.) (1985). *Denn ihrer war die Hölle: Kinder in Gettos und Lagern.* Cologne: Verlag Wissenschaft und Politik.

Eisen, G. (1988). *Children and Play in the Holocaust: Games among the Shadows.* Amherst, MA: The University of Massachusetts Press.

Ericsson, K. & Simonsen, E. (Eds.) (2005). *Children of World War II: The Hidden Enemy Legacy.* Oxford: Berg.

Flatsztejn-Gruda, I. (2004). *Byłam wtedy dzieckiem.* Lublin: Norbertinum.

Freud, A. (1967–1980a). An experiment in group upbringing. In: *The Writings of Anna Freud*, Vol. 4 (pp. 163–229). New York: International Universities Press.

Freud, A. (1974b). Child observation and prediction of development: a memorial lecture in honour of Ernst Kris. *The Writings of Anna Freud*, Vol. 5 (pp. 102–135). New York: International Universities Press,.

Freud, A. & Burlingham, D. (1982). *Heimatlose Kinder*. Frankfurt-on-Main: Fischer Taschenbuch Verlag.

Hammer, I. & zur Nieden, S. (Eds.) (1992). *Sehr selten habe ich geweint: Briefe und Tagebücher aus dem Zweiten Weltkrieg von Menschen aus Berlin*. Zurich: Schweizer Veragshaus.

Kris, E. (1956). The recovery of childhood memories in psychoanalysis. *The Psychoanalytic Study of the Child*, 11: 54–88.

Kuby, E. (1968). *The Russians and Berlin, 1945*. London: Hill and Wang.

Kushner, T. (1994). *The Holocaust and the Liberal Imagination: A Social and Cultural History*. Oxford: Blackwell.

Lange, H. & Burkard, B. (Eds.) (2000). Abends wenn wir essen fehlt uns immer einer: Kinder schreiben an die Väter 1939–1945. Hamburg: Rowohlt Taschenbuch Verlag.

Lessing, H. & Liebel, M. (Eds.) (1981). *Wilde Cliquen*. Bernsheim: Padex-Verlag-GmbH.

Lorenz, H. (2003). *Kriegskinder: Das Schicksal einer Generation Kinder*. Munich: List.

Macardle, D. (1949). *Children of Europe: A Study of the Children of Liberated Countries: Their War-Time Experiences, Their Reactions, and Their Needs, with a Note on Germany*. London: The Beacon.

Meyer, S. & Schulze, E. (1985). *Wie wir das alles geschafft haben: Alleinstehende Frauen berichten über ihr Leben nach 1945*, Munich: EBG-Verl.-GmbH.

Novick, P. (1999). *The Holocaust and Collective Memory: The American Experience*. London: Bloomsbury.

Paulsson, G. S. (2002). *Secret City: The Hidden Jews of Warsaw, 1940–1945*. New Haven and London: Yale University Press.

Petö, A. (2003). Memory and the Narrative of Rape in Budapest and Vienna in 1945. In: R. Bessel & D. Schumann (Eds.), *Life after Death: Approaches to a Cultural and Social History of Europe during the 1940s and 1950s*. Cambridge: Cambridge University Press.

Pines, D. (1993). *A Woman's Unconscious Use of Her Body: A Psychoanalytical Perspective*. London: Routledge.

Prenzlauer Berg Museum des Kulturamtes Berlin and Annett Gröschner (Ed.) (1996). *Ich schlug meiner Mutter die Brennenden Funken ab: Berliner Schulaufsätze aus dem Jahr 1946*. Berlin; Kontext.

Radebold, H. (2004). *Abwesende Väter und Kriegskindheit: Fortbestehende Folgen in Psychoanalysen*. Göttingen: Vandenhoeck & Ruprecht.

Rosenhaft, E. (1983). *Beating the Fascists? The German Communists and Political Violence, 1929–1933*. Cambridge: Cambridge University Press.

Rudashevski, Y. (1973). *The Diary of the Vilna Ghetto: June 1941–April 1943*. Tel Aviv: Ghetto Fighters House.

Schlumbohm, J. (1983). *Kinderstuben: Wie Kinder zu Bauern, Bürgern, Aristokraten wurden 1700–1850*. Munich: Deutscher Taschenbuch Vertag.

Scholz, S. & Singer, R. (1986). Die Kinder in Hadamar. In: Roer & Henkel (Eds.), *Psychiatrie im Faschismus: Die Anstalt Hadamar* (pp. 229–235). Bonn: Psychiatrie-Verlag.

Schulz, H., Radebold, H. & Reulecke, J. (2004). *Söhne ohne Väter: Erfahrungen der Kriegsgeneration*. Berlin: Christoph Links Verlag GmbH.

Sloan, J. (Ed.) (1958). *Notes from the Warsaw Ghetto: The Journal of Emmanuel Ringelblum*. New York: McGraw Hill.

Sosnowski, K. (1962). *The Tragedy of Children under Nazi Rule*. Poznań: Zachodnia Agencja Prasowa.

Stargardt, N. (1998). Children's art of the Holocaust. *Past and Present, 161*: 192–235.

Stargardt, N. (1999). Kinder zwischen Arbeit und Spiel. *Sozialwissenschaftliche Informationen, 2*: 123–130.

Stargardt, N. (2005). *Witnesses of War: Children's Lives under the Nazis*. London: Jonathan Cape.

Szarota, T. (1985). *Warschau unter dem Hakenkreuz: Leben und Alltag im besetzten Warschau 1.10.1939 bis 31.7.1944*. Paderborn: Ferdinand Schoenig.

Vassiltchikov, M. (1988). *The Berlin Diaries, 1940–1945*. London: Vintage.

Virgili, F. (2009). *Nait ennemi: Les enfants de couples franco-allemands nés pendant la Seconde Guerre mondiale*. Paris: Payot.

Warring, A. (1994). *Tyskerpiger: under besoettelse og retsopgør*. Copenhagen: Gyldendal.

Wierling, D. (2009). Kriegskinder: westdeutsch, bürgerlich, männlich? In: L. Seegers & J. Reulecke (Eds.), *Die 'Generation der Kriegskinder'. Historische Hintergründe und Deutungen* (pp. 141–155). Gießen: Pschosozial-Verlag.

Winter, B. & Hessen, L. (Eds.) (1994). *Verlegt nach Hadamar: Die Geschichte einer NS-'Euthanasie'-Anstalt*. Kassel: LWV.

CHAPTER ELEVEN

Social trauma

Michael Brearley

Introduction

We psychoanalysts have a unique kind of first-hand experience, which is a matter of, and derives from, working with patients in the consulting room. In thinking about individual trauma, we have our own resource in this kind of experience and expertise, which enables us to make important contributions to a broader account of the phenomena and the concept of trauma. When it comes to the nature of Society or of Culture, our knowledge is more indirect. With regard to our present topic, we lack the historian's or the journalist's or the social scientist's background knowledge as well as their conceptual apparatuses. I find myself relying a lot on the kind of knowledge that people like Nicholas Stargardt, whose chapter follows mine, have. Nevertheless, in this field too, psychoanalytic thinking adds a dimension to the general understanding.

Psychoanalytic accounts of trauma to the individual, as earlier chapters of the book illustrate (see also Garland, 1998), can be richly illuminating. But what can we say about social or cultural trauma? Is it even possible to speak properly of social or collective trauma? What might we mean by this? I don't think that social trauma is merely a matter of an accumulation of individual traumas. And can social trauma be overcome? Can the group be healed?

I should also say that this is a vast topic. The areas I will be focussing on are: first, I consider some aspects of psychoanalytic understanding of trauma. Second, I ask how far the concept of trauma is psychological, how far it implies environmental factors. I make a distinction between traumatic and traumatogenic elements. Third, I refer to Jonathan Lear's example of the Crow Indians' experience as an example of group trauma. Lear enables us to understand an aspect of the capacity to repair group trauma. Fourth, and leading on from my discussion of Lear, I discuss traumas involving language. Fifth, I mention the way historic events can be reconfigured according to current social beliefs and values, as has been the fate of versions of the death of the Zealots at Masada in 73–74 CE. Finally, I refer to the use of cricket by people in West Indies to transform what had been (largely) an instrument of repression into something acquired, owned and transformed in a way that modified trauma and restored and built collective pride.

Social trauma, like individual trauma, can be worked through and recovered from (by mourning, learning, and new routes to a positive identity). Play and symbolisation seem to play an important part in such repair and reparation.

Psychoanalytic concepts of trauma

A trauma is something that overwhelms the psyche in a more than momentary way, arousing fear or even terror, often a fear of death and a sense that life is not worth living. The ceiling falls in. Things are turned upside down. Trauma interferes with the capacity to symbolise. The traumatised person loses a sense of there being a containing figure, internally or externally.

With trauma, there may be depression or flashbacks, there may be over-sensitivity and a sense of grievance. There may be an impoverishment of the psyche in the attempt to keep away awareness of the associations to the trauma, such that the person becomes bland or insubstantial (Ingham, 1998, pp. 96–107). There may be confusion about what is one's own, and what comes from other people (for example, in the person who as a child was sexually abused). The person affected is unable to face and enjoy life as he could before or as he might have done without the trauma. He may have what is in ordinary parlance called a breakdown. He or she may well have a sense that no one properly understands what he has gone through (Garland, 1998, pp. 9–31).

Trauma often also has a delayed impact. For the individual as for a society, it is as Stargardt describes: "the full impact of the third Reich can be measured by the ways habits of thought remained intact long after its outward symbols and structures had been dismantled" (2006, p. 11). A patient speaks about the way physical pain may endure even when the physical causes a pressure on a sciatic nerve, say, is no longer in place. Something similar can happen with psychic pain.

Masud Khan's notion of cumulative trauma (Khan) contributes to our understanding of delayed impact. A small example: a young child asks his mother for juice. She has invited him to say what he wants, and seems disposed to try to satisfy him. But when he voices his not outlandish request, she refuses it curtly. If maternal tantalising is typical of life for this child, it seems to me that damage must be done to his sense that it is permissible for him to want things. There must also be a build-up of anger, perhaps not expressed or even known to him. The child may grow to identify with the aggressor mother, and impose similar frustration on others who depend on him. Here the trauma or wound to the psyche builds up gradually. It is "incremental and psychological rather than sudden and physical" (Stargardt, p. 240).

For Freud, until 1897 (1966, pp. 259–260), the basic cause of neurosis was trauma of a particular kind—the sexual abuse of the person as a child. This first theory was combined with the notion of deferred impact; something not felt by the small child to be hurtful is imbued with significance only when its sexual meaning becomes available to the growing adolescent, and it is then (or later) that it provokes hysterical symptoms—somatic displacements, tensions, pains, paralyses, and so on. From 1897, Freud developed what became a more fully psychoanalytical account, in which the psychic reality of the patient, his own inner world, which included wishes and desires of his own as well as passive experiences at the hands of others, underlies neuroses (as well as other states of mind). Such an account does not, of course, mean that abusive actions by others, including sexual abuse or interference, did not happen, or did not cause havoc; rather that, first, such interference is not a necessary feature, and, second, that even when it has occurred what is also significant is what such actions mean to the patient, what the patient makes of them in his unconscious and conscious fantasy.

Anyone who has read the earlier chapters in this book will know that traumatic impact has to do with individual personality structure, and with childhood experiences, which themselves continue to have an impact through unconscious phantasy. Thus if a traumatised person comes for consultation or ongoing treatment, the aim must be for him or her to come to understand the individual impact on the self, to give it, or to find in it, the full range of personal meaning. As the treatment develops, the analyst and patient come to address the whole person rather than the trauma by itself, as the links between the traumatic experience and other aspects of the person's inner life and ways of dealing with things become more apparent (Britton, 2012; Garland, 1998).

The abuser too may be traumatised by the abuse he commits. Power can be traumatic as well as powerlessness. In the film *Waltzing with Bashir*, almost all of which is in cartoon form, we encounter Israeli soldiers who had been complicit in the massacre of Palestinians at the camps in Chatila and Sabra twenty years before. The main character has to overcome his amnesia about these events. The film shows by means of the fragmentation of images in its cartoon form the loss of internal meaning and of coherence, both of which are typical of trauma, and the main character's reliance on others to restore his memory. Only at the end can things be experienced in a real, full way—a shift conveyed in the film by means of the representation of real people suffering loss— they are no longer caricature people in cartoon form. This is upsetting to the viewer, as it is, we presume, to the character.

How much should we emphasise the traumatic nature of the causal event and how much its personally inflected impact on the individual psyche?

How psychological a concept is trauma?

For an event to be traumatic, it must have some substance in external reality. For our patients, we try to provide a setting of regularity and constancy, both physical and personal. Some patients feel compelled to scrutinise the setting constantly; any sign of change may feel threatening, representing to them the loss of security that they expect and fear. One patient, for example, was overwhelmed when one day I uncharacteristically wore a suit for the session. We came to see that the suit meant to her that I had become a faceless, bureaucratic, and uncaring figure. We would be inclined, I think, to say here that it was not the suit that traumatised but what the suit meant; that her construction of my wearing the suit itself was a symptom of an earlier trauma, or of some particularly fragile, ongoing, mental structure. However, there is no sharp distinction between such cases and full-blown traumatic events; for the latter too, as we have seen, also depend for their individual impact on the personality structure and phantasies of the person affected, on what the traumatic event means to the individual.

It is hard to imagine of some events that they would not be traumatic to anyone who has human feelings. As has been said about moving house, if it doesn't drive you mad, you must already be mad. Exile, loss of parents or children, disasters, wars, racism, colonialism, cruelty—such events or ongoing situations cannot but be traumatic. But of course, the forms that traumas take vary with the psyches of the individuals.

And some people grow as a result of trauma. Sir Leicester Dedlock, a character in *Bleak House*, is a man accustomed to command all within his purview. He is condescending and elitist. In old age, an illness and a shocking disclosure of his wife's dubious past, which shatter his sense of omnipotence, lead him to face the fundamental dishonesty of his life, and to gain some humility. The illness confronts him with the reality of his impending death. It and the disclosure are traumatic, a rupture of continuity. But the shock acts as a stimulus to mental work, through which he is able to get some insight into his lifelong narcissism and sense of entitlement, and move towards a shift in his identity, in who he is.

There is some tension between (psychoanalytic) accounts of trauma which focus on the uniqueness of individual trauma, accounts which in other words focus on trauma as a psychological concept, and accounts which emphasise the intrinsically damaging nature of the events that disturb and disrupt the lives of individuals (focusing on trauma in its external aspect). I shall return to this when discussing cultural trauma as conceptualised by, for example, psychoanalyst and philosopher, Jonathan Lear (see below, section 3). It seems to me that both elements have to be taken seriously. We want to say both that we can grow from traumatic events, and that not everyone was traumatised by an event that was or would be traumatic for some.

There is also a wide range of concepts and cases to be considered, of losses, hurts and humiliations. Illness, disability, malnutrition, prolonged deprivation, emotional abuse, chronic humiliation, series of setbacks— how far are we inclined to think of these as actually or potentially traumatic? Death can come by a thousand scratches. It is also the case that patients, psychoanalysts and others may be over-impressed by some event of childhood, sexual abuse, for example, which may be used as a screen to keep out of sight other sources of pain and trouble, some of it more likely to be laid at their own door, just as national or group trauma may be used defensively and with polemical force. There is a risk of facile moral equivocation. As Stargardt says (p. 9), "the use of trauma as a quick concept forecloses curiosity and questioning". It may be tempting for people to see themselves as victims, to enlarge their own suffering, ignore that of others or that which they have caused, and find an excuse for all sorts of behaviour that would otherwise be unjustifiable: "I should be granted special disposition in the light of what I've gone through". We make different identifications, with and against those who treat us badly. Stargardt notes that in the German occupation of Poland boys played at liberating prisoners, but they were also observed acting out Gestapo interrogations, slapping each other's faces in this "wild" game. As reality invaded the make-believe, children were torn between the models of resistance and the power of their conquerors (p. 114).

As we have seen with Dedlock in *Bleak House*, a person may become better and stronger, more of a person, as a result of the working through of trauma and its associated penumbra of guilt, waste, failure, dishonesty, and so on. Trauma threatens our sense of identity, and may shake or shock us to do the emotional and mental work that enables us to strengthen and consolidate our individuality, our sense of who we are. Such processes, which we would call working through, can lead to new values and structure in the self. Development is full of such phases, starting with the crisis of birth itself, and including the proximity to the ultimate crisis, death. It is a matter of emerging from a narcissistic way of relating to more depressive position functioning.

Psychoanalysts support the idea that recovery from trauma has something to do with facing the facts, not only of the trauma, but of oneself, what one made of it. It includes remembering more honestly and self-appraisingly than we often do. It means recognising what we made of things that felt, and perhaps were, terrible, recognising, for example, how we may have nursed grievances, may have preferred to focus on what we didn't have rather than on what we did.

Trauma tends also to lead to an emphasis on revenge. In fact, I would say that it is almost inevitable that traumatised groups, like individuals, will go through phases in their reactions to trauma: in the case of sudden trauma, like that of 9/11, terror and panic come first, followed by anger, followed by a wish for revenge. In his book *Writing in the Dust*, Rowan Williams recognises this as humanly inevitable, but invites us to move on from such natural reactions to a more thoughtful and considered state of mind in which we ask wider questions about the causes of an atrocity. We need to use thought to pull back from our (universal) primitive wishes. If we fail to do this, we are likely to become stuck in settled attitudes and policy informed by grievance and self-righteousness. Grievances nursed oust grieving. On one side, there is the need for proper self-protection against real threats; on the other, there is an escalation of conflict via a subtle or crude projection onto those felt collectively to be responsible for the trauma. In the latter scenario, the abused nation or collectivity become, as in individual histories, abusers. This may take the form of an identification with the aggressor (like the children in Warsaw referred to above). It is tempting for those who have been traumatised to espouse or enact sadism. Nations or groups (like individuals) become unable to understand how much they are disliked in the world.

Another equally damaging response to trauma is passivity, fatalism, masochism, depression, or suicide. Victimised societies give up, turn in on themselves, become more narrow in aim and in sense of community. They may even invite further bullying or humiliation. There is a numbing of sensibility in relation to a calamity, a deadening of experience (cf. Ingham, 1998). Initiative is lost. People shrink into apathy. In more extreme ways, people can give themselves up to a living and then an actual death. In Auschwitz, the people referred to by other inmates as Musselmen became, according to Primo Levi (2000, p. 94), totally indifferent, impassive zombies, their condition predictive of imminent death. And death, as Saramago emphasises, "is the (ultimate) product of disorganisation".

It may also take a long time to begin to work through guilt. Around the time of the fiftieth anniversary of Kristallnacht, Lore Walb, a sixty-nine-year-old woman who was the daughter of convinced Nazis, and who had emerged from the war unscathed, wrote in her diary about a new dream she had (Stargardt, pp. 3–4). She had:

> in the course of this anniversary, found herself plagued more often than ever by dreams about the Jews. In one recurring dream: she

became a young student in Heidelberg during the war once more, when a Jewish classmate suddenly turns up on her doorstep, begging to be taken in, just for a day or two. Each time Lore Walb awoke from the dream, she had not made a decision.

Now, also in 1988, she dreamed:

a young woman once more, she found herself in the street walking alongside an older Jewish man clad in a long coat, broad-rimmed hat, his narrow, decent face sporting a goatee. Laying her hand on his bony shoulder, she leaned her had on it and said, almost weeping with relief and joy, "I am so glad that you are back".

Stargardt continues:

Like so many wish dreams, Lore Walb's posed the problem, not the resolution. The Jews had not come back and she could not ask their forgiveness. Instead of closing this chapter of her life ... she was embarked on what she called, "stations on the way towards the work of memory". She had to "deal with the guilt of having freely dedicated herself to Nazi precepts and goals". (ibid.)

As we will now see from Lear's account, the Crow Indians broadened and renewed their sense of cultural identity as a result (in part) of how they faced traumatic losses.

Social trauma: the Crow Indians

Lear's paper "Working through the end of civilisation" (2007), developed and reworked in his book (2008), helps clarify the notion of societal or cultural trauma, and makes plainer its relation to individual trauma. It also offers a way in to the notion of how a societal trauma may be healed.

Lear gives an account of an American Indian tribe, the Crow, who suffered the loss of concepts central to their existence. They also lost the social and physical environment in which such concepts could be lived out. Following Lear, we can see that there can be losses—of concepts, activities, and identifications—such that there is no possible place for the old traditional ways of belonging to, gaining credit in, or even seeing oneself as a member of, a particular culture.

The Crow were a nomadic tribe who hunted buffalo in the plains of America, sided with the United States in their fights with the Sioux, and then accepted being placed in a reservation. The disappearance of the buffalo, together with the restrictions of space, and the acceptance of the laws of the United States, meant that their traditional hunter-gatherer existence, with all the related paradigms of excellence, preparatory rituals, and many of the modes of belonging, became extinct. Lear shows, along the lines of Wittgenstein's theory of games (1953) (not explicitly mentioned by him), that, unless a cultural context exists, certain ways of life, or forms of life, become inconceivable—I mean this in a sense closer to logical than psychological inconceivability.

Lear goes on to describe ways in which the Crow managed to respond to major threats to its identity. He describes a dream had by a Crow boy called Young Plenty Coups, in 1855, at a time when the tribe was still vigorous, but when it was threatened with genocide (at the hands of their enemies, the Sioux), and when the white man was also becoming more and more of a presence. The dream was as follows:

> First, through a hole in the ground, all the buffalo disappeared. Out of that hole came strange spotted bulls and cows that gathered in small groups to eat the grass; they lay down in strange ways, not like buffalo. Second, Plenty Coups was told that the Four Winds were going to cause a terrible storm in the forest, and only one tree would be left standing, the tree of the Chickadee-person. He sees an image of an old man sitting under that lone tree and is told, in the dream, that person is himself. Finally, he is told to follow the example of the chickadee.

The dream was interpreted by the "wisest man in the lodge", Yellow Bear.

Bion showed (1961) that we function not only as individuals but also as group members expressing the life of a whole, whether (in Bion's terms) at work-group level or at basic-assumption level. Lear suggests, plausibly I think, that the boy, functioning at the work-group level, dreamed the dream on behalf of the tribe, picking up unarticulated anxieties relating to the loss of the buffalo and the culturally damaging "storm" that was on its way. The spotted cows were the domesticated cattle of the white man. The dream also offered a clue to survival and repair, in the form of the chickadee, a bird noted for its wily ways and its capacity to learn from others. Lear suggests that this can be understood as an indication of a new ego ideal, in the form of a canny openness—openness to experience, to change, and to learning. Such a new ideal would be necessary in the radically new context in which the traditional forms of admired courage—courage in battle and in hunting—would no longer have a lived place. The chickadee's qualities would, at least at this point in time, have to be open-ended, unspecific. Thus imagination was given an enhanced value by the Crow tribe. Lear links this situation to that of the patient who is offered an interpretation by the analyst at a time when he is not yet able to know what form the new personality structure that is beginning to form will take. The patient has to have a trust in the analyst and in the process, a sense that development will take place, that a new "form of life" will become gradually clearer; he has to have an energetic willingness to create and make the best of the bad job.

This crisis is similar to, and different from, the processes of growing up. The child or adolescent concerned, like the Crow, has limited capacities to imagine what the later stage of development will involve; but his or her elders have been through the development, unlike the Crow elders. The dream I would think also represents the young man's Oedipal conflicts. One might speculate on the bulls' and cows' lying down together being the parental couple, perhaps weakened (by their trauma or in other ways), and therefore not available to support him as he grows up into a man. He is then left alone, partly as a result of their weakness, partly too as a result of the force of his terrible storm coming from all points of the compass. It is harder for adolescents to grow up when there is a lack of strong figures to help, and the young Crow man is very much on his own. The dream may also indicate the need for each generation to stand alone, to dis-identify from their parents and from the older generation, as well as to identify with them.

A patient of mine felt stuck in a peculiarly philosophical way. He was aware of a kind of internal Cartesian demon who would question everything that he thought or felt. This young man was inhibited in many aspects of his life, in relationships, in work, in his artistic aspirations, not to mention in his therapy. He was perpetually and self-damagingly self-conscious. We had talked about this for some sessions. Then in one session he spoke of losing a folder, after which he had become a kind of false therapist to a girl in the pub. I interpreted his loss of parts of himself in such false functioning. He responded by telling me of moments of initiating things with a girl who attracted him. He had even kissed her, taking the first steps towards sexual engagement, thus being able to bear the risk of rejection. He went on to speak with more vigour of his plans, of his capacity to speak more fluently and passionately here, of his thinking of himself as a painter. It seemed possible for him now to inhabit his own wishes and his potential. It seemed there was still a shadow of the older opposition to wanting in the form of his thought that the girl was not so attractive after making love to her; a comment also, I thought, on the way in which he was inclined to diminish the value of the exchange with me by the end of the session. But this patient was beginning to find and/or create a self who could affirm his wishes, know some of his own qualities, and have a weight of self from which to live and act. He was moving from an omnipotent position (on which he has in the past got drunk) to one in which he began to relate to me more as a whole person, like the girl on whom he was beginning to depend. Neither of us knew at this point how it would all develop or end.

Lear notes that the concept of working through is enlarged by the realisation that we may not know in any detail how development will be lived out; at times, we work through not to ready-made values (ego ideals) but to values that we cannot yet fill out into imagined detail. Thus dreams can contribute to psychological structure.

What was traumatic in the Crows' predicament as a tribe was the loss of centrally important elements of their cultural and collective life. A way of life was, or was about to be, destroyed, with no indication of what might emerge from it or replace it. Destruction of this kind has faced hunter-gatherers across the globe as one by one they have been confronted with the immense expansionist power of the agriculturists with life structures and attitudes to the land that were so alien to their own. (Brody, 2001 and below).

What the dream underpinned—within a system in which dreaming and dream interpretation had (and could continue to have) a place and were themselves valued—was the valuing of qualities that would stand individuals and the tribe as a whole in good stead during a period of potentially cataclysmic change.

Lear's example helps us to see a distinction between situations in which the trauma is the loss of the good object (or objects), and situations where it is the loss of the possibility of good objects, loss of the possibility of good aspects of the self and good experience. In religious terms, the latter is the loss of God as the ground of one's being. It is the loss of meaning in the group's life, the threat of the extinction of that which has held the culture together, of that without which virtue and excellence struggled to find a place. Such shared cultural beliefs and practices are the container for a culture. They emphasise values, bind anxieties, and offer a shared framework for the members of the tribe. The loss of these represents the loss of a container—which parallels a feature stressed by Caroline Garland as present in individual traumas (1998, especially pp. 9–31), where there is a rupture in the sense of being held or contained internally.

Lear makes clear that there is a distinction between cultural trauma (meaning life-threatening wound to the culture as a whole) and an aggregation of individual traumas. In fact, one could say, as he is inclined to say without quite committing himself, that there was for the Crow a *cultural* trauma involved in various related losses—in the loss of land (and therefore activities), the loss of preparatory rituals (prayers, dances, propitiations), and in the loss of concepts (no room for traditional notions of bravery, etc.). We can see this without examining the no doubt varied psychological states of the individual members of the tribe. According to this line of thought, certain radical kinds of losses are themselves, intrinsically and necessarily, traumatic to the culture. Such a trauma may result in a chickadee-type response or alternatively in a self-pitying, passive, grievance-ridden reaction that might result in large-scale drunkenness, anomie, and depression.

Alternatively, one might keep Lear's distinction between trauma and loss, and coin a phrase like "traumatogenic events" to describe the fact that radical change is inevitably but causally disruptive, whilst recognising that, as with all other traumas, at every level, the existence of environmental factors may have very different trajectories and outcomes depending upon the susceptibilities and strengths of those affected. Nietzsche says "what does not kill you makes"—*may* make—"you stronger" (1884). As we have seen, there is the same tension in our use of the concept of trauma in relation to individuals; we may stress the extreme quality of the traumatogenic events, or we may stress more the individual reaction. However, Lear's paper offers us a way in to a notion of trauma in which structural losses can be of so radical a kind as to call for a major effort of reconstruction and rebuilding if the impact is not to be catastrophic. Perhaps a parallel at the individual level would be loss of sight or hearing, or the suffering of a stroke or other form of brain damage that lead to an inability to speak or think as one had been able before. I suppose too that for the individual whatever the outcome the loss of several members of his family in a disaster would constitute a trauma to his personal-relations map, which would require a massive reorientation and personal change for him to overcome, and be able to move on in life.

It makes a difference when traumatogenic events are encountered. We would expect there to be more disruption of thinking and feeling to such an event or loss which occurs in infancy, say, than to terrible events encountered when the individual has more internal resources to fall back on, and is more structurally developed and intact when meeting the disruption.

Language and cultural trauma

Language too, gets its possibility and meaning from shared activities and practices. So to lose one's language is to lose a form of life (Wittgenstein, 1953). One aspect of the cultural trauma perpetrated on hunter-gather cultures has been the colonial attempt to obliterate local language speaking, for example in Canada when the policy was to remove native (or "First Nation") children and put them in residential schools where they were punished if they spoke in their own languages (Brody). Enforced separations of children from their families, cruelty, the imposition of alien rules and habits, all these practices were also, of course, traumatic to these children and their parents. But, as Brody puts it (p. 186), "the fundamental, irreducible commitment of the undertaking was to eliminate ways of life, to do so through getting rid of peoples' languages. This was managed by brutal and corrupt institutions; but it is the intention, not the corruption or brutality, that is the deepest wrong." Brody questions the differences between a frontier where English was taught as an addition to existing languages and one where English was established and enforced as the only possible language. His answer is that the former was to do with:

> large sedentary populations whose mode of life was a version of their own, albeit one the British were ready to stigmatise as "native"; "savage"; and backward …. In a profound sense, the imperialists and those they conquered spoke the same language. They shared ideas about the exclusive ownership of small parcels of

land; they shaped and managed such land to grow domestic plants and support domestic animals; they built relatively durable and permanent villages; their societies were hierarchical .... In much of the New World, on the other hand, the newcomers encountered hunter-gatherers. ... human beings and social systems quite alien to them. The economic and material counterparts of these differences are central to the approach colonists in North America, Australia, and parts of Southern Africa took to the people they sought to conquer. (pp. 187–188)

Loss of language is, then, the loss of a central element in one's form of life, especially if the language is part and parcel of a cultural life that differs radically from that of the language (and cultural life that informs that language) that displaces it. It is a cultural or societal trauma, or, if that sounds too definite, it is a cultural and societal traumatogenic loss. (I am reminded too of the Pinter play *Mountain Language* (1988), which deals with a dictatorial prohibition on people speaking their own language.)

We might consider that loss of language associated with trauma might also be a way of speaking about the fact that, suffering trauma often means that we have no emotional language to describe it. We may be unable to find words for our experiences, which may contribute to our being reduced to somatic expressions of states in which underlying tectonic plates have shifted terrifyingly, so that we may find ourselves in a new internal landscape needing to learn a different, and as yet unknown, language.

To call an event socially or culturally traumatic, it is not enough that there be pain. Perhaps (as Lear suggests) it is not even necessary that there should be (felt) pain. What must be present is some damaging impact on a collectivity's sense of identity, a shake-up or convulsion in affiliation, in what it is to belong to the group/nation/tribe. Revolutions would have such an impact. Intellectually too, a new paradigm requires that the old paradigms be given up, or revalued and re-placed. In this regard, it is parallel to individual trauma, so that with the individual too what is traumatic is the rupture in one's object-map, or in one's conceptual coordinates. Sometimes, as with Lester Dedlock, what has been overwhelmed is a narcissistic and omnipotent structure. In other cases, it may be a healthier set of internal arrangements that have to be reconstituted or reconfigured. In each case, the loss of the good object (the loss of the buffalo in the dream of Young Plenty Coups) has to be mourned.

As with individuals, a cultural traumatic event may be either what used to be called in insurance policy documents an "Act of God" or it may be more or less man-made. As we have seen, both the impact and the acknowledgement of the impact may be instantaneous and/or delayed; in both the Soviet Union and post-war Germany, many people were able to talk about their experiences only to their grandchildren, not their children.

In what Garland calls "Given Groups" (1998, pp. 187ff), that is, groups that were themselves traumatised, as opposed to groups that come into being only because of a trauma (people thrown together by a hotel fire, for example), one sign of traumatic overwhelming is the loss of structured activity; healthy recovery may partly consist in a:

> move in the direction of *distributed functioning* again, *differentiated functioning*, characteristic of a working group, as opposed to one still in the grip of a trauma, in which every member is operating independently and autonomously and in multiply-overlapping ways .... In a group it is possible to move once more from passivity to activity, through being contained while in a helpless state to being part of the container for others' helplessness. (Garland, 1998, p. 195)

Groups suffering trauma are likely to become, then, disordered, scattered, less structured; and there is a tendency towards authoritarianism. *Blindness*, the novel by Jose Saramago (1987), depicts a contagion of instantaneous blindness, which becomes almost universal. Individual fates, individual traumas, of course; but the impact is clearly also social. Arrangements for dealing with the victims at first become cruel and suppressive, as the authorities try to eradicate the contagion by putting the blind in quarantine, but as the condition becomes more and more widespread, the whole organisation of society breaks down. "Death", Saramago writes, "is the product of disorganisation. Society needs government. Having organisation is the equivalent of having eyes" (pp. 279–280). And having eyes is the congruent with ego-functioning, which is, of course, thrown upside down in individual trauma.

Reconfigurations and trauma: the disaster at Masada

Lear's example shows in a stark way something that is harder to see in other cases, perhaps especially in individual traumas, namely, the centrality in trauma of the shattering of the subject's internal structure, the structure provided by concepts and/or that of object relationships.

A trauma is a wound that breaks the psychic skin that contains us—which is part of our internal structure. Of course, the outcome may vary. The wound may fester, or it may produce toxic effects that infect the whole system, or it may heal over and be even better than before.

As we have seen, explicit or implicit narratives form part of the structure of traumas; Gregorio Kohon, for example (Perelberg, 2007), shows how emphases in the telling of stories about a group's or a nation's past change over time—histories are revised according to later requirements. He writes about the differing accounts given by Jews about the (disastrous for the Jews) destruction of Masada: "Between 900 and 1000 children, women and men (all members of the sect known as the Zealots) died at the top of this mountain overlooking the Dead Sea, after a lengthy siege laid by the Romans." According to Josephus, by committing mass suicide they denied to the Romans "the exultation of victory anticipated by them". This episode has had various incarnations in the mythology of the Jews and of Israel.

Kohon mentions three main phases in the life history of this story amongst the Jews. First, there was the phase of its being, for eighteen centuries, generally "forgotten" by them. Second, "for the Zionist settlers of the early twentieth century ... Masada became a significant symbol: it stood as an exemplar of a heroic war of national liberation" (p. 119). It was a "patriotic symbol, a lesson to be learned by the Jews settling in Palestine .... Above all what needed to be stressed was the courage of the Zealots in defending their position... (these accounts) did not include any reference to the issue of mass suicide." The Holocaust further heightened the view of the settlers "that Palestine was the only possible safe homeland. Submissiveness was not a choice. They were ready to fight to the end, and die, if necessary a dignified death. Masada was thus reinforced as a model and symbol of national revival in Israel ... The ghetto fighters (in Warsaw) themselves spoke of their uprising as the 'Masada of Warsaw'."

The third phase occurred with the trial of Adolf Eichmann, and the trauma of the Yom Kippur war of 1973, which made Israelis feel— more than ever before—vulnerable and exposed .... Both Masada and the Holocaust should never be repeated. Now the fragility of Jewish survival was stressed, legitimising the current political concern for Israel's security.

Thus historical events may be scotomised; or they may be highlighted, but with different threads picked out from the past. The past is revised while the present is historicised. An event in the past has what Kohon calls an exploding reality; it of course is unchanged, it is what it was; but in the telling and in the experience of the group, it is transformed in the light of current or pressing needs and stances. This is exemplified in the varying versions of the last stand of the Jews at Masada. The story's use has changed, from something to be expunged from memory, to its being an emblem of heroic militancy equating with survival, to its becoming an image of embattlement and vulnerability that are to be avoided.

The same event, or long-term social change, or radical shift in conceptual framework, may be not only disruptive and traumatic, it may lead to exhilaration and a sense of freedom. Successful revolutions, whether in politics or ideas, may be causes for celebration as well as for traumatic disorientation, especially if what is good in the old can be mourned and, sometimes, recreated, re-shaped, or integrated within the new system (Einstein & Infeld, 1938).

We have seen one suggestion of how repair can occur in Lear's paper on the Crow. Here the resources of the tribe were marshalled or rather stimulated along new lines by means of access to and respect for creative dreaming. The unconscious was enlisted on the side of growth. Tribal leaders supported the significance of what one might call "social dreaming".

Other forms of leadership may also be helpful. The group/nation/ culture needs to be able to do certain things. Mourning has to be possible, and also the wish to make reparation. Memorials may help societies to mourn, as may artistic endeavours in all fields. A more truthful way of finding meaning is found, about the past as well as for the realities of the present and future.

The healing of traumas has to make use the similar means to that of the Jews to Masada. Other forms of repair and healing are also called for. Trauma can be countered, if not healed, by the capacity to make things better, sometimes in ways that had not proved possible before the disaster. One example would be the person dying of cancer who raises significant funds for fighting that type of cancer; or the relatives or friends may do this work. In such a case, the loss itself cannot be repaired, but meaning is given to the pain of the loss by the effort to save others threatened in similar ways.

In some cases, as Kohon indicates, the re-shaping may be not so much a reintegration as a persuasive definition, a re-telling to fit current values and priorities.

Slavery, colonialism, and cricket

I will give one final example of a process of healing, namely, the adoption in the Caribbean of cricket, a cultural value among the colonisers, by people who had been traumatised by slavery and colonialism.

This achievement epitomises the capacity of oppressed groups to recognise and make their own something good in the culture of their oppressors, even in the most appalling cases, as well as to take the opportunity to compete, symbolically, through play, with them. Stargardt gives a clue to such an attitude in his account of the children's homes in the Theresienstadt camp.

> "Against the odds, the children's homes worked. Child survivors have stressed the value of the daily routine, which contrasted sharply with the lack of structure for those children who remained in the adult barracks …. The children also formed intense attachments to their adult room leaders …. The cultural atmosphere animating these educational experiments was of a peculiarly central-European kind: an eclectic mixture of progressive German reform pedagogy, Zionist and Communist ideals of the collective, tempered with some admixture of Freud.

One of the children's room leaders, Valtr Eisinger, moved his bed into the dormitory to be with the children.

> This (the educational experiment) was an intellectual atmosphere in which he (Eisinger) had no hesitation in turning to the symbol of Goethe in order to explain to the children why they should

not reject Germans and German culture as a whole or hold them
collectively responsible for the persecution of the Jews. It was,
he claimed, impossible to "hate a nation that is one of the most
cultured in the world and to whom, to a great extent, I owe my
education". (pp. 204–205)

In the wake of slavery in the West Indies (Seecharan, 2006, passim),
racist attitudes involving stereotyping and projection were prevalent.
In the early days, blacks were not allowed to take part in cricket, one
of the culturally valued activities of the white colonisers. Gradually,
however, small inclusions were permitted. Blacks could retrieve balls
hit out of the ground. Blacks started to copy the whites with their own
informal play. They were needed to make pitches and ground. They
were useful as bowlers for the white players to practise against in the
nets. Clubs for black and coloured (according to the designations of
the time) players were founded, but these cricketers were kept out
of many other clubs, and were not included in representative teams.
Exclusion is a powerful form of splitting—they are not like us, we
do not want to play with or against them, but such exclusion had to
be rationalised; it was sometimes officially but dishonestly based on
the grounds that the blacks who might have been selected were professionals. (In fact, they were often ground staff, so, apart from the
prejudice against professionalism, there was a racism-serving logic-
chopping at work in this discrimination.) During the 1890s, Trinidad
was a partial exception, allowing their top black cricketers, fast bowlers "Float" Woods and Archie Cumberbatch, and batsman Lebrun
Constantine (Learie's father), to play in matches against visiting English teams. These bowlers were not, however, allowed to play in inter-
island matches.

One of the virtues of cricket is that because it is not easy to deny
excellence when it appears, it is not easy to keep good players out indef-
initely. Skill will out. In the West Indies, small integrations led to recognition of the qualities, personal and technical, of the trailblazers, which
in turn forced the extension of recognition to other non-white players.
Moreover, just as there were advocates of education, enfranchisement,
and human rights in the British West Indies—in Jamaica, for example,
there was a prominent advocate of Fabian socialism in no less a figure
than Sydney Olivier, who was governor of that island between 1907
and 1913, having previously been its colonial secretary. There were also

voices for cricketing inclusion amongst local whites, as well as from visiting MCC grandees.

Colonialism damages not only the bodies and living conditions of those who are enslaved or discriminated against, it also attacks, more insidiously, their minds. If one is treated terribly (and the ultimate oppression is slavery, where one is treated as a possession rather than as a human being, a subject), there are various psychological outcomes. Perhaps the most psychologically damaging is when a group takes on the identity that is attributed to them, and becomes in their own eyes worthless. The racist is internalised, as is the projected inferior parts of the racist oppressors; one treats oneself as an object only. (I am reminded of psychoanalyst Fakhry Davids' account of a young black boy in England who came to see the brownness of his skin as dirt that his mother should wash off (Davids, 2008)).

Since self-disparagement is one consequence of racial and other kinds of trauma, one gift of the cricketing pioneers in West Indies, men like Woods or Constantine, was to help build the self-respect of their fellows. The person in the street walks taller. The next generation may be stronger, more determined, more in touch with their proper pride. "There is no substitute for racial pride—as opposed to racism …—in countering self-depreciation and inferiority complex, the inevitable legacy of a history of subjugation" (Seecharan, 2006, p. 62).

It is remarkable, given the extent of the trauma, how forgiving the West Indians have been, and how much they have accepted and made their own from the colonial institutions of education and of cricket, with so little spilling over into reverse racism. In the field of cricket, they learned the game, decontaminating it from the mire of colonialism, and giving it their own style and character. They have not been timid in the way they have adopted the game. Their cricketers are far from being "mimic men". And they became, for nearly twenty years, between 1976 and the early 1990s, the best team in the world by far.

It seems to me that this is one element in the repair of cultural or social trauma: to take from your oppressors, to make what they give you your own, with your own style and emphases, and (preferably) show them your superiority in no uncertain terms. Becoming better than one's parents may also, as Hanna Segal says (personal communication), be a form of reparation, tribute, and love to them by making the most of what they have given you, and by forgiving them their failings and even ill-treatment towards you.

The development of a West Indian cricket tradition, then, offers a clear and even moving example of a culture being able to work through to a more depressive position functioning in its response to trauma rather than being stuck in a paranoid reaction (with all the possibilities of reverse racism), or endless grievance (depriving oneself of an opportunity for growth and success), or in masochistic submission. Part of the repair came through pragmatism—the Establishment wanted the best players on their side—partly through individuals making reparation for the terrible damage inflicted by slavery and post-slavery colonial attitudes. But most of the work was done by those who had been themselves traumatised; they took something good from authority figures and culture despite the latter's tyrannical superiority.

Conclusion

There is room for the concept of cultural trauma, and for the idea that cultures are capable of propagating the impact of trauma (or fail to recover from it), of shifting it in one way or another (think of the fate of the Masada story) and also of mitigating and recovering from trauma. Sometimes indeed they, like individuals, may be strengthened by this painful and prolonged process.

Acknowledgements

I would like to thank Eileen McGinley for her very helpful comments on the chapter, many of which I have incorporated in this final version. Also of course Nick Stargardt, whose book I read with great interest; we enjoyed the event at the Institute of Psychoanalysis, and our discussion, some elements of which we have included in the book. I am grateful too to Clem Seecharan, Hugh Brody, Fakhry Davids, and Jonathan Lear, for their seminal ideas and encouragement.

References

Bion, W. R. (1961). *Experiences in Groups*. London: Tavistock.
Brody, H. (2001). *The Other Side of Eden: Hunters, Farmers and the Shaping of the World*. New York: North Point Press.
Davids, F. (2008). Psychoanalysis and Racism. Lecture at Institute of Psychoanalysis, London.
Dickens, C. (1853). *Bleak House*. London: Everyman's Library, 1991.

Einstein, A. & Infeld, L. (1938). *The Evolution of Physics*. Cambridge: Cambridge University Press.

Freud, S. (1897). Extracts from the Fleiss Papers. *S.E. 1*. London: Hogarth.

Garland, C. (Ed.) (1998). *Understanding Trauma: A Psychoanalytical Approach*. London: Duckworth.

Ingham, G. (1998). Mental work in a trauma patient. In: C. Garland (Ed.), *Understanding Trauma: A Psychoanalytical Approach*. London: Duckworth.

Khan, M. (1963). The concept of cumulative trauma. *The Psychoanalytic Study of the Child, 18*: 286–306.

Kohon, G. (2007). The Aztecs, Masada and the compulsion to repeat. In: R. J. Perelberg (Ed.), *Time and Memory*. London: Karnac.

Lear, J. (2007). Working through the end of civilisation. *International Journal of Psycho-Analysis, 88*: 291–308.

Lear, J. (2008). *Radical Hope*. Cambridge, MA: Harvard University Press.

Levi, P. (1947). *If This is a Man*. London: Everyman's Library, 2000.

Nietzsche, F. (1889). *Twilight of the Idols*. New York: Dover, 2004.

Pinter, H. (1988). *Mountain Language*. London, *Times Literary Supplement*.

Saramago, J. (1987). *Blindness*. London: Vintage, 2004.

Seecharan, C. (2006). *Muscular Learning*. Jamaica: Ian Randle.

Stargardt, N. (2005). *Witnesses of War: Children's Lives under the Nazis*. London: Pimlico, Random House.

Williams, R. (2002). *Writing in the Dust: Reflections on 11th September and its Aftermath*. Grand Rapids: William Eerdmans.

Wittgenstein, L. (1953). *Philosophical Investigations*. London: Blackwell.

CHAPTER TWELVE

Trauma in culture and society

*Discussion between Nicholas Stargardt
and Michael Brearley*

Nicholas Stargardt

Among the things which Mike Brearley and I agree about, there is one which also sets us apart from many cultural historians who write about "collective memory". There is a prominent strand within this literature which sees the commemoration of the world wars, fascism, even the Holocaust, as entirely malleable and present-centred matters, moulded by contemporary politics and discourses. By contrast, Mike and I would both argue that violent social ruptures have long-running emotional and psychological consequences. And so we might both offer ourselves as members of a second, smaller group: scholars who would tend to depict the same acts of historical commemoration as a dialogue between contemporary concerns, and real affects which are often stubbornly resistant to efforts to shift the cultural significance ascribed to them. This way of formulating the problem begs a kind of chicken-and-egg question: where did that "original", rather immovable significance come from?

Let me take an extreme example, which is revealing because it is so far removed from contemporary, liberal ways of seeing things, in much the same way as psychoanalysts have often turned to pathological cases in order to reveal and isolate more typical, but also better concealed, mental processes. One of the insistent claims on the neo-Nazi Far Right has been that the murder of the Jews—if it happened at all— was certainly no worse than the Allied bombing of German civilians, and it is trumpeted in the slogan "Bombing-Holocaust" carried on the banners of Far-Right demonstrators marching on the anniversary of the bombing of Dresden since the 1990s. This claim duly featured in the libel action David Irving brought against Penguin Books and Deborah Lipstadt: she had alleged that he was a Holocaust denier and distorted history; the team of historians who traced his manipulation of statistical evidence to inflate the numbers of German victims and reduce the numbers of Jews provided important evidence for the successful legal defence against his charge of libel. The concomitant charge of relativising the Holocaust has lurked near the surface of recent German discussions of whether the Allied bombing was a a crime against humanity, a war crime, or indeed an act of genocide.

Most German participants to these contemporary discussions would, of course, prefer to keep the two issues separate, prefering a liberal, non-competitive way of talking about suffering, rather than the competitive victimhood of extreme nationalists, let alone indulging in a species of Holocaust-denial. What is interesting historically and culturally is that precisely this coupling of the bombing and the murder of the Jews was made in Germany at the time. References to Allied bombing as punishment, revenge or retaliation for "what we did to the Jews" were so frequent in the late summer and autumn of 1943 that it was not enough for the Nazi regime to demonstratively punish a handful of individuals for making such remarks: the Nazi press even went so far as to rebut this view. Hardly in a position to confirm or deny the reality of public rumours about the murder of the Jews, the press concentrated on telling its readers that the Jewish lobby in charge of Allied policy would have tried to wipe out the German nation whatever it had done. To the Nazi regime, popular identification of the bombing with the genocide of the Jews was uncomfortable because it expressed a sense of German guilt and a desire to get out of the war. According to public opinion reports, it was almost always couched as an impossible wish to put the war into reverse: "If only we had not…", then the Allied escalation would not have followed. This hardly chimed well with official propaganda which was trying to use the threat of "Jewish revenge" in order to rally the country for "total war" and escalate things further. To the handful of Jews still living in Germany in 1943 and 1944, like Victor Klemperer, these same sentiments were equally disturbing in a different way: when even old anti-Nazis made it clear that they believed that the Allied war effort was being directed by an all-powerful Jewish enemy, Klemperer and others worried about how deeply anti-Semitic propaganda had penetrated German society and drew ominous conclusions for their own chances of survival.

What is striking is that in none of these contemporary conversations was there any question about the appropriateness of the comparison. Indeed, even very high-placed and well-informed observers set rumours in circulation which estimated the death toll from air raids at many times what would eventually be established as the actual figure: in the May 1943 raid on Barmen-Wuppertal, 27,000 instead of 3,400; in the late June and early July raids on Cologne, 28,000 instead of 5,600 dead; instead of the 34,000 to 43,000 who died in the Hamburg raids of late July 1943—the highest toll for any German city in the war— rumours generated figures of 100,000 to 350,000. In the absence of official information, these figures were sometimes picked up by the Swedish press and spread further, re-appearing after the war in some West German publications. Like the identification of the bombing and Holocaust, attachment to these inflated death tolls at the time typified a barrage of criticism of the Nazi regime and an admission of German vulnerability and guilt. By the present, both the coupling of the events and the pursuit of statistical equivalence have ended up as political markers of extreme, neo-Nazi views and a species of Holocaust-denial.

But presumably for at least some elderly Germans, the associations have remained the same, because this was the form which they first used to give meaning to events which were terrifying, overwhelming and potentially beyond articulation. In other words, in breaking a Nazi taboo on talking about the murder of the Jews in public, ordinary Germans were also trying at the time to give a shape and a meaning to events which could otherwise have become still more disturbing by remaining inexpressible. The difficulty of erasing this way of seeing things also points up the fact that societies have ways of giving meaning to their moments of rupture and cataclysmic violence during or very soon after the events themselves, which may prove very hard to dislodge subsequently. So far, this sounds as if we are dealing with a similar kind of traumatic repression at an individual and a social level.

But I am not sure this is so. There is a difference between individual trauma and social taboo. The one defies expression, or, by its silences, shapes what else can be expressed. The other enforces its norms by moral censure or worse, silencing other, disagreeable views. And here I think we find that what often passes for the silence of a "collective trauma" is in fact the more active censure of a social taboo. Take, for example, the extreme reluctance to commemorate the Holocaust in Israel in the 1940s and 1950s. It was not that the survivors were incapable of giving expression to what they had gone through. There are many accounts of early plays about the genocide enacted in the Displaced Persons camps. Rather, it was with their arrival somewhere new that their problems began. One man who had survived Auschwitz and the death marches to Buchenwald as a teenager—told me how when he was settled on a kibbutz in British-ruled Palestine, he was called "soap" by local Jews of his age—as they mockingly refered to the myth that the Jews were turned into soap in the camps—and he felt he had prove himself to be a better soldier than anyone else in the 1947–1948 war, in order to get rid of the stigma of the genocide. As he and other survivors learned to talk about their experiences only with each other, the problem lay not with their inability to speak but with Israeli society's unpreparedness to listen: having modelled their new culture on a complete rejection of the "passivity" of the Shtetl, Zionists in Palestine horrified themselves with the image of European Jews who let themselves be "led like sheep to the slaughter". Nothing could be in greater discord with the notion of Israel as a self-confident and self-sufficient nation in arms. Not surprisingly, the first commemorations of the Holocaust focused on isolated instances of armed resistance. In similar fashion, from Poland to France, post-war Europeans prefered to celebrate acts of martyrdom or resistance, rather than probe the everyday moral ambiguities of "cohabiting" with their occupiers.

There is no question but that some memory and experience was being repressed in these examples, sometimes even before it could be publicly articulated. But in these simplified national cases the mechanism was not that of an individual trauma. Instead of the censorship occuring at an unconscious level, it appears as a social conflict in which one group succeeds in silencing another. This, of course, brings us back to the notion of national memory as a kind of political battleground so cherished by cultural historians of twentieth-century discourses. But it also reminds us how unmalleable the past is for those who lived it, and how much greater the cultural appeal of a particular "take" on that past may be amongst those who missed the critical moment altogether—like the generation of extreme nationalist students in inter-war Germany whose images of First World War heroism remained uncontradicted by any personal experience of the front. Theirs may have been a classic case of splitting and projecting their sense of failure and defeat onto scape-goats (Jews, socialists, communists, liberals, free masons), but it also released enormous energies.

I tend to avoid the term "trauma"—let alone "collective trauma"—when thinking about historical catastrophes, not because I think they start us on the wrong track, but because they often move us along it too fast in one secure direction towards a restorative "cure", so fast that we simply miss the many signs and turnings that lead elsewhere. There is a subsidiary danger here: especially once psychological language has itself become part of the rhetoric for staking public claims, it becomes difficult to deploy the same categories in order to analyse them. But at a deeper level, it is often not clear where the boundary of the "trauma" lie or what would constitute its cure. As Mike points out so eloquently, societies and cultures carry their pasts within them, often inextricably mixing restorative and destructive ways of dealing with them together. There are many new beginnings, but no utopian moment where their pasts are simply erased.

Michael Brearley response

I like what you write here, Nick. And starting with what you say at the end, I agree fully with you that there are risks of our using "trauma" to "move us along it (the wrong track) too fast in one secure direction towards a restorative cure"; I also agree there is "no utopian moment where pasts are simply erased".

To take the first point first: I agree, trauma is an elastic, even a slippery concept, and it can easily be used in slippery ways. It can be widened so that it applies to the trauma of being the abuser, as well as the abused. It can be abused in all sorts of ways. As you suggest with the Neo-Nazis, it can be used as a distraction and a covering to hide and diminish other aspects of history. It can be exaggerated, to make the group one is identifying with more victim than perpetrator. Social taboo can preclude, impede or delay one's dealing with terrible trauma (as your survivor in the kibbutz witnesses). My example of the fate of the story of Masada is an example of the way the past can be made to fit into current preoccupations, but this doesn't (as you also say) mean that there was no trauma to be dealt with. These may be ways of trying to come to terms with it, or they may be ways of avoiding it by distraction or by re-configuring what happened.

One might add other ways of dealing with guilt and with trauma that are defensive and evacuative, rather than genuine efforts to deal with such things. The contrite prisoner may confess as part of a genuine attempt to come clean and reform, or he may be doing so to get an early release; to play to an actual or imagined audience who admire and will be moved by his self-laceration; or he may be masochistically continuing his punishment. The Ancient Mariner couldn't stop telling people his story, endlessly, trying to get rid of his unbearable guilt. In all cases, as with the manipulation of statistics you refer to (re numbers of those killed in concentration camps and of those killed in Allied air-strikes) one important feature is exaggeration, crude or subtle.

Also denial. The play *The Fire Raisers* by Max Frisch depicts a bourgeois German family who are talking about the scandal of fire raisers getting into people's houses and eventually buring them down. The fire raisers come to their house, talk their way in by a mixture of threats and flattering, instal themselves in the attic, and bring in electrical wiring and cans of petrol. In the end, predictably but inexorably, the stage is filled with a lurid light as yet another house burns down. Here is the image of people complicit in their own destruction. We often play a part in the traumas that engulf us.

The mind is a subtle and often self-serving organ. We can evade or deny the infiltration of forces that are going to destroy or damage us; or we can indulge in catastrophe scenarios, "sexing up" situations to justify malpractice of one kind or another. We turn "defence of the realm" into "national security" in order to justify detention without trial, rendition, and complicity in torture. It is hard to tread a line between fanning the flames of potential disaster and pretending that all is well.

Nevertheless, if we're careful, we will keep paying attention to all these kinds of risk in the use of the term "trauma", and can attempt to make appropriate differentiations. Trauma, individual and collective, can readily be made use of and abused. One way of dealing with abuse is to become the abuser, to identify with the powerful (like the children playing games in occupied Poland, for example), and to be rid of the horrible predicament of being on the receiving end. But there are examples

of efforts to heal trauma; the most notable perhaps being the Truth and
Reconciliation Commission in South Africa. Here it does seem that at
an individual and collective level trauma was eased and mutual hatred
lessened by this painful process of publicly being heard, as well as by
the public admissions of the abusers. (I don't ignore the criticisms lev-
elled at the Commission on the grounds that former perpetrators made
their admissions in order to gain amnesty through their cooperation
from prosecution. Nevertheless, it seems that the process of healing was
aided by the process, however imperfect.)

This brings me to the second point you make at the end of your
discussion—'there are many new beginnings but no utopian moment
where pasts are erased'. I agree that there are many new beginnings,
some of them healing and attempts to be truthful, others manipulative,
evacuative, dishonest, and in the service of self-justification. But even in
the former cases, where people's efforts are primarily honest (perhaps
like the West Indian cricketers I refer to, or as with the victims of police
brutality under apartheid who gave evidence at the Commission), there
is no such thing as a "utopian moment" and certainly no erasure of the
past. Pasts may, however, be lived with more honestly and with less
interference with the capacity to live life as fully as one might have been
able to without the trauma. One aspect of the Truth Commission was to
lessen that common feature of trauma, the reluctance or even taboo on
discussion of it with others, as indeed often happens within the family
(think of child sexual abuse) or in society. So, I see social taboos not only
as a continuation of the trauma on the traumatised individual, but also
as part of the society's way of construing things in order to deal with
its trauma.

This leads me to my last point. I think that in our discussion when
the papers were first given, you asked the question: "where does social
trauma end and individual trauma begin?" When things happen in
groups, there are always two ways of looking at them. One is: here is
an individual event, produced by individual factors and characteristics,
which may have an impact on, and be in its outcome affected by, the
group's behaviour. It may also, in contrast, be seen as a symptom or
expression of something in the family, the group, the society. Both ways,
it seems to me, are likely to have truth in them, and neither is reduc-
ible to the other. So, sexual abuse of a child by a priest says something
about sex, society, and the priesthood, as well as about the individual(s)
concerned. So though we have to be careful here too, it seems to me that

the difficulty is not one that is overcome by avoiding the concepts either of collective trauma or of individual trauma. There seem to be good reasons to speak of both. The important thing is to be aware of how easily slippage occurs. As John Wisdom, the philosopher, used to say: "Say what you like; but be careful".

INDEX

223